TANK MAN

THE LIFE AND TIMES OF CAPTAIN BERT BAKER

JONATHAN BAKER

First published in Great Britain in 2023
by The Tank Museum

Registered Charity 1102661
Registered Company 4962619

ISBN 978-1-739354-73-2

Designed and produced for The Tank Museum
by JJN Publishing Ltd.
Production Director: Nigel Clements
Editorial Director: Jonathan Falconer
Art Director: Jud Webb

Maps by Jed Wright

Most of the photographs in the plate sections are
reproduced by permission of the
Baker family and The Tank Museum.
Cuinchy, France, 1915 – Imperial War Museum
Photographs of old Kirdford reproduced by
kind permission of Kirdford Parish Council;
Cowkeeper shop, 1825 – Wellcome Library, London;
Victorian East Dulwich – Southwark Archives;
United Dairies, Uttoxeter –
Staffordshire County Council Archives;
Milk Train – courtesy of Hannah Velten.

FOR MY GRANDFATHER,
WITH ADMIRATION AND RESPECT

AND FOR MY FATHER,
WITH LOVE

CONTENTS

ACKNOWLEDGEMENTS

I am grateful first and foremost to The Tank Museum at Bovington for the help and support that made this book possible, through access to my grandfather's papers, records relating to G Battalion and their extensive picture archive. In particular, I must thank the museum's Curator, David Willey, for his encouragement and enthusiasm when I first floated the idea of a memoir, and the energy and perseverance with which he helped bring the project to fruition. David Fletcher, perhaps the world's leading authority on the tank, and himself the author of more than 30 books, did me the honour of reading the manuscript and putting me right on a number of points. All proceeds from the sale of this book will go to The Tank Museum.

Amanda Gillett, Chair of Kirdford Parish Council (KPC), arranged for me to have access to the parish records. I am grateful to the KPC for allowing me to reproduce photographs of the village as it would have been around the time George Baker and Emma Braby were growing up there.

Members of the Dulwich Society helped with details of late Victorian East Dulwich, and I owe a particular debt to Sharon O'Connor, who helped me run a number of important details to ground and was also kind enough to go through my draft of the chapter on East Dulwich.

Thanks also to the various members of the extended Baker family who scoured their memories, photograph albums and attics to help me with all sorts of information, and in particular what happened to Bert's siblings in later life. Special thanks to another of Bert Baker's grandchildren, my cousin Claire Higgott; a notably enthusiastic supporter of the project from the start, her own researches were invaluable in keeping me on the right lines as we tried to get a grip of events of 150 years ago and more.

I thank Jed Wright for the excellent maps he created especially for this book, Marjolijn Verbrugge of The Tank Museum for her help in researching many of the images, and Jonathan Falconer of JJN Publishing for guiding me through the publishing process.

Jonathan Baker
Autumn 2023

INTRODUCTION

Every day, ordinary people do extraordinary things. When confronted with pressure, stress or threat, they show resources of courage, enterprise and resilience of which they had not previously thought themselves capable. This is never more true than for those coming face to face with the ultimate experience of pressure, stress and threat: an enemy on the battlefield.

So it was for the hundreds of thousands of young men who streamed into recruiting offices in the autumn of 1914 to sign up to fight the Kaiser. They had little inkling of the horrors and the terrors that lay in store, nor were they especially well equipped to handle them. They were ordinary men, some not much more than boys. Yet so many would perform extraordinary feats of heroism, valour and self-sacrifice.

Each would have his own story, heroic or otherwise: a million and more of them. Most will forever remain untold. But thanks to the resurgence of interest prompted by the centenary of the Great War, and to the amazing resources now available online, many more have come to light in recent years. This, the story of Albert George 'Bert' Baker, is one such.

Bert Baker would not have regarded himself as anything other than an ordinary person. He had spent the first 25 years of his life working for his father in a small family dairy in south London. And although he had shown signs of ambition, and a determination to better his situation in life, he was no more prepared for the demands of the Great War than anyone else. Yet he was one of those who proved to be capable of great things. His story is of particular interest because of the small part he played in the revolution that took place between 1914 and 1918 in the way wars were fought. It was a revolution brought about by the mechanisation of warfare, through the artillery shell, the machine-gun and, later, the aeroplane – and the tank.

Bert's wartime story is inextricably bound up with that of the tank – a machine that did not exist in 1914 and yet helped bring the war to an end four years later. The tank had a difficult birth and painful infancy. Its dismal showing in the early actions in which it was involved brought it perilously close to the scrapyard. There was no shortage of people in the British High Command who thought Kitchener had hit the nail on the head when he dubbed the tank 'a pretty mechanical toy'.

That the tank was able to survive these early vicissitudes and establish itself as a frontline weapon of power and potential was very largely the result of two very different actions in 1917. In the first, a small exploit known as The Cockcroft, the tanks gave notice of their potential, if properly used. In the second, deployed in their hundreds at the Battle of Cambrai, they were the spearhead of a spectacular advance that finally overcame the doubts of most of the sceptics.

Bert Baker, my grandfather, featured in both of these decisive actions. He distinguished himself in both, winning a Military Cross in the first and a bar to it in the second. He could therefore claim to have made a small but not insignificant contribution to the seismic changes that would define how this and all subsequent wars would be fought.

One might think he would have wanted to pass his story down through the generations. He was a gregarious and energetic man, moulded and shaped by the Great War. But that did not happen. Once he was demobbed in early 1919, Bert Baker returned to his new wife and his old job, and settled down into a comfortable and uneventful middle-class existence in rural Staffordshire. His son John would follow him into the tanks in the next war, but John seldom talked of either his father's experiences or his own. Bert Baker died in 1958, so even those of his grandchildren who had been born by then are too young to have any real memory of him. He was, in consequence, a rather shadowy figure in our family history. His wartime exploits were not spoken of, perhaps because by the time his children were born, the war was already starting to pass into history. In 1991, my father donated all Bert's papers to The Tank Museum at Bovington in Dorset. As far as I am aware, he had never shown them to anyone.

My own interest in my grandfather's war record stems from the moment I came across his medals in a drawer while on a visit to my parents in the 1990s. There was a full set of medals, and a smaller, dress set, for attaching to mess dress or a dinner suit. I took the main set away and framed them as a gift for my father, along with the medal citations from the *Tank Corps Book of Honour*. Those citations were brief and yet strongly redolent of the drama, chaos and colour of the battlefield. My father was delighted with the medal display, and also enjoyed a first visit to The Tank Museum, where a German field gun captured by his father was on display. Towards the end of his life he wrote down a little of what he knew of his father's career as part of a few pages of autobiography.

In 2015, I was contacted by The Tank Museum in connection with a special exhibition being planned to commemorate the centenary of the tank the following year. The exhibition was to feature eight prominent early tank men, and Albert Baker would be one of them. I was astonished. I had had no idea that my grandfather's accomplishments were such as to be considered worthy of such prominence and recognition. The museum wanted to know more about Bert Baker's life both before and after his war service. Only as I undertook the research for the exhibition did I begin to appreciate the scale of his achievements, and what a wonderful story was waiting to be brought back into the light. I provided the museum with a few pages of information about Bert's early and later life, which duly formed part of the exhibition and the souvenir booklet published to accompany it. The exhibition was formally opened by HRH The Princess Royal in March 1916. Each of the eight tank men was accorded an individual stand and display setting out his achievements. Bert Baker's exhibit referred to 'a man of understated courage and military skill'.

I wanted to investigate further. But once I embarked on the project, I was quickly overcome with the regret, familiar to many amateur genealogists, that I had not started sooner. Sixty years after his death, there was no one left alive with any useful memory of Bert Baker the man. If I had begun a few years earlier, I could have interviewed living witnesses, and would doubtless have cleared up some of the mysteries that have proved so frustrating. On the other hand, the delay meant that I had at my disposal the most powerful research tool imaginable, in the shape of the internet. Through genealogy websites and other records, it offered access to the documents that record the milestones in all our lives: the dates of births, marriages and deaths, Census returns, in some cases military records or dates of schooling.

It is an astonishing resource, although it can be infuriating, since every answer it yields tends to raise a whole series of further questions. In the case of Bert Baker, it even proved difficult to pinpoint his year of birth. Here, and elsewhere, there were discrepancies between official sources, each of which on its own might be considered authoritative. There are still gaps in this story and questions that remain unanswered. I have tried to steer clear of assumptions, and speculated only when the evidence has seemed to justify it. For the most part, I have preferred to acknowledge the difficulties and leave the questions open, rather than indulging in conjecture for the sake of a tidy narrative.

The quest has also taken me down a number of unexpected alleyways, such as the agricultural depression of the 19th century, the late-Victorian development of London's suburbs, the ins and outs of running an urban dairy and the decades-long efforts to produce milk that was safe to drink. I have included some of the fruits of those peregrinations here: they are the 'and times' of The Life and Times of Albert Baker. I have willingly gone off at tangents. But I hope they will be of interest, and serve to fill out context and background and an understanding of certain aspects of Bert's life and career, and the times in which he lived.

Much has been written about the tanks, both in the immediate aftermath of the Great War and at regular intervals since then. I have drawn most freely from the near-contemporary writings of those who were actually involved in the creation of these machines and their early deployment. Military historians have also published yards of books about the tanks and their impact on the theory and practice of warfare. This book is not an academic study, and does not aspire to add to that scholarship; it simply offers a new perspective on the story, the eyewitness perspective of one of those at the sharp end, one of the first men to command a tank in battle.

This is a resource that has not previously been published or studied in detail, so perhaps Bert's story can claim to make a modest new contribution to the study of the early tanks. His papers included his own handwritten record of his wartime service, his part in, and responses to, the momentous events that were happening all around him. The Tank Museum has described it as 'one of the most complete and well-preserved documents of the history of one man's service with the Tank Corps'.

The principal document is a writing pad, the size of a reporter's notebook. 'The Upwood Writing Tablet' it says on the cover, and for convenience it will be referred to throughout this account as 'the Tablet'. There is no other handwritten source material – no diaries, no letters, just this one record, page after page written in pencil in a neat and even hand, an account of the main events of the war years as he experienced them. Importantly, it is not a memoir, but a series of extracts of what he actually wrote at the time.

This curious document was compiled at some time after the conflict: there is no indication of exactly when, or indeed why. One of Bert's purposes appears to have been to provide himself with a reminder of his movements throughout his time in the military. In this it is extremely detailed – virtually every move is recorded. By cross-referencing with official sources, it is possible as a result to trace exactly where he was and what he was doing at any given time between September 1914 and January 1919. This cannot have been an effort of memory: the level of detail is such that he must have been referring to diaries or some other form of record maintained at the time. But why not just keep the diaries, rather than painstakingly transcribing page after page of them? Perhaps his records were scattered across many scraps of paper, and he wanted to bring them all together in one place.

Large sections of the Tablet are extracts from letters he sent home to Miriam Potter, whom he had met just before the outbreak of war and whom he married when on leave from France in the summer of 1918. In the passages that he chose to preserve, the emphasis is once again on the factual. There are few endearments; that doesn't mean of course that the original letters were not affectionate in tone, merely that he chose not to reproduce that part of them in his record. Even so, some evidence of a more sentimental side occasionally emerges. He tells Miriam at one point that he is sending her a brooch he has had made from one of the buttons of his army greatcoat. When he and some of his fellows hire a boat for the day, he is pleased to note that it is called Miriam. When he is posted to a camp near Mansfield, he calculates how far he is from where she is living. And in a note to Miriam telling her of forthcoming leave he signs himself 'your own Bert'. But these are the only semi-romantic glimpses we have. And apart from a couple of mentions of his brother Len, also fighting in France, there is nothing at all about his mother and father or any of his other siblings.

It seems the Tablet had a functional purpose rather than anything else, as a sort of *aide memoire*. And yet some of the things he thinks worthy of recording seem random, trivial even. One is left wondering why he included them – and, more tantalisingly, what he left out, and why. The Tablet is disappointingly light, for example, on descriptions of the actions in which he was involved, or how he reacted to them. There are no extracts from any of the replies he received from Miriam. And he adds no later remarks or reflections to the contemporary record as he reproduces it, editorial comment made with the benefit of hindsight. What we have are reproduced fragments of what he wrote at the time, with no gloss or commentary. Therein lies much of their value to the historian.

At this distance, one of the surprising aspects of Bert's record is how little time in four years of continuous service he actually spent in action on the frontline. Periods of intense activity were interspersed with much longer periods of hanging about doing not very much. Such has always been the lot of the military man. There were the usual soldierly preoccupations with the quality of his billet and where the next meal would be coming from. Most of his days were occupied with training or just moving from one place to another. This is true of his time both as an infantryman, and later as a tank man.

Our image of the Great War is of wretched Tommies splashing through rat-infested trenches with no respite either from the rain or what Wilfred Owen called 'the monstrous anger of the guns' – the incessant artillery bombardments. This is indeed what conditions were like for many on the Western Front. But soldiers did not spend extended periods in the most forward trenches; they were rotated in and out on a frequent basis. And in the early days at least, as is evident from Bert's account, the war was exciting, even enjoyable. Until people were worn down by the grinding attrition of it all, and the numbers of dead ran into the hundreds of thousands, the whole thing was a bit of a lark for young men who had never before ventured beyond the bounds of the parishes where they had been born. The songs they sang were full of humour, often gallows humour admittedly, but very different in mood from the later narrative set by the war poets and memoirists, the narrative that still dominates today.

The prevailing tone of Bert's recollections is upbeat and positive, even when things are at their toughest. To that extent, the Tablet reflects a fleeting mood that has perhaps been somewhat forgotten in the century that has passed since these remarkable events took place; a time when ordinary men did extraordinary things.

1
KIRDFORD

Generations of Bakers had populated the villages of West Sussex since the Middle Ages. People tended not to stray far from the parishes of their birth, and they also had large families. So, by the mid-19th century, the Bakers had multiplied considerably. They lay especially thickly on the ground in the small and picture-perfect farming village of Kirdford. The 1851 Census shows that the parish had a population of around 1,850. Of those, no fewer than 75 bore the Baker name, spanning several branches of the family: only the Puttocks and the Pullens could boast the same degree of fecundity.

On the face of it, Kirdford – pronounced as if it were two words – looks like an idyllic place in which to grow up. It was, and remains, a charming and peaceful village. Today, only about a thousand people live there, although the wider parish, the largest in West Sussex, includes a number of surrounding villages swelling that figure to about 4,000. Many of those living in Kirdford today are actively engaged in opposition to planners who would like to despoil it with new housing developments. The village centre is a conservation area, with around one-fifth of the houses having Grade 2 listed status. It lies amid beautiful countryside on the edge of the South Downs National Park.

Kirdford is at the centre of a group of villages, with Plaistow to the north, Wisborough Green to the east, Fittleworth to the south and Northchapel to the west. It is connected to all of them by B roads and narrow country lanes, and is not close to any through roads that might make it a rat run for commuters. As such it retains a pleasing sense of remoteness and tranquillity. The nearest town of any note is Petworth, and much of the parish was at one time within the Leconfield estate, which includes Petworth House.

Nairn and Pevsner found it an attractive spot, calling it in their *The Buildings of England*, 'a gracious place.... the centre of the village is a small oblong green, not much more than a wide street, with the church at the south end. What makes it special is the grand formality of the row of big horse chestnut trees up the centre. The effect is of a French place done on purely English terms.'

David Arscott was similarly impressed in his *County Guide of West Sussex*: 'This entirely satisfying village centre is tucked away off even the quiet lanes that characterise the Weald. The road enters alongside a village green and then seems to be part of a small town square, so compact is everything around it, with inn, cottages and church bordering on three sides. A row of immense horse chestnuts marches up to the churchyard forming a splendid processional way. Beyond the church the land dips down into a gentle valley, providing a fine view from the churchyard and increasing the impression of smug compactness.'

Nearly everyone who lived in Kirdford in the mid-1850s was engaged in agriculture or its allied trades. In the Middle Ages, the area had been notable for its iron industry and glass making, but these had gradually given way to crops, and most of the land was given over to arable farming. The tithe map of 1884 records that just under half the land was arable, about one third woodland and the rest meadow or common land. There were around 70 farms, mostly belonging to the Leconfield and other estates and farmed by tenants. There were some smallholdings. Kirdford had its blacksmiths, grooms, gardeners, millers and wheelwrights, but more than 95 per cent of the inhabitants worked directly on the land. The farmers kept as many livestock as they could afford to feed over the winter, but the main business was in growing wheat and oats.

Earning a living from the land has always been a hard and unpredictable business, and this was especially true in the 1850s. At the root of the difficulties British farmers were experiencing at that time, and in the decades that followed, was the controversial repeal of the Corn Laws. The laws had imposed taxes on imported grain, and their abolition in 1846 meant free trade, which it was believed would cut prices. In the event, it opened the door to cheap imports from the United States, where vast expanses of land were going under the plough as the American pioneers moved westwards. Railways were springing up everywhere to bring the grain to the ports, and cheap steamship travel bore it onwards to Europe. The cost of transporting a ton of grain from the American mid-west to Liverpool fell by nearly two-thirds in the 1870s. That was a decade of poor harvests in Britain. The American grain undercut prices at home and overwhelmed British farmers no longer protected by the Corn Laws. It was the start of what became known as the Great Depression of British agriculture.

Kirdford did not escape the effects, and it became increasingly difficult for agricultural labourers to scratch out a living for their large families – each averaging between three and six children. One such family was that of George and Mary Baker.

The Bakers of Kirdford, though numerous, were generally poor. There was the odd tenant farmer among their ranks, but most of them worked on the land as labourers. They did not share the fortunes of another branch of the family, living only half a dozen miles to the west, in Northchapel. The Bakers there were landowners with aspirations to join the gentry. Over the previous two centuries they had steadily acquired farms and land in the area, such that by the 1840s, the three Baker brothers of Northchapel owned 4,000 acres, and property in Hampshire and Surrey as well as Sussex.

Well might George Baker have envied the fortunes of his distant relatives down the road. He was one of at least nine children of Benjamin Baker and Ann Napper, who lived at Scratchings Farm a couple of miles outside Kirdford. It is still there today. Like so many of his brothers, uncles and cousins, George grew up to be a farm labourer. He married Mary Hammond in Kirdford in 1843, and they lived in several properties around the village over the next few years, as they began raising a family of their own. By the time of the 1861 Census, they were living in Streets Cottage with their five children – Emma, James, Jonas, Mary Ann and George junior. Young George, then aged five, will play a prominent role in our story, as Albert Baker's father.

Living a couple of miles west of Kirdford, and a contemporary of George Baker, was George Braby. Braby appears to have lost his parents when he was small, and to have been brought up by his uncle and aunt, James and Mary Peacock, at Great Allfields Farm in the hamlet of Balls Cross. By the time of the 1861 Census, George had married, and had taken over the tenancy of the farm. His wife was Elizabeth Peachey, the eldest daughter of a farmer turned grocer, George Welland Peachey, and his wife Amelia. The Peacheys also lived in Balls Cross, and some branches of the family were much higher up the social scale. Peacheys had built Ebernoe House near Balls Cross in 1786, and owned ten farms.

The first of George and Elizabeth Braby's four children, Emma, was born in 1857. Emma would become Albert's mother. The 1861 Census records Great Allfields as being a farm of 320 acres, employing seven labourers and four boys. A lot of the tenanted farms in the area were smaller than that, at around 120 acres – just about big enough to support a family. The Brabys were certainly in a stronger position economically than the Bakers in Kirdford, although even with his larger farm, George would probably not have regarded himself as particularly well off. West Sussex is one of the most heavily wooded parts of the country, so it would not have been possible to cultivate all of the land. The heavy clays of the Low Weald were capable of producing good crops, but were notoriously difficult to manage, and depended on the right amount of rain falling at the right time for sowing in the autumn. In wet weather, the clay became sticky and formed clumps that provide challenges even for modern machinery. If dry for prolonged periods, the ground became hard and cracked, such that only plants with deep roots could survive. Yields in the 19th century would in any case have been low by today's standards.

The farms were spread over an extensive area, and if you wanted to visit someone, you walked or hitched a lift on a cart. We do not know how George Baker and Emma Braby came to meet, though in a small community, most people would have known each other and come together for festivals and important dates in the calendar. A village school was built in Kirdford in 1819. They might both have been pupils, although there is no guarantee that either or both of them would have attended with regularity. By the time they were of school age, the government had just introduced regulations tying central funding for schools to annual exams and good attendance records. The ambition at that time was simply to give children an elementary mastery of reading, writing and arithmetic. But many parents still thought education a waste of time, and certainly of less value than the passing down of skills and practical knowledge by which their children might earn their living. Boys would be expected to contribute to the family economy by the time they were about eight, and girls might be kept at home to help with household chores or mind younger siblings. Everyone was expected to lend a hand with harvesting and haymaking. So, schooling was a hit and miss affair. Parish records of the time show a large proportion of couples signing the wedding register with a mark because they were unable to write their own names. George and Emma were of one of the first generations for whom illiteracy and innumeracy would become the exception rather than the rule.

We have a few outlines of what life in Kirdford was like when George and Emma were growing up there in the 1860s and 1870s. There were more shops in the village then than there are now. There were two general stores – Irelands and Thompsons; a Post Office standing next to the Half Moon inn just a few yards from the church, and Mr Enticknap's boot and shoe shop. There was a grocery shop for a time at Pound Common, at the western end of the village, not far from the other pub, the Forester's Arms.

In the 1930s, the *West Sussex Gazette* published some portraits of elderly residents of Kirdford who were by then in their 80s, and as such contemporaries of George and Emma. They recalled their early lives in Kirdford. George Stevens had begun work as a farmer's boy and spent his entire life on the land. Jane Pennicard, one of 12 children, had started working in the fields at the age of 11. Her hours were eight to four, her wages fourpence a day. James Enticknap had attended the village school but left before he was 11, and served as Kirdford's blacksmith for 34 years.

It was a tough life, but there were occasional moments of enjoyment. One such was a fete held at Ifold House in 1861, a colourful account of which appeared in the *West Sussex Gazette* in September of that year. Ifold was the local country estate, and the house was one of the main residences of Kirdford. It was owned by John Napper, who lived there with his wife and their nine servants. Their fete was a grand affair, to which all the local gentry and villagers were invited. The invitation extended to old and young alike, and it seems very probable that George and Emma were among their number on what sounds like a memorable day:

> Not only did the company comprise a numerous gathering of the nobility and gentry of this and the adjacent county, and the tenantry of the estate, but the good things of this life were unsparingly distributed to a large number of schoolchildren, and of the inmates of the Kirdford and Wisborough Green Union workhouse bearing in their hands flags and banners inscribed with 'My Happy Day & etc etc', and when they arrived they were met by the word 'Welcome' in large letters as well as a warm reception and a hearty shake of the hand from the amiable lady of the house, whose condescension and affability was the admiration of everyone during the whole of the day, her study being to make everyone happy.
>
> Soon afterwards the schoolchildren from Wisborough and Kirdford made their appearance headed by their respective tutors and patrons. At half past 12 they sat down to a good old English dinner in a spacious booth to the number of 155... the old men were given pipes and the weed and home-brewed ale. The tenants were all regaled to their hearts'

> content, while the children were enjoying themselves at cricket or riding upon a run-around hired for the purpose. Here and in the parklike grounds adjoining, where the refreshment marquee for the children and old people was erected, there was afforded every facility for enjoyment in the form of a variety of outdoor games and amusements. The contents of a booth literally full of presents adapted to the taste of the juvenile and aged guests, were distributed by Mrs Napper, amidst unequivocal manifestations of delight on many happy faces. Several races were run by the schoolchildren – both boys and girls – and none were allowed to depart without some token of regard from Mr and Mrs Napper, in the shape of prayer books, reward cards etc.

Days like this were the exception, and it is easy to see why many sought an escape from a life of near poverty on the land. Others had left before them, when times had been equally harsh. Even so, by 1830 the population of Kirdford had risen to around 1,600, living in only 200 dwellings, which suggests large families and probably several families living together. But productivity had not kept pace with the increase in population. The relative agricultural prosperity of a generation earlier had collapsed after the Napoleonic Wars, bread prices had risen and there was extreme hardship in nearly every rural parish. In the words of a local history: 'The parish welfare systems could not absorb the large rise in population, and farm worker pay could not pay the high prices for the wheat, which had trebled during the Napoleonic war; men were struggling to support a family on 6s a week or less; men in rags, anxious to work, were found dead in ditches, their stomachs full of only dandelion leaves.' There were outbreaks of rioting, and the situation became one of national concern.

One escape route lay in the New World. Lord Egremont of Petworth House helped finance the Petworth Emigration Scheme, which provided passages on ships sailing from Portsmouth to Montreal every year between 1832 and 1837. There were 600 people on the first two sailings in 1832, carrying 58 people from Kirdford and many others from surrounding parishes such as Northchapel and Lurgashall. That figure of 58 included a number of the Bakers of Kirdford.

What little we can discover of George Baker junior, born in 1856, can be deduced by what is known of his actions. As he entered his 20s in the mid-1870s, he decided that agricultural labour was not the life for him. He was capable and resourceful and unafraid of hard work, but he could see no future for himself in Kirdford. He determined to head for London and try his luck in the big city.

Tens of thousands of others across the country had the same idea. George became part of a large migration from the countryside to the big urban centres. The 1881 Census showed that the number of people describing themselves as agricultural labourers had fallen by more than 90,000 since the previous Census ten years earlier. The number of urban labourers had increased by 53,000 over the same period, many of them former farm workers heading to the cities to find work. It was the beginning of a long trend. In the last 30 years of the 19th century, the population of England and Wales rose by more than 40 per cent, but the number of male agricultural labourers dropped by more than a third.

At some point, we do not know exactly when, George Baker resolved that the time had come for him to make the break. By this time, he and Emma Braby were attached, if not actually engaged. Perhaps George's timing was influenced by the fact that in 1881, Emma's father had taken up a new tenancy at Kilsham Farm, several miles from Kirdford on the other side of Petworth. The new farm was much bigger – 480 acres. George Braby would remain there for the rest of his working life, and it would hold a special place in the affections of his children and grandchildren. But it was too far from Kirdford to allow George Baker and Emma to meet very easily. When he asked her to go to London with him, she agreed. In fact the whole Braby family seems to have been infected with the appeal of the move, because Emma's siblings decided to go too. Indeed, her brother George might already have left, because he was not at Kilsham when the 1881 Census was taken. It was a bold decision, and one that must have disappointed George and Elizabeth Braby, who were suddenly seeing all their children disappearing from home. But with agriculture increasingly in decline, and so many labourers hovering near the poverty line, it was a decision that multitudes of others were taking as well. Some time around 1881–82, the Braby children set off for London to join George Baker, and to embark upon a new life. Their eventual destination would be a small but growing community a few miles from central London called East Dulwich.

2
EAST DULWICH

When George and Emma were growing up in West Sussex, East Dulwich was a small rural hamlet only about the size of Kirdford. Although its main thoroughfare, Lordship Lane, was barely six miles from the City of London, it might as well have been sixty. East Dulwich in 1850 was a community of only a few hundred, with poor transport links to the city – always assuming its inhabitants had any cause to go there. Few did. But by the time George and Emma arrived and began to put down roots there, it was well on its way to becoming a busy London suburb. The transformation was completed over a single generation, in the last quarter of the 19th century.

The first signs of the encroaching tentacles of the metropolis were agreeable country villas, erected by members of the emerging commercial classes growing prosperous on the back of Britain's mighty manufacturing strength and a global empire that was still expanding. The newly-rich were moving out of their inconvenient and cramped houses in the insalubrious and teeming streets of central London. They scattered in all directions, and several found their way to East Dulwich. The new arrivals built their houses, mansions in some cases, around the open spaces of Goose Green, towards Peckham. But with no easy access to central London, development was desultory.

It was in the late 1860s that the real building boom began, and continued for a dozen years or so before pausing, and resuming in the 1890s. The main driver was the astonishing speed of population growth in the capital. Immigration from the countryside was one of the key causes. London – already the world's largest city – was also consolidating its position at the centre of global trade. The population of what we now call Greater London was around three million in 1850, very heavily concentrated in the centre. By 1900, that had risen to more than eight million; but a far larger proportion – nearly a quarter – now lived beyond the centre. The population of this outer ring of boroughs grew by about 50 per cent every ten years. In the 1880s, the four fastest-growing districts in the country were all London suburbs. In the process, many a rural backwater was transformed into a dormitory town.

East Dulwich was swept along on this tide of expansion. More than 5,000 houses were built in the decade after 1871, mostly for members of the lower middle classes – such as the army of clerks and bookkeepers who kept the wheels of commerce and empire rolling. They were upwardly mobile, seeking to climb the social and financial ladder on the back of unprecedented national prosperity. A smart and spacious terraced house in the fragrant suburbs met their aspirations to perfection. Commuting from there to their desks in the City was made possible by the coming of the railways. Stations were opened during the 1860s at Herne Hill, West Dulwich, Sydenham Hill, East Dulwich and North Dulwich. In the energetic and earnest way of the Victorians, the newcomers set about founding all sorts of clubs and societies and in no time created vibrant communities.

All the other building blocks of Victorian urban development came with them: churches, schools, a hospital, public baths, and of course, shops. The clerks and their young families need to be served by the retail trade, and traders of every stripe were soon opening their doors on and near Lordship Lane.

The area was made more attractive still by the relocation in 1854 of the Crystal Palace. Built to house the Great Exhibition of 1851, the vast glass structure had rapidly become one of the wonders of the world, attracting hundreds of thousands of visitors to Hyde Park to celebrate British ingenuity and invention and to view the latest in technological and scientific advances. It was three times the size of St Paul's Cathedral, and it contained more glass than any building that had gone before. Once the exhibition was over, it was decided to move the entire structure to the new suburbia of south-east London, not far from East Dulwich.

With the arrival of the Crystal Palace, the area suddenly was made more fashionable, as well as creating a major tourist attraction. On Easter Monday 1883, more than 60,000 people flocked to the site. All of this brought with it commercial possibilities, new jobs and further development, and accelerated the already-rapid programme of house building. That meant opportunity, and George and Emma were not slow to seize it. Their experience of farming in West Sussex might have been of limited value to them, but there were plenty of unskilled jobs available in the new retail businesses. Why they settled on East Dulwich is unclear, but it was there that their son Albert would spend the first 25 years of his life. And it is there that we next find an official record of what they were doing.

We can surmise that George came to London first, although we do not know when, or where else he might have spent time, if anywhere, before he made his home in East Dulwich. Emma was still living at Kilsham Farm outside Petworth in 1881, but she and her siblings appear to have followed him to the city around then, or shortly afterwards. On 9 September 1883, George and Emma were married at St John's Church in East Dulwich, with Emma's brother and sister acting as witnesses. Both bride and groom gave the same address on the marriage certificate: 24 The Pavement. And they both gave the same occupation: greengrocer.

The Pavement was a run of terraced properties on Lordship Lane that typified the piecemeal nature of the development of the area. In 1883, Number 24 was a greengrocery and general store run by William Cooper, so it seems fair to assume that both George and Emma were employed in the shop, and lodged (separately, to be sure) in the rooms upstairs. In time, The Pavement would disappear as a separate name, and the houses would simply become numbers on Lordship Lane. What was the Cooper grocery at 24 The Pavement is now a shoe shop.

The newlyweds did not stay there long, as by the time Albert was born at the end of 1884, their address had changed to 2 Dulwich Rise. This was another terrace of a few houses, very newly-built – indeed, probably only numbers 1 and 2 had been completed by 1884. It was only a short walk down Lordship Lane from The Pavement. Dulwich Rise was another name that would disappear within a short time, Number 2 becoming 215 Lordship Lane.

Although thousands of houses were going up, nearly all of them were being built in small blocks of anything from five to 25 properties, each block being given a separate name. In time, they would be joined up and become whole streets of terraced houses. Around 70 per cent of the construction companies working in the area were small firms, each of them building fewer than a dozen houses. In one road alone, Barry Road, there were about 50 different builders at work. A walk around the streets of East Dulwich today brings the visitor into contact with the extraordinarily varied range of styles and external trimmings that resulted. All the builders added their own distinctive touches to satisfy the Victorian mania for decoration. Two-tone brickwork, with the bricks sometimes laid at angles, elaborate bay windows and porches with coloured-glass doors, tiled porches, plasterwork fruit and flowers or gargoyles embellished the exterior of even the most basic terraced house.

George and Emma remained at 2 Dulwich Rise for ten years, and began to raise a family there. At some point soon after their marriage, in circumstances that are not clear, George became associated with the dairy trade that would provide his livelihood for the rest of his working days. How and where this happened is not known. It is possible that Number 2 was itself a dairy, and they were working there and living above the shop, as they had done at The Pavement. But I have not been able to find any conclusive evidence of this, and viewed today, the building appears too small to accommodate a dairy, and has limited access to the rear of the property from the street.

The mystery even extends to the birth of their first child, Albert George, the hero of our story. His birth certificate states that Albert, or Bert as he would be known, was born on 28 December 1884 at 2 Dulwich Rise. However, in some later official documents such as Census returns, Bert's year of birth is usually given as 1885. Census data are not always 100 per cent reliable, and the discrepancy could be explained by the fact that his birth was not actually registered until January 1885. However, Bert himself deepened the mystery in one of the earliest entries in his wartime diary, made on 28 December 1914. He would have turned 30 on that day. But the diary record states: 'My 28th birthday'. For that to be the case, his birth date would have had to be December 1886. Given that his younger sister Nellie arrived in April 1886, simple maths suggests that he must have been mistaken in this entry. His birth date was given as December 1884 when he was registered as a new pupil at Heber Road School in 1892. The 1891 Census, taken in the spring of that year, before his birthday, gives his age as six. Coupled with the birth certificate also saying 1884, this seems conclusive. Yet, it is strange for someone turning 30 to be unaware that they were marking a milestone birthday. It may be that because the Tablet in which he transcribed his wartime movements was not written until some years later, he made a simple error when transcribing this early entry.

Assuming that 1884 is the correct date, George and Emma must have moved the few hundred yards from The Pavement to Dulwich Rise sometime between their wedding in September 1883 and Albert's birth in the December of the following year. And it was during this period that the association with dairying began, because by Christmas 1884, George was a grocer no longer. He registered his occupation on Bert's birth certificate as 'dairyman'.

Although we do not know what occasioned this move, it seems to have been a beneficial one in terms of the Baker fortunes. The dairyman was able to support a growing family: Bert and Nellie were followed in September 1888 by Lily Lavinia, and in December 1890 by Ernest Reginald. He also had the means to employ a domestic – the 1891 Census showed that 19-year-old Eda Nicholson lived with the Baker family as a servant. Bert, then aged six, was missing from Dulwich Rise in this record. On the day the 1891 Census was taken, he and his Aunt Ellen, Emma's sister, were staying at Kilsham Farm in West Sussex with his grandparents, George and Elizabeth Braby. We can perhaps take from this that although the Braby children had moved to London, they were still in touch with their parents in West Sussex and made regular visits to see them.

By 1891, George Baker was doing well enough in the dairy business to consider branching out on his own. Again, the circumstances are not clear, and we have to consider a range of possibilities. If there was indeed a dairy at 2 Dulwich Rise, it could be that over the decade he lived there, George rose to become head of the business, and by the early 1890s was ready to move to larger and more convenient premises. If he was still working as a waged dairyman for someone else, it could be that over these ten years he had saved enough money to be able to strike out on his own. In any event, he now began to look for a suitable location to establish his own dairy.

He did not have far to look. Development to the east of Lordship Lane was moving on apace. Road names had been registered, and their outlines had been marked out on the map by the late 1860s. But it was some time before the building caught up and houses began to appear. Stanford's Map of London for 1877 showed very little development in East Dulwich apart from the area around Goose Green. The builders were creeping slowly southwards from East Dulwich railway station, then named Champion Hill. But they had not got very far, and were still five or six streets north of Dulwich Rise. Indeed, in 1877 Dulwich Rise had itself yet to be built. Pellatt Street, as it was then called, around the corner from Dulwich Rise, had a single terrace of ten houses on it.

The road names in the area appear random, but there were some themes. One of the most active builders of the ten years or so after 1873 was Ezekiel Bailey. Bailey hailed from Derbyshire, and borrowed the names of towns and villages in his home county when naming the streets he was developing: Ashbourne, Chesterfield, Derwent, Melbourne and Colwell. Other roads, for no obvious reason, were named after bishops: Goodrich, Heber, Underhill and Whateley. Still others were named after famous people – recently deceased – with local connections. Barry Road commemorated Sir Charles Barry, architect of the Dulwich Estate and, more famously, of the Houses of Parliament. Pellatt Road was named after Apsley Pellatt, sometime MP for Southwark. Pellatt had owned a glass factory in Southwark and developed an innovative process for the enclosure of ceramics within glass.

It was the development of Pellatt Road that was of particular interest to George Baker. It was literally on his doorstep – its junction with Lordship Lane was only a few paces from his front door. Building in the 1880s had left Pellatt Road with several clusters of buildings, each block named individually. A walk along the road would have taken George past Frederick Terrace, Rose Villas, Poland Villas, Pellatt Terrace, Claremont Villas and Alfred Terrace. Gradually, the piecemeal developments would be joined up, and street numbers would replace these names. The property on which George Baker had his eye was Landcroft House, at the corner of Pellatt Road and Landcroft Road, and 100 yards from the main shopping area of Lordship Lane. It is likely that this was a new property, and that George, Emma and their children would be its first occupants.

The family appears to have taken up residence at Landcroft House by the time a fifth child, Leonard, was born in mid 1893. George appeared on the electoral roll of 1894, listed simply as a resident of Pellatt Road. In time, Landcroft House would become 75 Pellatt Road.

By early 1895, the family was completed with the birth of Winifred Emma, and the Bakers were fully established in the house that would provide them with a home and an income for more than 30 years. The shopfront of the dairy they built there is still clearly visible, with display windows on both Pellatt Road and Landcroft Road, and the entrance door between them. There were two upper floors, offering more living space than they would have had at Dulwich Rise. A few paces along Landcroft Road was the entrance to the back yard and the dairy itself.

It was a good location for a dairy, and George and Emma were not the only ones to see its potential. At the next junction down Pellatt Road was a corner property with an almost identical footprint. Another dairy already existed there, run by one Albert Gower, aged 36, and his wife Emmeline. As we shall see in the next chapter, small urban dairies were springing up everywhere to supply the rapidly-increasing local population. There were at least a dozen within a short walk of 75 Pellatt Road, all competing for a share in this new market. Many were on corner locations, favoured because they had direct access from the back yard to the street, which most terraced houses did not have. This allowed for storage of the carts used by the roundsmen to deliver the milk, and, in many cases, for the keeping of cows on the premises. This in turn enabled the dairymen to boast of the freshness of their product. Customers who came into the shop could purchase their milk more or less straight from the cow.

The farm labourer from Kirdford, brought up on the breadline with little in the way of career prospects, was now in his mid-30s. He had done well. He had a wife and six children, and had created what would become a modestly prosperous business in a growing London suburb. All this would surely have seemed impossibly out of reach to the young lad growing up in poverty in the remote farmlands around his home village. And indeed it is difficult to understand exactly how he managed it; how he could afford the considerable step up represented by moving into a new house and starting a new business.

George and Emma were almost certainly renting 75 Pellatt Road. Only about one person in ten was a freehold owner-occupier. Number 75 was a seven-roomed house of a sort that might be rented for £30–60 a year. Prices were more affordable than they might have been, because for a while in the 1880s, supply outstripped demand. Of those 5,000 houses built in the 1870s, about a thousand lay vacant for some time and others were only partially let. The Bakers perhaps gambled on the dairy delivering enough income to make the new property affordable. If they already had a stake of some sort in a dairy business, they might not have had the extra expense of purchasing new livestock and other equipment: but there would surely have been significant expenditure involved in building a shippon for the cows and other parts of the dairy. Perhaps they had saved enough in the previous ten years to be able to afford these costs; perhaps Emma's father was in a position to help them; perhaps they were able to take out a loan.

This assumes that the Baker dairy was an end-to-end operation – the milk going from udder to counter – or delivery cart – all on the same premises. We believe that this was the case but cannot be sure. It was certainly common for urban dairies to keep cows on the premises: there was one such in Shawbury Road, only a short distance from Pellatt Road, the original frontage of which can still be seen. As late as 1916, a dairy advertising its wares in Camberwell considered it a selling point that the milk came from cows living on site. But other dairies ran a retail business and a milk round, bringing in supplies daily from one of the outlying farms. Before cooling and refrigeration were possible, it would have been difficult to do this and deliver the milk fresh and on time; and the profit margins must have been very tight for dairymen not producing their own milk.

On the 1901 Census form, George described himself as a Dairyman/Shopkeeper. This would seem to imply an enterprise that was something rather more than a simple retail business. But even given this and everything we have noted about the suitability of 75 Pellatt Road for a larger enterprise, it is possible that George Baker sold the produce of others and kept no animals himself.

One reason East Dulwich's new houses had been slow to find tenants among the commuting class was that communications with central London were still not very good. The railway station at Champion Hill, as East Dulwich station was first known, was not well served. A complainant in 1888 pointed out that only 37 trains stopped there on a weekday, less than a sixth of the number that stopped at Rye Lane (now Peckham Rye). The quality of the roads was poor, and although tramways would be coming, the network was not completed until 1908.

Even so, the new suburbs were producing a fascinating demographic mix, older established and sometimes genteel residents crowded out by the new lower middle classes and the trades and shopkeepers that served them. In the new streets, all rubbed shoulders daily, yet the character of a locality could vary from street to street.

We know so much about the social make-up of turn-of-the-century London because of the inquiring mind and deep pockets of Charles Booth, business tycoon turned social reformer. Booth was born into money as the son of a wealthy Liverpool shipowner and corn merchant. He made a good deal more of it through his own business ventures, notably the Booth Steamship Company he set up with his brother. Moving to London, Booth became increasingly interested in social conditions. He was suspicious of claims that a quarter of Londoners lived in abject poverty, and felt that the Census returns provided inadequate information about the real extent of want in the capital. Towards the end of the century he set in train a massive survey, funded by the profits from his shipping business. The exercise eventually ran to 17 volumes, published serially, the whole finally brought together in 1902 as *Life and Labour of the People of London*.

Booth employed teams of researchers to undertake a methodical street-by-street investigation of the social conditions of Londoners. The results were recorded in handwritten notebooks, now held in the library of the London School of Economics. They were also transferred onto a colour-coded Poverty Map. Booth's survey was subsequently criticised for its methodology, but no one ever doubted the richness of its descriptive detail, and it had a profound impact on the development of the discipline of sociology.

A number of those who walked the streets with a Booth notebook went on to become distinguished public servants. They included George Arkell and George Duckworth. In 1899, the two Georges were assigned to survey East Dulwich.

Booth's researchers accompanied local policemen walking their beats, getting a knowledgeable first-hand account of the nature of each area, noting the social class of virtually every household and recording their own impressions at the same time. While containing a mass of fascinating local detail and colour, their findings also fed into the bigger picture that would help create the Poverty Map. For these purposes, each street was given a colour to denote the class of its inhabitants. Its definitions of class, and the colours assigned to each, were as follows:

Lower class	Vicious, semi-criminal	Black
Very poor, casual	Chronic want	Dark Blue
Poor	18–21 s a week for a moderate family	Light Blue
Mixed	Some comfortable, others poor	Purple
Fairly comfortable	Good ordinary earnings	Pink
Middle class	Well-to-do	Red
Upper middle/upper class	Wealthy.	Yellow

Armed with these definitions, Arkell and Duckworth sallied forth on two walks around East Dulwich in the affable company of Police Constable 'Taffy' Jones. 'PC Jones is a big beefy man of 40 with a full, jolly-looking face and a fund of humour and contentment that nothing can disturb,' their report of the first walk began. 'He is a Norfolk man and has 17 years' service in the East and West Dulwich sections. He was examined for promotion 12 years ago but failed to pass and is now looking forward to his pension. Although not a scholar, he is a shrewd sensible man with a good record – only one caution during his service.'

The second walk, which took them along Pellatt Road, took place in rain that became so heavy the expedition eventually had to be abandoned. Taffy Jones was as imperturbable as he had been on the first excursion. 'PC Jones is a cheery fellow whom even a drizzling rain cannot damp,' his companions reported. 'He talks freely as we walk along. Today the conversation turned to the drink question. He is not an abstainer, likes the occasional glass. He would like to see the public houses closed on Sunday, also the clubs. It would be no use to close the pubs without the clubs. The men would simply go to the clubs to drink. Now they go to the clubs in the morning and as soon as the public houses are open they are into them.'

The evil of drink would be a theme that cropped up repeatedly in their interviews with churchmen in the area. But the main task of the researchers on these two walks with PC Jones was to note down the characteristics – and colours – of each street in and around the vicinity of George Baker's dairy in Pellatt Road. These are some examples of what they found:

Lordship Lane
The east side between Whateley Road and Pellatt Roads is three-and-a-half-storey houses with a few shops at the south corner. Two or three families in each house, more in some. Looks poor, and is the poorest part of the Lane. **Purple**.

South of this to Heber Road are a few 3-storey shops and 2- and 2-and-a-half-storey houses. Comfortable – some own their own houses. **Pink**.

On west side between Melbourne Grove and Colwell Road are 2-storey cottages. All working class, sweepers etc. **Pink**. A few shops and then 2-storey houses to Townley Road. 2 families. Comfortable but no servants.

Landcroft Road
2-storey houses on w side and part of east side. 3-storeyed by Silvester Road. 2 or 3 families in each. Houses in bad condition: walls cracked. Look poor – proximity to Whateley Road keeps respectable people away. **Purple to pink.**

Landcroft Road (Pellatt to Goodrich Road).
From Pellatt Road southward the road rises and the houses are better on this slope. 2-storeyed with bay windows. Look comfortable. **Pink**. Some 3-storey houses on west near Goodrich Road with a family on each floor. In Goodrich Road an 8-room house is to let at 15 shillings a week.

Whateley Road
On the north side near Lordship Lane there are some 2-and-a-half storeyed houses occupied by costers and a very rough set of others. About

3 families in houses – street doors open. Almost as bad as Rye Buildings. **Light blue to dark blue.**

Pellatt Road
A few 3-storey shops on south side near Lordship Lane. Rag dealer, grocer. [And a dairy, although there is no specific mention of it.] **Pink**. East of Landcroft Road are 2-storey houses. North side is new and much better than south. Some of the people are buying the houses. **Pink.** Other side is poor and poorest near Crystal Palace Road.

Crystal Palace Road (Whateley Road to Jennings Road)
South of Pellatt Road to Jennings Road the houses are 2-storey semi-detached with about 7 rooms. Most are owned by the occupiers. Were sold a few years ago at £290 each. Ground rent £5. All comfortable, doctor, builder, laundress. **Pink**.

Woodwarde Road
A few shops and good two-storeyed villas with gardens in front. Two doctors, schoolmasters, surgeon, builder. All keep servants. **Red**.

The research said little about the nature of occupancy. It did reveal that the houses on three floors were usually occupied by more than one family, perhaps as many as three, one per floor. Some would have been run as boarding houses with several lodgers.

Most of the streets around Pellatt Road were classified as purple or pink – that is, 'some comfortable, others poor' or 'good ordinary earnings'. Nowhere was wealthy enough to merit the designation 'yellow', denoting wealthy residents. At the other end of the scale, only one road was 'light blue to dark blue' – that is, chronic want or low salaries. That was Whateley Road, the next road to Pellatt moving north up Lordship Lane. There was a range of social conditions therefore, but for the most part the houses were occupied by lower middle-class workers or shopkeepers.

The interviews with the clergy of the various churches serving the area offered more insights. Booth's investigators did not enjoy their visit to St John's Church, where George and Emma had been married in 1883. When they wrote to arrange an interview with the vicar, Dr Strickland, they were told 'Dr Strickland was away hopelessly ill and the next news they expected to hear of him was of his death.' They interviewed his curate instead, a Mr Joyce, who painted a picture of a parish in complete disarray because of the vicar's long-term illness. 'I never knew such a muddle.' Joyce said the average Sunday morning congregation was 450–500 – enormous by today's standards, but unremarkable then. The churchgoers he described as mostly being of the same class – lower middle.

The researchers made it clear in their report that they did not like Mr Joyce very much. The Reverend F.F. Kelly, vicar of St Giles Camberwell, was a different kettle of fish altogether, though they did not fully take to him either. 'The living is one of the plums of the English Church,' they reported. 'A real and substantial living with an income of £1,600 a year and a quite palatial vicarage. He is a worldly-minded man, and he shows a strong taint of snobbery. But he is not a fool, he appears to have a kindly heart.'

Mr Kelly told them the population of the parish was about 14,000. A generation earlier it had been barely a thousand, an indication of just how extensive had been the growth of recent years. According to the vicar, roughly one third of them kept servants, a third were middle class people without servants, and a third were working class. 'Among the working classes there is no great poverty: nearly all are in work.' Churchgoing was falling off – even the vicar's own children attended seldom or not at all. The reporter noted that the pious member of the family was Mrs Kelly.

Mr Kelly did not seem much impressed by his wife's devotions. 'I daresay you have discovered,' he told the researchers, 'that most holy women are fools'. When asked about levels of prostitution, however, he bowed to her superior knowledge. 'My wife tells me there is a great deal more than anyone would suspect'. As for drinking: 'I think there is less, but I don't think I really know.'

The clergy were not emerging too well from this investigation. The Reverend H.C. Jennings of St Clements could have been expected to demonstrate greater insights into the nature and habits of his flock. He had been the incumbent ever since the establishment of his church 17 years earlier.

He offered a rather different analysis of the social make-up of his flock. About a third are lower middle class, clerks and shopworkers. None are wealthy: even in the best streets such as Barry Road many of them dread quarter day. They have just enough to enable them to keep a black coat on their shoulders and avoid sending their children to the board school, but no margin. The remaining two-thirds of people Mr J. described as "mainly unemployed". He considered his parish the poorest in the neighbourhood and one of the poorest in south London, although it need not be that way. "The fact is that the men are content to be poor; they loaf about the public house and gamble while the women work."'

Jennings was also gloomy about the seamier side of East Dulwich life. 'Drink: a great deal in all classes. Even church workers attend meetings, not drunk but excited. The idea of hospitality here is to produce the whisky bottle.
Prostitution: Mrs J. tells her husband that Rodwell Road is full of prostitutes.

Crime: none serious but a great deal of street gambling. Marriage: nothing like number of illegitimates there used to be, but still a great deal. They are not well pleased with a girl who has a child before marriage: they are not well pleased with a girl who goes "big" to church. Health is not good. It is an intensely damp and rheumatic district. God Almighty meant it for rearing cows/corn not children. Diphtheria and scarlet fever are never absent.'

A slightly cheerier tone was adopted the Reverend E.A. Tydeman, Minister of Lordship Lane Baptist Church. 'The congregation are nearly all better-class working people – warehousemen, printers, postmen, young men who are clerks in the City. No one has independent means and scarcely any of them keeps a servant.' In common with other churches, the Baptists had a Temperance Society to discourage excessive drinking. But the meetings were not well attended, in spite of the offer of free teas. They were now planning hot suppers, in particular aimed at the 'public house loafers' who hung around on Whateley Road.

'There is a good deal of drinking. We do not see much of the police. The minister told he had followed a drunken man into a public house on Lordship Lane and prevented the landlord from serving him. Marriage tends to be to "their own people". Prostitution is unknown in this area.'

The overall picture that comes across – and can be seen reflected on the poverty map – is of a district most heavily populated by the lower middle classes: the London clerks and the shopkeepers who supplied them. There were some posher areas, and some rougher spots to be avoided. Although the temperance movement was still very active, plenty of people, mostly men, still drank heavily when they got the chance. There was some prostitution, some poverty and some crime, but East Dulwich was probably no more vicious than anywhere else, and most of its citizens had jobs of some sort and aspired to respectability.

Many of the newcomers would have been migrants from the countryside, like George and Emma Baker. Some were able to put their backgrounds to good use and work as gardeners, catering to the Victorian passion for shrubberies and formal flower beds. The women would frequently go into service, or work in dressmaking or other crafts. In the larger houses, there might be as many as ten servants. There was no stigma attached to being in service – indeed, it probably kept many people out of the workhouse.

The Baker children were able to benefit from the 1870 Elementary Education Act, which created an infrastructure to provide schooling for all children aged 5–12. Not everyone thought mass education was a good thing – some considered it positively dangerous, and that it would make the workers uppity. But there was a feeling that Britain needed a more educated workforce to maintain its supremacy in manufacture and trade.

Under the Act, local authorities had to calculate from Census returns how many school-age children lived in their areas. If there were insufficient school places for them all, a school board would be established to make sure that extra provision was put in place, paid for out of the rates. As a result of this, the London School Board opened Heber Road School in East Dulwich in 1879, originally for 500 pupils, later expanded to 1,000. The school was only a stone's throw from Pellatt Road, and when they were old enough, the young Bakers trooped along there to lessons each morning. Bert began school at Heber Road in March 1892, when he was seven, and was there until January 1899, when he had just turned 14. Intriguingly, the register says that he had been 'privately schooled' before that – which could just mean that he had done some early learning at home. Nellie, Lily and the others followed him to Heber Road by way of the infants' school. How much any of them learned is a matter of conjecture. When Bert first went to school, he was one of more than 160 boys and girls recorded on the roll as starting that year. Classes for infants might contain 100 pupils.

According to the fragments of memoirs left by my father, George and Emma had ambitions for the education of all their children, but not the means to pay for it. They therefore made a choice to invest in the future of just one of the six. It sounds arbitrary and heartless, but was by no means uncommon. The favoured child was their fourth, Ernest Reginald, known in the family as Ernie, but to later generations as 'Uncle Reg'. One can see how they probably came to this difficult conclusion. Albert, the eldest, could not be spared from the business: his future as a dairyman was mapped out for him. It probably didn't take George and Emma long to skate over the next two possibilities. Nellie and Lily were both girls: a different future lay ahead of them, and it was not one that would require an extensive education. Len and Winnie were probably still too small to be part of the calculations. So Ernie was the chosen one.

As far as he was concerned at least, the money was well spent. In due course, Ernie qualified as a civil engineer and went abroad. He spent much of his working life building roads and bridges in British North Borneo.

The teenaged Albert must have watched his younger brother's progress with mixed feelings. He was a bright young man himself, and he had aspirations of his own. Whether or not he articulated them, they did not involve a lifetime of selling milk. Opportunity of a sort beckoned in the form of 'continuation classes' that were established at Dulwich Hamlet School to allow 13-year-old school leavers to acquire new skills. For a couple of shillings a term they could take what we would now call evening classes in practical and technical skills such as carpentry, machine drawing and building construction. In addition, children from surrounding schools were able to attend weekly science classes at Friern Road School, learning physics and chemistry. The idea gathered pace from 1900 when science and arts classes became more freely available. The impetus seems to have come from a fear that better-educated Germans and Americans had much greater technical and scientific knowledge than their British counterparts, and might start elbowing them out of jobs. Bert was in his mid-teens at about this time, ready and keen to learn. We cannot know for sure, but it seems likely that it was through one or more of these channels that he was able to acquire some scientific learning and ultimately some qualifications in chemistry – qualifications that would offer him a passport out of Pellatt Road, and the chance of the sort of career upon which young Ernie was about to embark.

This was the environment in which Bert and his brothers and sisters grew up. The earliest picture we have of them is a posed family group photograph with their parents, probably taken in the early 1900s. They look appropriately serious in the fashion of the time, but well-dressed and relatively prosperous, too. There would not have been many such opportunities to escape from the 24/7 demands of running a dairy. Their leisure time, such as it was, might have included the occasional trip out – perhaps a visit to the Crystal Palace, a daytrip by train to the seaside or a boat ride on the Thames, where steamers ran to Margate. There are some surviving pictures of Bert, Nellie, Ernie and friends on one such day out in

1906. But such treats were the exception. The work of the dairy was demanding and relentless. It would have occupied most of the family, young and old, most of the time.

3
DAIRYMAN

From his earliest years until his retirement, the dairy industry formed a constant backdrop to Bert Baker's life. He would have been helping his father with the cows in East Dulwich almost as soon as he could walk. When he left the family business, it was for a job as a chemist with a dairy company. After an enforced break for service in the Great War, the study and analysis of milk quality would occupy the rest of his working life. And during that span of years, from the late 1880s to the early 1950s, almost everything about the production and distribution of milk, including its very content, would undergo a series of profound changes.

The industry in which Bert's father George found himself in the mid-1880s, whether by choice or chance, was already in a state of flux. All aspects of life and work were being turned upside down by the effects of the Industrial Revolution and subsequent advances in scientific discovery. When George Baker opened his doors at 75 Pellatt Road, there were still plenty of people who could remember buying their milk from milkmaids, tripping around the public parks with a shoulder yoke bearing two heavy pails. By the time he closed them in the late 1920s, the business had been refrigerated, pasteurised, sterilised and homogenised, and was under the control of a handful of very large dairies operating across the whole country. And by then, the job of his eldest son was to ensure that the milk on sale to the public was of a quality and purity undreamed of half a century earlier.

George Baker's dairy was itself an indicator of the changing nature of milk consumption and distribution. Domestic dairymen like him now appearing on the High Street were soon as common as greengrocers or bakers. They were the tangible symbols of changing habits in changing urban and suburban landscapes.

Anyone who wanted to make a living selling milk had a fundamental problem: it was highly perishable, and went off quickly. If it was to arrive at its destination in a drinkable state, it could be transported only a short distance. The time and the physical distance between production and consumption had to be as short as possible.

One simple consequence of this was that practically all the milk produced in England went into the making of butter or cheese. Relatively few people drank it on a daily basis. It was very far from being the cheap staple we know today. Before the imaginative genius of the Victorians started to get to grips with the problem, very little milk travelled from the countryside to the cities in liquid form, because it went sour long before it arrived.

This had been less of an issue for the urban dweller at a time when cities were still quite small. London, which was several times larger than any other metropolis, still had a population of less than a million in the early 1800s. The milk had only a short journey to travel from the grasslands on the outskirts of town, fields rented by cowkeepers for grazing their herds. These pastures were not far from the city centre, in districts that have long since disappeared under concrete – places like Edgware, Islington and Paddington. There were about 8,500 cows in pastures around London at the start of the 1800s.

One of the biggest of the dairy farms that ringed London was at East Dulwich. Friern Manor Farm acquired a reputation as a beacon of good agricultural practice through its methods of recycling liquid manure, spreading it directly across the farm's 200 acres of arable and grassland. The resultant yields were seen as remarkable, so much so that the farm was the subject of an admiring feature in the *Illustrated London News* in 1853. The magazine reported that there were 186 cows on the farm, milked twice daily by a team of 14 milkers, at 1.30am in the morning and again at 10.30am. Each cycle took more than three hours, with the milk ready to be transported into London for early morning and mid-afternoon deliveries.

Friern Manor was regarded as a model farm in 1853. But within 20 years it was gone, swallowed up by the urban spread. It was divided up into 200 lots and sold to the British Land Company for development. The cowkeepers were being pushed further and further outwards, or disappearing altogether. Yet as supply diminished, there was ever-increasing demand from the expanding metropolis. The new railways were beginning to bring milk into the central London termini, but they could not meet that demand fully, and had still to solve the problem of transporting it any appreciable distance before it went off.

In an academic paper on London's milk supply in the second half of the 19th century, David Taylor attempted to put some numbers on all of this. He drew on contemporary research, while cautioning that there was little hard evidence to go on. He suggested that the highly-fed cattle of the London cowhouses might each produce as much as 750 gallons of milk per year. Londoners were not consuming much milk in the middle of the century – only nine gallons a year, barely a glassful a day. But with a population of three million, that still added up to around 27 million gallons a year. Taylor concluded that London cows could not possibly meet this demand, and that – imperfect though it was – several million gallons of milk must have been coming in by rail even at this early stage.

Although there might still be some larger herds on the outskirts of town, these urban cowkeepers with perhaps a dozen cows, located on the High Street and serving a hyperlocal market, began to meet more and more of the domestic demand. The loss of grassland meant that the cows now lived in an urban environment, and barely left their stalls. They were usually cooped up in filthy and overcrowded sheds within the communities they served. The cowkeepers acquired a well-deserved reputation for keeping their beasts in insanitary and dirty conditions and adulterating the milk itself by watering it down.

Several observers railed against the disgusting conditions and corrupt practices that characterised the dairy trade of the mid-19th century. 'None of the cowhouses are properly constructed or ventilated,' wrote William Harley, a Glasgow cowkeeper who was regarded as a shining exception to the usual rule. 'Nor are the cattle kept so clean as they ought to be.'

Another observer wrote of 'the miseries which cows endure in London, and the evils which result to the community in consequence'. He went on: 'All who dwell near a cowkeeper know the abominable smell which proceeds from his sheds and pollutes the atmosphere, besides the unnatural gloom, confined space and want of drainage.'

Writing in 1850, a Dr Rugg agreed, and was one of the first to understand the nature of the consequent threat to public health: 'The cowhouses are pest houses of the most abominable nature. The stench arising from the filth, muck and manure contained therein is almost insufferable. Two large cows are allowed only 6ft in width. What is the result but disease of the lungs, consumption – there is scarcely a drop of milk in London without a trace of tuberculosis.'

Dr Rugg could not understand why the cowkeepers did not take more care of the creatures that provided their livelihood: 'It really is astonishing that the cowkeepers do not see that the cause of their losing so many cows by disease is from these close, filthy, unventilated, damp, badly-drained and ill-constructed sheds.'

The cows were fed mainly on brewers' grains – the fermented by-products of the brewing industry. Beer was the economic basis of many a cowkeeping enterprise. A London cow might consume as much as nine tons of brewer's grains every year. The connection between brewing and milk production was so strong that many breweries established their own herds.

Another contemporary commentator believed that an excess of brewers' grains in the diet might be good for yield but not for quality – and was also mindful of the implications for human health. 'Although it may improve the quantity, it cannot improve the quality of the milk. When we consider what an important part milk is of the food of young children, it will seem to be a matter of great importance.'

To modern sensibilities, the idea of cows kept permanently enclosed in this sort of squalor is a horrific one. But this was a different age. Cows were not being singled out for cruel treatment. Life was in its own way every bit as fragile, unpleasant and perilous for everyone, including humans. Medicine was in its infancy. Tuberculosis was widespread and killed thousands. Infant mortality rates were high, and poorer children who did survive found themselves employed in dangerous manual labour from an early age. The physical abuse of servants and apprentices was commonplace, and minor crimes were punished by transportation or death. In this altogether more vicious age, the maltreatment of urban cows did not stand out as particularly barbaric.

Even so, many wondered about the nutritional properties of milk produced in such conditions. Adulteration simply made matters worse. Estimates about the amount of water added to milk – which is 85 per cent water to begin with – ranged from 25 to 50 per cent. William Harley said he knew of only one cowkeeper that sold unadulterated milk in locked pitchers. The rest could not resist the temptation to resort to 'the cow with the iron tail' – the water pump. And pump water was often full of impurities as well.

It wasn't just water that was mixed in with the milk. In an effort to add body and flavour, all sorts of ingredients were thrown in: flour, starch, chalk, the water from boiled carrots, even the brains of animals. The food colouring annato was often added to the naturally white milk to give it a yellow tinge. Yellow milk was thought to be richer.

The dishonesty of the cowkeepers was common knowledge. 'Few ever make the effort to be honest,' according to another contemporary account. 'No dairyman in London sold cream except in measures of 25 per cent short.' Street hawkers bought skim milk at a farthing a pint, watered it down and sold it for twice as much.

But the growing city needed to be supplied somehow, and by the mid-19th century there were an estimated 24,000 cows in London, even if their milk was produced in conditions of filth, and was of a highly dubious quality. It was a disaster waiting to happen, and the disaster duly came in the mid-1860s in the form of a plague known as rinderpest. Cattle went down with it in their thousands, and 80 per cent of the bovine population was slaughtered in an attempt to get on top of it. Unsurprisingly, it was attributed to poor hygiene and the filthy conditions in which so many cows were kept. This was only partly true. Rinderpest was a virus; its spread was more likely to have been the result of overcrowding than a lack of cleanliness, although the two went hand in hand.

It was a wake-up call. Foot and mouth disease, rinderpest and pleuro-pneumonia would remain endemic in London cowsheds for another 50 years, but now the Victorian instinct for control and regulation came into play. The sanitary reformers who began to emerge identified a direct connection between the conditions in which the capital's food was produced and the effect on public health. It was not surprising that the business of urban milk production, disease-ridden, filthy and noxious, should rapidly attract their attention.

Among the early reformers was John Simon, Medical Officer of Health in the City of London. Ten years before the outbreak of rinderpest, he had introduced by-laws regulating various aspects of cowshed design: minimum space for the animals, drainage, water supply, ventilation, lighting, and provision for the removal of dung. A system of licensing followed soon afterwards.

Baseline standards were codified further by the Metropolitan Board of Works in 1879. The Board's regulations listed 22 specific requirements for the construction and cleansing of cowsheds and dairies. They stipulated a breathing space of 800 cubic feet in most sheds, 600 if there was good ventilation. The cowkeepers complained that these were unreasonably restrictive and would increase their costs to the point that the business would become unviable. This is what happened to some of them, and it might have happened to more had the regulations been enforced strictly. New sheds might conform, but old ones that did not were often tolerated. In 1894, fully 15 years after the start of centralised control, and about the time George Baker was dipping his toe in the market, the average cubic space per cow in London was reckoned to be only around 625 cubic feet.

George Baker was a product of the evolutionary change that had helped the urban herd recover over the two decades after rinderpest, and maintain the potential profitability of the trade. Rather than sell their milk to a larger dealer, the cowkeepers became producer-retailers, selling it themselves at the point at which it had been produced, or distributing it door-to-door through the development of milk rounds. The small-scale, localised urban and suburban dairy was born. The sale of milk could be profitable because production costs fell more than prices. Even in the early 20th century, three quarters of the retail outlets for dairy products in London were single-shop enterprises. There were 500–600 cowkeepers in London in the 1880s, by now selling as much milk as they had in the years before rinderpest. They began to call themselves dairymen, and diversified into making butter and cheese if space allowed. The kings of this new way of working were the Welsh, arriving in London in large numbers after fleeing agricultural depression at home, and keeping labour costs down by sending home for more members of the family once a foothold had been established. All George Baker's children helped in the business as soon as they were old enough.

We have no record to suggest what George Baker's dairy was like, but enough is known about the trade during this important period of its development for it to be possible to make some educated guesses. The property he moved into at 75 Pellatt Road was in many ways ideal for his purposes. It was only a few paces from Lordship Lane, the main shopping street of East Dulwich. It was a substantial building, enabling him to set up a cowshed and retail outlet on the ground floor, while still having enough living space for his growing family on the floors above. There was access to the street on Landcroft Road, for the prams or carts that would take the milk out on its delivery rounds.

The idea of a High Street shop selling milk or anything else is one that is familiar enough to us. Less easy to imagine is that the producers of the milk – the cows – were actually kept on the premises. Cows are noisy and smelly animals, and milking would be done in the early hours in order to be ready for the morning delivery round. It is hard to see a modern urban dweller tolerating the idea of being woken before dawn each day to the sounds and smells of a functioning dairy farm.

It was tolerated 150 years ago because the co-existence of people and animals was commonplace in any urban environment, and had been from time immemorial. The food chain was a short one – in the early 1800s, 30,000 sheep were driven through the streets of London each week on their way to and from Smithfield Market. The technical advances of the Industrial Revolution had not meant that machines had suddenly replaced animals. Horses were no longer required to walk in endless circles to power grindstones; but they were in huge demand as draught animals, hauling carts all over London and beyond. Few could afford a horse as a means of personal transport – they usually walked. But the demands of the coal, beer and construction industries in particular meant that there were more horses in London after the Industrial Revolution than there had been before.

It wasn't just on the streets that people had direct contact with animals. Those who could afford it kept a pig and a few hens in their back yards, or even in the house. In the middle 1800s, pigs outnumbered people in London by three to one. Animals played a key role in the economy, and no inhabitant of London could walk more than a few yards without coming into contact with their physical presence, or the noise and smells – or excreta – that accompanied them. Even in the new suburbs like East Dulwich, with their aspirations to middle-class gentility, there was nothing remarkable about a cow house on a residential street. There were at least ten of them within a short range of 75 Pellatt Road. They had become, simply, a feature of late 19th century urban life.

This was the commercial environment in which George Baker set up shop in Pellatt Road in the 1890s. Cowhouses, or dairies as they were now more generally known, had cleaned up their act significantly as the result of three decades of regulation and oversight since the rinderpest outbreak. But conditions were by no means universally good, and the cows still lived out most of their lactating lives without ever moving beyond the doors of the dairy. They might occasionally be taken out to stretch their legs, since many developed stiff joints and problems with their feet as the result of this static and restricted regime. But even in a model establishment, it must have been a miserable existence. Once they could no longer produce milk, the cows would be sold for meat and replaced.

We do not know how many animals George Baker might have kept in his new dairy. But, like David Taylor, we can make some rough calculations. The manager of one of London's largest milk contractors told Charles Booth's researchers in 1895: 'A small dairyman who works the business with his wife and one boy must sell 30 Imperial gallons a day to make a living.' This exactly described George Baker's situation at that time. A daily output of 30 gallons works out at around 11,000 gallons a year. Taylor's conclusion that an urban cow might produce 750 gallons of milk a year, would suggest that our typical dairyman would need to have about 15 cows in production if his business was to be viable. We can deduce from this that these dairies would need a lot of space to house their cows if they were to satisfy the new regulations – hence the preference for corner properties with larger yards. We can also understand more easily why so many smaller cowkeepers went out of business when they found themselves unable to comply with the new sanitary stipulations.

The footprint of a typical cowhouse might include the following: a shippon, the area in which the cows were kept and milked; a space for storing their food; a midden, where the muck was kept prior to collection; a dairy, for making butter – though probably not cheese, which required much more storage space; a cellar for keeping produce cool; a shop for selling directly across the counter; storage space for the delivery carts, known as perambulators, or 'prams'.

The shippon would have consisted of a series of stalls, 6 to 7 feet wide and about the same length, divided by partitions, each housing two cows. The animals would be tethered on either side, leaving space for the milker to operate between them. At the back end there would be a channel to collect waste. Food and water would be at the head end, possibly accessed by a passageway.

In terms of labour, hands were required to milk the animals twice a day.

It would probably take two experienced milkers the best part of a couple of hours to milk a herd of 15 to 20 cows. Then there was the constant battle to muck out and dispose of the solid and liquid waste produced by the animals. A single cow might produce nine tons of manure every year. Young Bert would doubtless have been expected to help with both milking and mucking out from an early age.

A number of roundsmen would be employed to make the doorstep deliveries, although some milk was sold over the counter in china urns, and some would be made into hand-pressed pats of butter. In 1880 it was estimated that a roundsman with a pram could sell as much as 30 gallons of milk a day.

Usually, it was a man doing the milking and delivering. The women of the household would make and sell the butter and cream and any other products, and collect the eggs produced by hens if they had them. The women were also in charge of cleanliness and hygiene. It was an important role: in many areas the shippons were subject to their own regime of inspection and licensing, and had to be ready for examination at any time. That meant keeping them clean, ventilated, drained and supplied with water. The walls had to be limewashed annually.

Each day all floors were supposed to be washed, all work surfaces scrubbed, all utensils and vessels involved in milk production scalded with boiling water. Any space that was used for the preparation, storage or sale of dairy products could not be used as living space, or even be directly connected to living quarters.

It was a hard life, and there were no days off. Milking began in the early hours, typically around 5.00am, so that the milk could be loaded on to the delivery prams in time for every home in London to have a delivery by around 8.00am each morning. A second milking took place in the early afternoon, and a second delivery began at about 4.30pm. This was sometimes called 'the pudding round' as cooks and housewives emerged to buy supplies for the evening meal. Some dairies did a third delivery. The roundsmen carried two large churns on their prams, and dispensed the milk directly into the customers' own jugs using a measuring ladle or 'dipper' for any quantity between a gill (a quarter of a pint) and a quart (two pints).

Dealing with the muck produced by the cows was a never-ending and unpleasant task. A herd of 20 cows might produce a staggering five tons of manure every single week, more than 1,000 tons annually. By the 1860s, London's cows were producing a quarter of a million tons every year. The smell must have been all-pervasive: you would never be far from evidence of a cow. However, the muck sold for a few shillings a ton, and provided a profitable sideline for the dairyman. It was gathered in the midden ready for collection by the muck merchant. From there it went to outlying farms or market gardeners who used it as a fertiliser.

It all sounds like a well-ordered system, free from the corruption and abuse of half a century earlier. Needless to say, the picture was by no means as rosy as that. Charles Booth's indefatigable researchers, working in 1895, found that in many places old habits were dying very hard – and the purity of the milk being produced still left a great deal to be desired.

As well as studying the social make-up of late Victorian London, Booth's men also carried out a detailed examination of its commercial side, interviewing scores of businessmen and shopkeepers across the capital. Questionnaires were sent out to try to collate statistics about the state of each trade, the numbers it was employing and the wages it was paying. Booth's team sent out questionnaires to 33 small London dairies in May 1895.

Grocers and the bakers, who were among those also canvassed in this way, sent back a huge volume of information, which would be invaluable to anyone researching those trades in this period. The dairymen, sadly, were nothing like as assiduous in responding. Barely half a dozen did so, and those from dairies of such different size and scale as to make meaningful conclusions difficult to draw. But they did offer some pointers, and there were probably just about enough returns for us to make some valid observations.

The urban dairies that returned questionnaires employed between them 179 people. Of these, three-quarters earned between 20 and 25 shillings a week, and 90 per cent earned below 30 shillings. That is the equivalent of £100–£150 today. Most had an allowance of milk, and roundsmen could earn commission from bringing in new custom. Competition was unrelenting. The trade was so saturated in some areas that there might be four or five dairies operating a round in the same street.

Wages for some comparable trades such as confectionery and baking were higher. But in the grocery business, more than half of those in the survey earned less than 10 shillings a week. Women earned significantly less than men, and wages were lower still for 'boys' or 'lads'. This might have been a function of the differing nature of the work for men and women, or it might have been an early example of the arbitrary wage gap between the sexes. Cream Dairy Limited of Faringdon Street, for example, employed five men at between 24 and 30 shillings, six women and girls at between 13 and 16 shillings, and ten lads on wages of between 6 shillings and 14 shillings. This latter range probably reflected the different ages of the boys, but the numbers also suggest that the dairy was heavily dependent on child labour in all aspects of the business.

The researchers also conducted face-to-face interviews with the some of the smaller businesses, about the size of George Baker's, and with the bosses of some of the big wholesale dairies that were now beginning to eat into the trade of the local dairymen. One of Booth's men made a visit to the East End. 'I visited about half-a-dozen cowkeepers,' he reported. 'In each shed there were 10–20 cows. No doubt they were kept as clean as possible, but both to the eye and nose they were certainly offensive.'

Life for the deliveryman was not easy. Mr J.A. Hattersley of the Aylesbury Dairy Company told Booth's team: 'we try as hard as possible to let each man have one day off in a month.' Another milk seller reported that 'in the small dairies where no extra hands are kept, a man may often do two or three rounds a day for years on end without a break. He can only get a holiday by paying someone else to do his work, and the Master usually objects to this.'

Mr S.J. Pocock, of Freeth and Pocock in South Lambeth Road, the largest wholesale milk contractors in London, painted a slightly rosier picture. 'Wages plus commission would give a wage of 25–35 shillings a week and good tips. Many of them save money and start for themselves in the retail trade.' Perhaps, this is exactly what George Baker had been doing throughout the 1880s.

Mr Pocock also explained how urban producers were increasingly under pressure because of the volume of milk now arriving from outside London by rail. The problems of keeping it fresh during the journey had been solved, partially at least: 'Twenty years ago, there were probably three times as many cowsheds in London as there are now. At that time the country milk service was not properly organised, and it was very difficult to get the milk from the country in good condition. That is now reversed. The milk trains run regularly and punctually and owing to the milk coolers the milk arrives in good conditions.' The milk cooler, Pocock explained, was an appliance that trickled the milk over a surface under which water was running, and which reduced it from a temperature of 90 degrees to about 60.

This was a big change. For the first time, consumers were beginning to find unregulated country milk sweeter and fresher than that produced locally. Mr Pocock attributed this to the failure of the small urban cowkeepers to instal milk coolers themselves, and the conditions in which their animals were kept. Even in 1895, 40 years after rinderpest and the resultant drive for hygiene and sanitation, some London dairies were still not being run in such a way as to produce good milk. 'Cowsheds are always filthy places and the cattle get no fresh air, they are unnaturally fed on prepared foods, cabbages etc,' Mr Pocock was reported as saying. 'In fact the conditions under which they live are such as to make it impossible that they can give good milk.' He concluded by telling his interviewer: 'I would not drink a glass of milk out of a London cow if I were paid for it.'

That these old problems persisted was borne out by the testimony given to the researchers by Mr H. Tuck, an inspector for the London County Council also interviewed in 1895. 'Many of the small dairies are not at all what they should be,' the interviewer recorded him as stating. 'The floors are often covered with dirt and the utensils are seldom properly cleaned. The large businesses keep a special staff for cleaning, but in the small businesses this is not done. The master and the men have to do the cleaning where they can, with the result that the utensils, even if kept decently clean, are seldom scalded at all.'

Mr Tuck also made it clear that the other old problem, of adulteration, had not been abolished either. 'The amount of adulteration in small dairies and among milk hawkers is very great,' he said. 'It is an exceedingly common practice even in good dairies to colour the milk with annatto to produce a yellow colour. The natural colour of milk from cows of nearly all breeds is white, but Alderneys, Guernseys and some Norfolk cows give milk with a slightly yellow tinge. This milk is certainly richer, and the public knowing that yellow milk is the richest often refuse to buy white milk with the result that it has to be coloured for them.'

The opinion was now taking root that the reason milk was very often impure was less the result of the state of the cowsheds, and more to do with the actual content of the product itself. Victorian science began strenuously applying itself to the examination of milk. The emerging field of nutrition had identified it as a health drink, and safe and pure milk was increasingly seen as vital to a good diet. Public health officials were pushing for its consumption as a food staple, especially for children, because the calcium and phosphorous it contained were essential to healthy bone growth. One of the local farms that supplied milk to some of the retailers of Dulwich was Potash Farm, run by John Woodhams. By 1886, Woodhams was advertising his wares in the *Sydenham, Forest Hill and Penge Gazette* under the heading: 'Have you delicate children or invalids?' His ad went on to trumpet the benefits of fresh milk, with the claim: 'Specially Recommended by the Medical Faculty.' But as the medical faculty were all too well aware, milk was also highly prone to infection by pathogenic bacteria, and more likely to cause disease than any other food staple.

Efforts were intensified to keep milk drinkable for longer and stop it from spoiling. This was achieved by the addition of chemicals and other additives designed to slow down the process of souring. It appeared to work, and was in popular use from the 1870s. But it actually made the underlying problem worse. The preservatives kept the milk useable for longer, but they did not kill the harmful bacteria present in most of it. As a result, people drank contaminated milk in the mistaken belief that it was healthier.

It was some time before it was established just how effective milk could be as a vector of bacteria, and in particular the bacteria that caused one of Victorian Britain's greatest killers: tuberculosis. Milk was the perfect vehicle for transmitting infectious diseases and viruses to humans. Everything about the way it was produced, kept and distributed offered opportunities for contamination. It was a silent assassin. As Hannah Velten wrote in *Milk: a Global History*: 'Milk was definitely "the white poison"on many levels: it was produced from poor cows, in dirty dairies, diluted, adulterated, made toxic with preservatives and transported and stored without regard for cleanliness or coolness.'

Just how much bacteria loved milk, and the public health dangers associated with that relationship, had been suspected for some years. The pioneering chemist Louis Pasteur established in the 1860s that milk could be transmitting not only tuberculosis, but also typhoid fever, scarlet fever, diphtheria and septic sore throats. Connections were made between milk consumption in infants and the still high levels of childhood disease and morbidity, although the very young faced a wide range of other health hazards as well. It was now accepted that the main danger presented by milk was disease in the cow that produced it. As late as 1895, only a year after George Baker had opened his doors in Pellatt Road, a Royal Commission stated categorically that tuberculous milk contributed to the spread of tuberculosis in humans.

The difficulty facing science and public health bodies was now laid bare. On the one hand, the nutritional benefits of milk for growing children were well established. Milk contained fat, carbohydrate and protein and important vitamins; it was rich in mineral salts. The problem was how to ensure that children and others could continue to benefit from the high nutritional value of milk without becoming ill; or, to put it another way, how to eradicate the risk of disease without affecting the nutritional quality. This dilemma would not be resolved finally for many more decades.

A new test that could identify whether tuberculosis was present in the cow served only to demonstrate just how big the problem was: testing in the United States between 1906 and 1910 found tuberculosis bacteria in eight per cent of urban milk. The same was true in the UK. A bacteriological examination of 50 samples of milk arriving at St Pancras station in London in 1899 found that only one third of them could be classified as 'normal' in content – in other words, free of disease. One in ten samples contained bovine tuberculosis. Others were contaminated with excess leucocytes, showing that the cow had been fighting an infection.

The scientific analysis of milk was developing fast, and would have huge implications for the later career of young Bert Baker as he helped milk and muck out his father's cows in East Dulwich. The key work built on the foundations laid by Louis Pasteur, and would eventually result in the process that bears his name – pasteurisation.

Pasteur had discovered that microbes in beer and wine could be eliminated by a process of heating and then cooling. In 1886, the German chemist Franz von Soxhlet proposed applying the same principle to milk. After experimentation, this led to the High Temperature Short Time method that is still the basis of today's pasteurisation. It required the rapid heating of a flow of milk to a temperature of 161 °F/72 °C for 15 seconds, followed by rapid cooling.

Some argued that the process would affect the nutritional value of the milk. Dairy farmers objected on the grounds of cost and said the scientists, not being farmers themselves, didn't know what they were talking about. Take-up was painfully slow. The Americans moved more quickly than the British, to the extent that most milk on sale in Britain at the time of the Great War would have been considered unfit for human consumption if put on sale in New York City.

Because of the time it took for pasteurisation to take hold, the effects of all this scientific enterprise on the small urban dairies was limited. Eventually the big dairy chains would swallow them up, but for now they carried on pretty much as before. Standards of cleanliness and sanitation were more strictly enforced, but otherwise it was business as usual. A collection of advertisements appearing in Camberwell in 1916 included almost a dozen placed by small local dairies, most emphasising the purity and freshness of locally-produced milk. One, Thomas Marshall, thought it worth underlining this with the further reassurance: 'Cows kept on the premises at Camberwell Grove'. It would be a while yet before the residents of suburban streets no longer shared them with live cattle.

George Baker was not among those advertising his wares in 1916. We know very little about his business, but we can draw some inferences from the few bald facts at our disposal. The dairy at Pellatt Road was established in the mid-1890s, by which time regulation was well developed, and more steadily enforced.

George ran the dairy for 35 years before his retirement in 1928, managing to keep it viable through the Great War and in spite of the increasing dominance of large-scale commercial dairies, which by then were producing the bulk of London's milk. Their prices undercut those of the independent dairymen, but there was still a niche, albeit an ever-narrowing one, for localised businesses.

The family photograph of George and Emma and their six children, taken in the early 1900s, seems to suggest that the business provided them with a reasonable standard of living – assuming the clothes in which they were posing were their own, and had not been provided for them by the photographer. They looked prosperous enough. George and Emma – now both about 50 – were beginning to succumb to a comfortable middle-age spread. When George came to retire, he had enough money to buy a piece of land on the south coast and build a house on it. All this suggests that the dairy was well-run and relatively profitable, and the Baker family were respectable members of the local community. But whatever profits the dairy yielded were certainly fully earned. George himself described his success, such as it was, as the result of many years of careful living and hard work.

Not many years after the family portrait was taken, seismic changes took place within the Baker family. The 1911 Census showed four of the six children still living with their parents at 75 Pellatt Road, all of them – and Emma too – described as 'assisting in the business'. It was very much a family concern. Lily was not at home on Census Day, but this may have been a temporary absence: she would not leave home until her marriage in 1916. Ernie was abroad. All seemed calm enough.

But Bert was about to drop a bombshell. He had worked for his father in the dairy for more than 20 years, from almost the time he could walk. As the oldest, he was probably the one George leaned on most heavily, and the one expected to take over the business at some point in the future. But Bert had other ideas: he announced that he was leaving the dairy, leaving home, and leaving London.

We have already seen the way that Bert, whose education would have been basic, was keen to better himself by taking advantage of evening classes. He clearly had a scientific bent, and did well enough to gain some sort of qualification in chemistry. It was this that provided the possibility of advancement. With his lifelong experience of the dairy industry, he was ideally placed to take advantage of the emerging need for chemists able to use the new science around milk to analyse samples and ensure quality control. It was not an opportunity he was about to let pass. Perhaps he had actively chosen to study chemistry, being aware that with all that was happening in the dairy industry, a qualification in this field would offer the best means of advancing himself.

At some time after the spring of 1911 and no later than the end of 1913, Bert Baker landed a job as a chemical analyst with the dairy firm of F.W. Gilbert of Derby. This was a massive lifestyle change and career shift for a young man who had spent the first 25 years of his life working in his father's dairy in a London suburb, and – as far as we know – seldom venturing more than a few miles from its doors. The move represented a much bigger step into the unknown than would be the case today. Derby was 150 miles from East Dulwich, but it would have felt almost like another country. Most people still lived and died within a very short distance of the place they were born. Even if excited by the prospect, he was making a big leap, and must have been apprehensive about what lay ahead.

He had no connections in Derbyshire, and no particular reason to go there, so the move from Dulwich to Derby contains an element of mystery. It may be that he answered a number of job advertisements in the trade press, and that the application to F.W. Gilbert was the one that came up trumps. It could also be that he made a personal connection with Frank Gilbert, the founder of the company, at the London Dairy Show.

The show had been staged in Islington, north London, in every year since 1876. It was one of several such trade shows established by different branches of the food industry at about that time, partly in response to complaints that products were of generally suspect quality and frequently adulterated. By the early 1900s, the Dairy Show had become a major shop window for all aspects of the dairy trade, its awards carrying considerable prestige.

Frank Gilbert had established Burnaston Dairy at 248 Uttoxeter New Road, Derby, in 1907, and was soon competing regularly at the London Dairy Show. The letterhead on his company notepaper trumpeted that he had won a Silver Medal for his cream. It is possible, probable even, that Bert Baker and his father would sometimes make the trip across London to visit the show and catch up with the latest practices and techniques of the dairy business. It was a big event, attended by thousands: but it might also be possible that Frank Gilbert and Bert Baker somehow came into contact with each other at one of the shows, and that Gilbert was sufficiently impressed by the background and energy of the young man to offer him a job. This might seem fanciful, although in some ways it feels like the most plausible explanation for such a fundamental watershed in Bert's life.

How the news went down at home is something else about which we can only wonder. It must have been a heavy blow for George to lose his right-hand man from the business at a time when his thoughts might have been turning towards an easier life. Was he disappointed and resentful at the disloyalty of his firstborn? Or did he see something of his own earlier self in Bert, a young man keen to get out into the world and better himself? Bert was leaving a much more secure and comfortable family hearth in East Dulwich than George had done in Kirdford 30-odd years earlier. But he was bright and outgoing: could his parents blame him for aiming for something higher than a life spent mucking out cows in a suburban street?

Again, the evidence on which we might draw to answer these questions is frustratingly scant. Bert's wartime diaries referred to brief visits to East Dulwich during the odd day's leave, but he never mentioned either his mother or father by name. His parents did not attend his wedding; but it was arranged at a few days' notice during a period of leave from the Western Front, and took place in Derby, so there might be no significance in that – although his sister Winnie was there as a bridesmaid. Bert took his family on holidays to Bosham on the south coast once his father had retired there in the late 1920s, which might suggest that if there was a coolness, it had been smoothed over by then.

Frank Gilbert's family had been in the milk trade for 40 years or more. As well as that Silver Medal at the London Dairy Show, his company notepaper boasted 'Sixteen Highest Honours for Dairy Produce. Genuine New Milk of Guaranteed Purity delivered twice daily. Fresh Butter, New Laid Eggs, Cream, Cream Cheese, Dressed Poultry and all kinds of Dairy Produce.' It was an environment in which Bert would have felt at home, albeit that the diary was clearly set up on a much larger scale than his father's. As chief chemical analyst, it would be his job to make sure that the claim for 'Genuine New Milk of Guaranteed Purity' was no idle boast.

Although we do not know when he made his momentous move to Derbyshire, it is clear that Bert Baker had established himself as a valued member of staff at Gilbert's by the time war came in September 1914, at which time he immediately joined the army. The company thought enough of him to pay him a small pension during the war, to lay on a special dinner for him when he came home on leave in 1918, and to promise to keep a job open for him until it was over. This last pledge was honoured, even though by the time he was demobilised the company had been taken over. All this suggests that he must have been working there at least a year by the time war came, and to have been regarded as a valuable employee.

In his few pages of memoirs, Bert's son John described his father's job at Gilbert's as 'looking after their milk supplies and the cheese-making activities at their various factories.' He added: 'F.W. Gilbert was a dairy company with a retail dairy in Derby, and cheese factories at Weston, Ecton and Hartington. Frank Gilbert owned two large herds of pedigree British Friesian cattle at Chellaston and Weston, and was one of the foremost breeders in the country. He exhibited at all the well-known shows including the Royal Show and County Shows all over Britain.' Chellaston, the home of one of the herds, was then a village of about 800 people on the outskirts of Derby. It was there, in summer of 1914, that Bert met the woman who would become his wife.

Miriam Potter was 26 when her family moved to Chellaston in the spring of 1914. She was the youngest of five children of John Holland Potter and his wife Leah – four girls and a boy. She had been brought up first in Spondon outside Derby, and then in Rolleston-on-Dove, near Burton-on-Trent. In the early 1900s the family had moved some 20 miles to a farm in the village of Heather in Leicestershire.

John Potter was a farmer and well-known breeder of shire horses. He bred Harold, one of the best-known and most celebrated of all shires, named Champion of England for ten successive years. John Potter had already decided to retire from the farm when he died suddenly in early 1914. His widow went ahead with their retirement plans. In March 1914, Leah and her adult children moved to Chellaston, and a house called Oaklands.

Chellaston was five miles from Burnaston Dairy, but when Bert returned to his job after the war, he gave the address of his workplace as 69 Derby Road,

Chellaston. It would appear that as well as keeping a herd at Chellaston, Gilbert's maintained a satellite operation there, perhaps one dedicated to laboratory work analysing samples. The Derby Road address was barely half a mile from Oaklands, Miriam's new home. Bert's lodgings, assuming he was based at Derby Road in 1914, might have been closer still. The two of them would have had plenty of opportunities to be thrown together, which is what happened very soon after the Potters took up residence in Chellaston.

It must have been quite the romance, because they had known each other only a matter of weeks when Bert left for the army, and their meetings after that were restricted to brief days together when he was on leave. They wrote to each other very frequently, however, and were sufficiently sure of each other to marry before the war ended.

Bert had good reason to be pleased with his prospects when the outbreak of war changed everything, for him and for everyone else. By his own efforts he had gained a qualification and used it to secure a good job higher up the social scale, a job he was bound to consider more convivial than the rigours of life as a dairyman. His professional prospects were good. And he had fallen in love.

In the absence of any written evidence, what can we say about Bert in the autumn of 1914, at this watershed moment in his life? He was 29 years old. Photographs show a young man of medium height with sandy hair. We know he had a winning smile – two of the letters he received from old comrades in the years after the war remarked on it as something they particularly remembered about him. Like his father at the same age, he was a young man with ambition and imagination, who wanted to make something of himself and was prepared to put in whatever effort was necessary to succeed. He had had the courage and resourcefulness to take a big leap into the unknown by uprooting himself from everything that was secure and familiar to him and moving to the Midlands. Although his schooling had been sketchy, he could express himself well and his Tablet is written in a neat and pleasing hand. As we will see when he began to record his wartime experiences, he had a positive outlook on life, and was prepared to embrace its possibilities and throw himself into its challenges. He was to demonstrate qualities of courage, resilience and leadership, but there was no hint of swagger about him. There was no pressure to enlist when he signed on for the army in the autumn of 1914 – the war was only a few days old. But he did not hesitate. He may have looked on it as his patriotic duty – but also as something exciting and full of possibility. Many others entered the fray with the same enthusiasm, but understandably struggled to maintain it during the horrors that would unfold over the next four years. Bert Baker, to judge by the fragments of writing he chose to leave behind, never seems to have lost his basic optimism and positive attitude. It would be severely tested in the conflict to come; but it would serve him well in the challenges that lay ahead.

4
CHARLES AND WILLIE

The tank she was a monster, designed for strength not speed
Her form was fierce and terrible, as even Huns agreed
If only all that might and power
Could move, say, twenty miles an hour
A swift avenging avalanche on whirling wheeling treads!
And some they chewed their pencil ends, but most they shook their heads.
(Anon)

Bert Baker's military career would always be bound up with his exploits in the tanks. But when the newly-enlisted Private Albert George Baker made his way to Surrey to join his regiment in September 1914, no such machine of war even existed. Its distant relative, a tractor mounted on caterpillar tracks, was pulling heavy ploughs across fields on the very few farms that could afford to own one. The idea of a mobile fortress that could roam the battlefield as freely as a warship on the waves existed only in the minds of science fiction writers and fantasists. Private Baker and his friends would suffer many route marches, and dig many holes across southern England, and the war in France would have long since subsided into a grim impasse, before practical notions of such a beast began to surface. When they did, there would be months of fitful development before the first of those leviathans was ready to be thrown onto the killing fields of the Somme. During that time, Baker completed his military training, was twice promoted, learned how to fire a machine-gun, and survived a three-month tour of the trenches on the Western Front.

This part of our story, then, has a dual narrative: Baker's early service as an infantryman – we will refer to him as Baker rather than Bert in a military context – and the development of the tank. They will unfold in parallel until they come together in the early part of 1916. By then, the tanks were enough of a reality for it to become necessary to recruit the men who would take them into battle. And by then, the newly-commissioned Second Lieutenant Baker offered the ideal profile to be one of those entrusted with the task.

Baker

The Royal Fusiliers, also known as the City of London Regiment, raised no fewer than 47 battalions for service in the First World War. Bert Baker was placed in the 21st (Service) Battalion on its formation in September 1914, and made his way to billets in Ashtead, near Leatherhead. In one of the earliest entries in the Tablet, the notepad into which he later transferred extracts from his wartime diaries and letters, he reported being issued with a uniform, given vaccinations that left him with a sore arm for three weeks, and notified that his pay would be seven shillings a week. Most of these early days were spent in and around Ashstead, either marching or digging. There were many references to digging parties, none of them containing any hint of what it was that was being dug. But this whole area became a sprawling training ground for the army, so it is not difficult to imagine the sort of work involved in creating the camps in which the men would live.

The physical demands would not have come easily to those who had so recently been in soft work on Civvy Street. They also had to become used to the frequent organisational foul-ups. New Year's Day 1915 was spent digging at Woldingham, near Caterham. '3 hours in rain on platform waiting for train, owing to a mistake,' said one of the early entries in the Tablet.

Perhaps the most gruelling of these exercises was a ceremonial event, blown off course by the weather. On 22 January 1915, Baker was one of more than 20,000 members of the so-called New Army to gather on Epsom Downs. They were to be inspected by the Secretary of State for War, Lord Kitchener, accompanied by the French War Minister.

The soldiers were on parade in the dark by 5.00am and set off without breakfast to a rendezvous already under almost a foot of snow. It started snowing again at six o'clock and did not let up. Kitchener was not due to arrive until 11.00am. The troops were told to keep moving, or to mark time to stave off the bitter cold. But by mid-morning, some of them were passing out. A Lieutenant Hamilton wrote in his diary: 'Just as Kitchener arrived, I fainted. Dash nuisance!' He was one of several taken to hospital, one of whom later died.

Kitchener and his French counterpart spent only a few minutes reviewing the troops before deciding the weather was too bad for a full inspection. Since the intention of the day was to impress the French, this might have been a blessing in disguise: few of the thousands of men on parade were carrying any weapons. They could muster only about 100 drill and practice rifles between them, all of which were prominently displayed in the front row. This may have been in Kitchener's mind as he suggested curtailing the inspection at the end of a rapid walk along the foremost rank. After several hours standing in the freezing cold, Baker and his fellows could be forgiven for being unimpressed. 'K looked very fat and big,' was his verdict on Britain's greatest warrior.

At about this time a machine-gun section was being set up within the Fusiliers, and Baker was one of 16 men chosen to be a part of it. It was the first fateful step on a road that would lead him to the command of a tank in battle two and a half years later. His earliest view of the Maxim guns then in service was at Caterham in mid-January, at a demonstration by the Royal Naval Air Service. '4ft long on a tripod,' he noted. 'Fired live cartridges at 500 rounds per minute.' The first day the group was involved in actual fieldwork with a gun did not go well for Baker: he tripped and twisted his ankle in a rabbit hole. The injury was not bad enough to stop him spending the following weekend in London, where he saw his brother Len, who was preparing to leave for France. But when he got back, the ankle kept him away from full duties for another ten days or so. Soon after that he had to take to his bed for 48 hours after a reaction to a vaccination. He recovered in time to go home to Derby for a weekend's leave. The midnight train from Derby back to London on the Sunday evening was packed with soldiers. He had only 15 minutes to get from Euston to Waterloo to catch his next train. He made it with seconds to spare after sharing a taxi with seven others.

After that it was back to the soldiering – more digging at Woldingham, one of the many temporary camps that had sprung up in the area. In March there was a 16-mile route march. By now he had been issued with a rifle. He suffered only small blisters on the march, though reported that several men fainted with exhaustion on their return to Ashstead. He also noted that he had sent Miriam a brooch made from a button of his greatcoat.

Swinton

Who was the father of the tank? The question was actually the subject of an official investigation after the war, a judicial inquiry conducted by the Royal Commission on Awards to Inventors. Among those giving evidence was Winston Churchill, not himself a claimant but certainly one of the first to have seen and supported the potential of the weapon. The Commission's verdict was clear: the main credit for the invention of the tank lay with the two men who had actually designed and built the first machines. It awarded them £15,000 each. But it made a handful of smaller awards too, to those who had brought the project to the drawing board and had some claim to paternity. Like all such enterprises, the tank was the product of many hands, sometimes working together, sometimes in complete ignorance of the parallel efforts of others.

The author H.G. Wells was not credited as an inventor – a conclusion with which he indignantly took issue. His claim was built on his 1903 science fiction short story *The Land Ironclads*. The narrative had been set in a future war, in which armoured vehicles roamed the battlefield on tracks and jousted with each other in combat. But no direct line can be drawn between this tale and the real ironclads that emerged in 1916. Indeed, some historians trace the lineage of the tank back to Roman chariots and medieval knights in armour. But there were more obvious and very recent forbears of the machine that began to emerge through 1915. Most of them had their derivation in the increasing mechanisation of the farming industry. In 1902, Bramah Joseph Diplock – one of the many unlikely names that pepper this story – invented something he called the Pedrail, essentially a box mounted on tracks. In the United States, Benjamin Holt was also experimenting with linked tracks, and cannily trademarked the name 'caterpillar'. Richard Hornsby was doing similar work in England, but could not find financial backing and sold his patent to the enterprising Holt. All of them were aiming to develop a machine that could traverse and plough broken ground. All would seek to achieve it by dispersing the weight of the machine over the largest possible footprint, using a track rather than a wheel. There was nothing very organised happening, and no military interest whatsoever. An Australian with another unfeasible name, Lancelot de Mole, had sent the War Office a plan for something that looked much like a tank in 1912. It had gone straight on to the shelf marked 'crackpot schemes'.

Any account of the birth of the tanks cannot but give a prominent place to Ernest Dunlop Swinton. He might not have been the first, or the only, person to spot the possibilities of tracked vehicles, then mostly used in agriculture; but with his first-hand experience of conditions on the Western Front in 1914, he was quick to understand how such vehicles might be adapted for the battlefield. He had high-level contacts that enabled him to push the idea forward, though not without resistance. And he was the first to try to set down in writing some tactical analysis of the strengths and drawbacks of the new weapon, and how it might be used most effectively. It was not his fault that no one in the War Office or in the field took much notice of this document, and came to the same conclusions only in the light of bitter and costly experience.

Swinton was a military thinker. He had served in the Boer War as a captain, and become an expert in railway construction, while also taking a keen interest in military tactics, fortifications and the development of new weaponry. He had been official British historian of the Russo-Japanese War of 1904–5, where the machine-gun had for the first time been an influential weapon. When war broke out in 1914, he was sent to France by the War Minister, Lord Kitchener, who had known him slightly in South Africa, to act as an official war correspondent. Newspaper reporters were banned from the front, and had to rely on dry despatches stitched together by a cabinet committee. This only encouraged Fleet Street's finest to produce a succession of lurid unofficial stories that appalled Kitchener. The appointment of an official war reporter was his response. Although he was a government employee and his reports were censored, Swinton was the only journalist allowed on the Western Front, and his despatches – filed under the byline 'Eyewitness' – represented the only first-hand reporting available to the British press.

In this role, Swinton roamed the battlefield in late 1914, and watched as a campaign of movement rapidly subsided into one of defensive attrition – what soon came to be known as trench warfare. The line of fortified trenches would eventually stretch 400 miles from the English Channel to Switzerland. In this new form of combat, the advantage almost always lay with the defenders. As a result, the conflict rapidly descended into a stalemate from which it would not fully emerge for another four years.

One day in October 1914, Swinton was driving from the British base at St Omer to Calais on his way back to London. On the journey he ruminated on the state of deadlock and played with some embryonic ideas about how it could be broken. There suddenly flashed into his mind the memory of a letter he had received in July from a South African mining engineer, Hugh Marriott. The two had met during the Boer War and remained in contact, Marriott occasionally passing on news of technical developments that might have military applications. Marriott's letter had told Swinton of a machine he had seen demonstrated in Antwerp before the war, the Holt Caterpillar Tractor – built, as we have seen, in the United States. Its primary agricultural use was to drag a heavy plough through marshy soil. But it had shown a striking capacity to cross difficult ground, including narrow ditches and large holes.

Swinton had passed the letter on, and thought little more about it at the time. Neither did anyone else. But on the road to Calais, he recalled it with a start. 'It was as if a ray of light had struck a sensitised plate,' he said in his autobiographical book about the tanks, also called *Eyewitness*.

'Since I had been at the front, all the information I had gathered had seemed to me consistently to bear out the fact that apart from his artillery, the main strength of the enemy resistance lay in his skilful combination of machine-guns and wire. Throughout this time, I had been racking my brains to discover an antidote; and within the last two weeks my vague idea of an armoured vehicle had definitely crystallised in the form of a power-driven, bullet-proof, armed engine capable of destroying machine-guns, crossing country and trenches, of breaking through entanglements and of climbing earthworks. The idea flashed across my brain – the American Caterpillar Tractor at Antwerp!... The key to the problem lay in the caterpillar track!'

An excited Swinton wasted no time in repairing to see his old boss at the Committee of Imperial Defence, Maurice Hankey. As secretary of the Chief of the Imperial General Staff (CIGS), an influential body in controlling the conduct of the war, Hankey had access to everyone and acted with the authority of the Prime Minister, Herbert Asquith. Swinton found in Hankey a willing listener and later described their discussions as, 'the sowing of the first seed – the first constructive step in the conception and evolution of what came to be known as the Tank'.

Swinton had to return to France before getting the chance to put the idea before the War Minister, Lord Kitchener, who in Swinton's view was at that time 'the greatest driving force in the country'. But once back in St Omer, he planted a second seed by seeking out the army's Engineer-in-Chief. Here, his pitch fell on stony ground. He was not surprised. Swinton's view – widely shared – was that the military had an inbuilt bias against new ideas, especially if they came from the lower ranks. To the men at the top, such presumption had the whiff of subordination about it, and might perhaps come to be a threat to their own positions.

Kitchener vetoed the idea when it was duly put in front of him. But Swinton kept plugging away at Hankey, who was by now Secretary of the War Council. In the last week of 1914, Hankey sent a memo to the Council, setting out the bones of the idea. One of its recipients was the First Lord of the Admiralty, Winston Churchill.

This was exactly the kind of scheme to fire the imagination and enthusiasm of the First Lord, whose reputation was yet to be tarnished by the disaster of Gallipoli. With his customary impetuous energy, he immediately fired off a letter to Asquith, urging that the idea be taken up and lamenting that several months had already been lost.

'It would be quite easy in a short time to fit up a number of steam tractors with small armoured shelters, in which men and machine-guns could be placed, which would be bullet proof,' Churchill wrote:

> Used at night they would not be affected by artillery fire to any extent.

> The caterpillar system would enable trenches to be crossed quite easily, and the weight of the machine would destroy all wire entanglements. Forty or 50 of these engines, prepared secretly and brought into positions at nightfall, could advance quite certainly into the enemy's trenches, smashing away all the obstructions and sweeping the trenches with their machine-gun fire and with grenades thrown out of the top. They would then make so many *points d'appui* for the British supporting infantry to rush forward and rally on them. They can then move forward to attack the second line of trenches. The cost would be small. If the experiment did not answer, what harm, would be done? An obvious measure of prudence would have been to have started something like this two months ago. It should certainly be done now.

With these words, Churchill articulated exactly the idea that had come to Swinton on the road to Calais. Unbeknown to Swinton, the First Lord did not wait for a response from Asquith, but acted on his own initiative. He set up a technical committee on landships, as the prototypes were inevitably named by the Admiralty. He signed off an order for the building of experimental pedrails and wheeled landships. He also sent a three-man fact-finding team to France to report on requirements. They were cold-shouldered by the army, and returned empty-handed, a further sign in Swinton's mind of the superior attitudes and tunnel vision of the commanders. The pedrail was soon abandoned as impractical. Work concentrated on the caterpillar option, although without much headway being made.

Baker

In March 1915, Baker's company was in huts at Woodcote near Epsom, which offered more in the way of protection from the weather, if a good deal less in the way of privacy. There were 54 men to a hut, each hut with two sergeants, a corporal and two lance corporals. He had become a lance corporal, and as such was excused the more menial tasks. 'My stripe gets me off swabbing huts, fetching food from cookhouse (¼ mile away) etc.' There was no escaping brigade inspections though. 'Fearful lot of scrubbing and polishing – 30 buckles, all free from dust and shining bright, also boots, rifles etc had to be super.' In between times, he managed to get to East Dulwich for the day to see his family, and also to top the platoon ratings in rapid firing tests, as well as being in the first five as a marksman. The Tablet entries show Baker to have had a strong competitive streak, which made him ambitious both for himself and for the company as a whole. He was one of 23 men picked out for a potential command in the Sherwood Foresters (the 'Notts and Derbys') but did not make the final selection.

As always, there was constant speculation as to where they would be going next, and when. The camps were always full of rumours, almost all of them without substance. At the end of March, Baker said they expected to hear something soon, and the options he listed underlined the dearth of hard information: 'To be told in one week what is to happen to us – Egypt, France, England – or N Pole?'

What fate actually had in store for the Battalion was a gruelling four-day march, beginning at the village of Rusper in West Sussex – not many miles from Kirdford, where his parents had grown up. There were 1,100 men in the battalion, and the officers let it be known – no doubt with some relish – that they expected half of them to drop out before they finished the course. It was not an inviting prospect.

Baker's description of this exercise was the most detailed and lengthy entry in the Tablet, and appears to have been copied from a letter he sent to Miriam telling her about it. He was obviously pleased, and with good reason, with the way he came through the ordeal – especially as it got off to a difficult start for him: he was on sentry duty the night before it began.

> I was in sentry – 7pm, 1 hour on, 2 hrs off, two at a time (standing in a field) until 6 am. Some cold stew to eat at 10 o'clock. They had a difficulty in finding us. Raining on and off – till 12 o'clock, then fine and beastly cold. No packs or kit to be removed for lying down between duties. Just got close together for warmth – most miserable night.
>
> Back to camp at 6.30 and on parade at 7.00 to march to Ockham. Bread and meat for breakfast (in a few minutes) no time for a wash even, and some vile coffee. Then 25 miles over hilly country. The other companies had had a warm billet and food for the night and got boots and packs off to sleep. By 2 o'clock we reached Shere – sent you a PC. An ambulance followed and picked up the men falling out, took them to nearest station and train to camp. They started to fall out after ten miles. Tom Forman fell out at Gomershall (blisters and strained tendons).
>
> 1½ hours at Shere – everyone's boots came off to attend to blisters. You never saw such feet as some had! I was all right, although tender, and went round the village foraging for food.
>
> We had 9 miles to do to Ockham. Never felt so done up in my life. 40 or 50 must have dropped out after Shere. We marched into Ockham Court – the seat of Countess Lovelace (a friend of the Colonel's). We were drawn up to attention in front of the house and fellows fell out left and right. I was busy with the brandy flask going round the section to revive them. Dr gave them sal volatile. In the meantime the Coy had marched off to their billet in a farm (1½ miles away!).
>
> I had to get a gamekeeper to show me the way with my crocks, we were lost. We had tea on the farm and just lay down where we were – you never saw such blisters! Like eggs. Those who had none, (including self) were so tender footed that it was agony to stand. We put our feet in cold water troughs and slept with heads on packs on the stone floor of the barn. Feet so hot that couldn't sleep for a bit.
>
> Parade at 5 am, breakfast and marched to Woodcote (12 miles) arrived 11.30 am. After the usual 5 mins halt per hour no one could stand

upright for 500 yards!

70 miles in 4 days, night duty and food chronic. New food kitchens in use for first time. Cooks didn't understand them.

Feet nearly normal next day.

In spite of the dire predictions of the officers, only 80 of more than 1,000 men fell out over the course of the exercise. 'Very good,' Baker noted approvingly.

After this, the training seems to have become more focused on battlefield conditions, with exercises involving mock attacks and defences. The machine-gun training continued, too. Baker called this 'a soft time' but it did not last long. Soon they were off to a different part of the country entirely.

The land occupied by Clipstone Camp, north of Mansfield in Nottinghamshire, had been offered for military use by the Duke of Portland, and rapidly developed into an extensive training camp that, at its peak, could accommodate 30,000 men. Baker and his comrades in the Royal Fusiliers were the first to occupy it. Though noting with satisfaction that his new base was only 26 miles from Miriam in Derby, Baker also reported the inevitable teething troubles: 'May 11. Left Woodcote 3am arr Clipstone 2pm. First in camp. Very little food, no beds and raining hard – all wet through – kit bags also. Huts smaller than Woodcote, not so good. No lighting or roads made in camp.'

His spirits never seemed to be dampened for long though, and a fortnight later there was something to celebrate – promotion to full corporal. A field day with the Notts Yeomanry was described as 'good fun', although they got very hot waiting to be inspected by General Henry Lawson, head of Northern Command, who did not endear himself to them by arriving half an hour late. Another VIP, the Inspector General of Infantry, watched a practice attack on the moors, also on a very hot day.

News filtered in from the outside world. His brother Len, serving in the East Surrey Regiment, was now in the trenches in France, and would soon be in action, during which he survived a German gas attack. And although Baker's former work as a chemist must now have felt as though it had happened in another life, there was news on that front, too. A number of big dairy firms, including F.W. Gilbert of Derby, had amalgamated to form United Dairies. Frank Gilbert was on the board of the new company. Baker was probably giving little or no thought to a post-war career, but the news would have been a little unsettling nonetheless. Gilbert's clearly felt a strong duty of care to their man though, and paid him a small weekly allowance while he was serving. It was a generous gesture which he much appreciated.

With his sergeant away on a gunnery course in July, Baker was in sole charge of the machine-gunners. He took the section out on exercises and did well. Ever ambitious, he also applied unsuccessfully for a commission in the Northumberland Fusiliers.

Swinton

In London, politics had taken a hand. In May 1915, Asquith was forced to take his Liberal party into coalition with the Conservatives. Part of the price demanded by the Tories for their cooperation was the removal of Churchill from the Admiralty. Memories of his defection from the Conservatives to the Liberals a decade earlier clearly still rankled. Churchill was, and would remain, one of the most steadfast and tenacious supporters of the tanks. But now, though still in government, he was no longer in a position to give substance to that support. In the meantime, without Swinton's knowledge, the War Office had received – and failed to act upon – recommendations that it set up a special technical committee to explore the possibilities for the new machines. It had, however, organised a trial involving a loaded Holt Tractor and an obstacle course. The exercise had been a failure. The official report sounded the death knell for the project: 'no modification of the engine would make it possible for these obstacles to be crossed. Any use of the caterpillar for the attack of trenches seems to be out of the question.' The project was as mired as the armies in France.

Swinton's stubborn belief in the possibilities of the landships would not permit him to give up the cause. On 1 June, he was formally relieved of his role as official war correspondent, as a Press Bureau had now been established to accredit journalists from the national newspapers. On the same day, he played what he described as his last card, submitting a lengthy memorandum setting out how he thought the landships could and should be developed.

He argued that along the miles of trenches, it was the machine-gun that was the biggest obstacle to a successful attack on the German lines. He formally proposed the construction of an 'Armoured Machine Gun Destroyer', capable of travelling at 4mph and crossing ditches of up to 4 feet without climbing. The machines would be built in secrecy, surprise being a critical feature of their deployment. He suggested an attack formed of 50 Destroyers, spaced at distances of 100 yards over a three-mile front. Advancing at dawn on the German lines, they would crush the wire and the machine-gun emplacements, drawing fire and allowing the infantry to follow up. While they were doing so, the Destroyers would turn right and left and rake the next line of German defences, a practice known as enfilading. He also described how the Destroyers might be used in a defensive capacity as a weapon of counter-attack.

The paper was a summary of Swinton's thinking. In his view it could have been written at any time over the previous six months, and his purpose in submitting it now was to try to galvanise someone into doing something before the idea was forever consigned to oblivion. The document was sent to the Army's chief engineer, General Henry Fowke, for his assessment. Fowke thought the idea implausible, raised a series of objections, and concluded with the words, 'before considering this proposal we should descend from the realms of imagination to solid facts'. Fowke died in 1936, so he had 20 years to rue a sarcastic response that was to put him on the wrong side of history.

Swinton, now back in France wrapping up his Eyewitness commitments, noted wryly that his idea had by now failed to find favour with the War Minister, the Director of Fortifications and the chief adviser in military engineering. Undeterred, within a week he had put together another paper addressing the objections raised, with reference to feasibility, speed, steering and weight.

This time, his efforts were to bear fruit. His proposals found their way on to the desk of Sir John French, Commander-in-Chief of the British Army in France. French read them, and sent them on to the War Office with a covering letter demonstrating that he had quickly grasped the potential of the destroyers in a way that others, by accident or design, had failed to do. 'There appears to be considerable tactical value in this proposal,' his letter ran. 'It adapts the peculiar qualifications of the caterpillar mode of traction to the transport of a species of armoured turret across cultivated and uneven ground, especially in connexion with the trench warfare, which is the feature of the present operations; and particularly if the production of these machines be a surprise to the enemy.'

French requested that a commercial manufacturer be approached in secret to advise if such machines were available, or if not, could be built. He also referred to the experiments he understood to be taking place in the Admiralty, and suggested efforts be pooled.

His days as a war correspondent done, Swinton returned to England to replace Hankey as secretary of the Dardanelles Committee of the Cabinet. It was a post that opened every door to him, and presented the ideal opportunity to discover what, if anything, was happening in response to French's letter. On only his second day in the job, he went to the War Office to find out, and for the first time received hard information to confirm what French had said: that the Admiralty, on Churchill's initiative, had already been experimenting with the idea of landships for some time.

There had been some vague talk of bringing together what little expertise had been gained so far by the separate efforts of the War Office and the Admiralty. French's letter now made it happen. As Swinton said: 'such a communication could not be ignored'. A joint naval and military committee was duly formed. Swinton was advised to go and see its chair, the Director of Naval Construction, who rejoiced in the name of Eustace Henry William Tennyson d'Eyncourt. From there he was referred to the secretary of the new committee, Albert Stern.

Swinton learned from Stern just what the Admiralty had been doing on the landship project. Before leaving his post as First Lord, Churchill had put d'Eyncourt in charge of a technical committee and authorised the spending of £70,000 to finance the pedrail and caterpillar experiments. That Churchill was prepared to spend the navy's money on a weapon for the army was, to Swinton, further evidence of his vision and foresight. Churchill and David Lloyd George, head of the newly-formed Ministry of Munitions, had watched a modest demonstration at the end of June – a week after French had put his weight behind the project. Lloyd George was infected with Churchill's enthusiasm and was to become another staunch supporter of the idea. He was an important ally: by the end of 1916 he would be Prime Minister.

But the formation of the Ministry of Munitions meant that there was now a third party with an interest in the scheme, with roles and responsibilities yet to be defined. Swinton procured from Asquith permission to call an inter-departmental conference to coordinate efforts. For the first time, all three departments sat at the same table. The meeting decided to leave the Admiralty to lead on experimentation and design, based on requirements laid out by the War Office; and when the work was sufficiently advanced, the Ministry of Munitions would take over.

At last, by a mixture of perseverance and networking, Swinton had got the project more or less up and running. It was this work that most supported his claim to fatherhood of the tank. The Royal Commission would award him £1,000 for his efforts. Its only other significant award beyond those to designers was to d'Eyncourt, who received the same sum. After all the rejections, Swinton had sold the vision to the Prime Minister and the Commander-in-Chief, among others. Through his efforts, through the forcefulness of Churchill and the support of Hankey and others – politicians rather than soldiers – he had got the show on the road. Swinton's influence would remain great; but now – arguably several months late – it was time to bring in the technical brains and explore whether the vision could become a practical reality.

Baker

Clipstone Camp was filling up as new battalions arrived – four of them on a single day in late July. But the machine-gunners were heading out. On 4 August they relocated to the Wiltshire village of Perham Down, near the military base at Tidworth and the big training grounds of Salisbury Plain. The move intensified rumours that they would soon be on active service abroad. But where? In early August, Baker recorded: 'rumoured we leave in four weeks for 1) France, 2) India or 3) Dardanelles'. Although none of these things happened, the speculation was doubtless fed by the issue of new boots and clothing, and the news that their Maxims were to be replaced with Lewis guns. Two officers were sent to Hayling Island to learn how to use them, after which they returned to train the rest of the battalion.

In early September 1915 the war was a year old, and Baker was recovering from a 24-hour spell in trenches dug on Salisbury Plain to simulate conditions in France. 'Very uncomfortable, but good experience,' he recorded with his usual upbeat tone. He had just been made a lance sergeant, and as such would stand in for his sergeant in his absence. It was a sign that his potential had been recognised. But the window for possible commissions had gone; they had been told there would be no more until after they travelled.

Everything that happened now seemed to signal that their deployment was coming ever closer. After his brief exposure to the trenches, Baker had a few days of what he described as 'final leave', and when the troops were addressed by General Sir Arthur Paget, commander of the Salisbury Plain training area, he told them they would be going very shortly. For the first time, there was confirmation of their destination. As they had suspected, it was to be France. Baker wrote that

Paget had told them, 'our Div, the 33rd, was one of the best in the 4th Army, and would be one of the first to go'. He spent that weekend in London with his friend and fellow Fusilier Ted Loxley, and went to East Dulwich to say goodbye to the family.

The pace now began to pick up. The following week there was a two-day exercise, and in the absence of his officer and sergeant, Baker was in charge of a party of 33 men, and seven mule carts. 'Looking forward to it very much,' he wrote the night before – further evidence that for him, at least, the first year of the war had been a largely interesting and enjoyable experience. The scale of the slaughter in France and elsewhere had yet to register fully at home, and for tens of thousands of those who had volunteered 12 months earlier, personal experience of the horrors of life in the trenches still lay ahead. The mood was still enthusiastic. For many, the war had opened doors that would have remained firmly closed to them in peacetime. That might be as basic as the provision of warm clothing, regular food and a roof over their heads – even if that roof was often made of canvas. For others the war meant excitement, variety, opportunity, comradeship, travel, a regular wage, the learning of new skills and disciplines and the prospect of heroic action. For these men, disillusion and despair had yet to set in. If they thought of death at all, they would have imagined a glorious end for themselves, falling with their faces to the foe. The war was still a huge adventure, and they looked forward eagerly to playing a part in it. Baker wrote: 'We are all very excited and keen to get a move on.'

One of the features of army life Baker appeared to enjoy most was the fellowship of men of his own age, and the friendships and good-natured banter that went with it. Long hours helping in the dairy, and evenings spent studying chemistry, would probably have limited such opportunities back home in East Dulwich. The same might have applied to chances to meet the opposite sex. Once released from those shackles when he took up his post in Derby, it was not long before Baker had acquired a serious girlfriend in Miriam. It is evident from his writings that he was a sociable and gregarious person. He clearly revelled in army life, was tolerant and relaxed about its privations and determined to make the most of the chances the war had presented to him. In all the pages of his notes that survive, there is barely a word of complaint. The reference to the vileness of the coffee on an exercise is about as critical as it gets.

Another thing he acquired at some point along his military journey was a new name. All the soldiers gave each other nicknames, and for some reason, he became universally known among his fellow infantrymen as 'Charles'. The name was to stick with him throughout the war, and friends writing to him years later would always address him as 'my dear Charles'. It did not catch on at home, where he was always known as Bert.

Nicknames have all sorts of origins, but are often conferred on people who share the same surname as famous figures of the time, say in entertainment or sport. There is one potential candidate for the nickname of Charles, a man who was active in both those fields. Charles Shaw Baker was a well-known player in the golden age of county cricket in the early years of the 20th century. He was on Warwickshire's books for 15 years, and scored more than 9,000 runs for them. A left-handed middle-order batsman, he was a member of the Warwickshire team that had unexpectedly won the County Championship in 1911. He somehow combined this with a career on the stage at the music halls, accompanying such stars as Marie Lloyd with a sketch act. It might be stretching fancy too much to suggest that a follower of Warwickshire cricket or an aficionado of the music hall was among Bert Baker's fellows in the Royal Fusiliers; that he christened him Charles, and the nickname stuck. Perhaps. It is pleasant to think so. Charles Shaw Baker became a cartoonist for the *Daily Express* and died in Cornwall in 1976, at the age of 93.

Back at the camp, 'Charles' Baker's stewardship of men and mules on the exercise went well, although the weather was very wet. 'The Col complimented me on my positions covering the company flank,' the diary noted. Two days later there was a 23-mile route march with full packs. This time it was very muggy. A week later came a big divisional operation involving 25,000 troops and artillery – 'everything roped in'. By now it was cold and frosty and they had to walk about during the night to keep warm. Daylight brought more rain for the attack exercise. They would certainly be prepared for whatever the French weather could throw at them.

Once dried off and back at base, Baker and a couple of the others organised a company dinner to celebrate the anniversary of their formation at Ashstead 12 months earlier, though it must have felt very much longer. 'Rather rough and ready, but very enjoyable. Major Stanley presided and he got very drunk.'

More rifle and machine-gun training on the Lewis guns. More divisional training, including a big exercise supported with aeroplanes. Baker was kicked on the thigh by a horse, but suffered only stiffness. More signs of their imminent departure: 'all sorts of new equipment being served out – new greatcoats and floppy hats, new boots etc.'

A further instruction afforded them hours of harmless amusement: 'All heads have to be shaved. Having mine done by degrees. Already feels draughty.' He takes a more brutal approach with others: 'I borrowed some clippers and shaved half the heads of the MG Section. I loved doing it. Caused no end of fun. We laughed at each other for hours. Cowleshaw's hair was the longest in the Section and we took every bit off – he looked a scream.'

When he was not scalping his men, he was lecturing the machine-gun reserve on the use of the Lewis gun and using up what remained of the practice ammunition on the range. 'Had a good time loosing off thousands of rounds.' It is difficult not to conclude that Lance Sergeant Albert Baker was having the time of his life.

Swinton

Sir John French had recommended that a commercial manufacturer be brought in to advise on the possibilities for the landships. But such manufacturers were few and far between. In fact, only one company was at that time making caterpillar-tracked vehicles on a commercial basis. So it was that the relatively obscure firm of William Foster and Co of Lincoln suddenly found itself at the heart of a top-secret military project, commissioned to build the first prototype landship. In Lincoln we find the tank's true fathers – William Tritton, the chairman of Foster's, who would become the production engineer; and Walter Wilson, an engineer, inventor and naval officer assigned to work with him. Wilson had designed aeroplanes and cars, and was an expert on gearings. The Royal Commission on Awards to Inventors named Tritton and Wilson as co-creators of what would become the tank. Every First World War tank was built to their designs. Poles apart in temperament and background, they made a formidable combination, rapidly turning a basic concept into a functioning machine.

By September 1915, Tritton and Wilson had a working model to demonstrate at Lincoln. Officially known as the Number One Lincoln Machine, it was soon nicknamed, 'Little Willie'. It was almost literally a tank – a huge rectangular box placed on top of caterpillar tracks. The tracks represented one of the early fruits of the collaboration between Tritton and Wilson. Swiftly realising that the imported American tracks were not up to the task, they had produced a design of their own within a matter of days. Swinton was there for the demonstration, with d'Eyncourt and other members of his committee. Little Willie performed disappointingly. But the trip was not fruitless. After the trial, Tritton and Wilson took Swinton across to an outbuilding to show him something else they had been working on. Inside was a full-size model of a completely different design – one that would potentially overcome the deficiencies of Little Willie. This, inevitably, was 'Big Willie'.

It was Wilson who had made the imaginative design leap necessary to move the project forward. Little Willie was essentially a big box on tracks. The most striking feature of Big Willie, then officially called His Majesty's Land Ship (HMLS) *Centipede*, was its rhomboidal, or lozenge-like shape. It looked a little like a flattened diamond, with the tracks running on rollers round the whole outer structure of the hull on either side, rather than being beneath it. This would prevent it becoming top-heavy and would lift the nose for climbing. It would be able to climb 5 feet vertically, and because of its length, would be able to span gaps of up to 9 feet.

When they took him into the shed to see the model, Swinton must have felt as though he had entered Aladdin's Cave. It was almost literally a dream come true. He was elated. 'I felt that I saw in front of me – though only in wood – the actual embodiment of my ideas and the fulfilment of my specification. Dinner on the train on the return journey to London was a joyous occasion.'

A fortnight later, HMLS *Centipede* was brought down by lorry to Wembley Park, the experimental station of the Trench Warfare Department, to be displayed to a wider audience. It was decided to proceed with the construction of a prototype. One issue to be settled was what armaments to use and how to locate them within the new shape. The first was decided by what happened to be available. The navy offered 100 spare Hotchkiss 57mm quick-firing (QF) 6-pounder (pdr) guns, with barrels 7½ feet long and a maximum range of 7,500 yards. These guns would be heavy enough to knock out enemy machine-guns, one of *Centipede*'s principal functions. A naval solution was also applied to the question of where they should be placed. A gun turret on top of the vehicle would raise its centre of gravity too high, and its position above the engine would make conditions intolerable for the gunners. Instead, each gun would be mounted in a swivelling unit called a sponson, one on either side of the machine. The landships would also be equipped with machine-guns of their own.

No further progress could be made until the first fully-operational *Centipede* was available for inspection and trials. The workshops at William Foster had many weeks of toil in front of them before that would be possible. In the meantime, Swinton turned his mind to some of the practical issues that would arise if the project was a success. In yet another document, he addressed the question of who would pay for the mass manufacture of the machines. The Ministry of Munitions seemed the obvious place. Although the War Office had not borne any of the costs of the experiments to date, the landships would become part of the army.

Men would have to be found to operate them. As Swinton made clear in this latest paper, these would not be just any men. 'It will necessitate the enlistment and special training of special officers and men of technical qualifications, each of whom will have to perform the duties of a mechanic, an expert motor driver and a QF [Quick Firing gun] and machine gunner. It will be no easy matter to obtain men of this class.'

Swinton's paper went before another inter-departmental meeting on Christmas Eve 1915, which again brought together all the parties with an interest in the project. The Admiralty confirmed its offer of 100 6pdr guns and suggested ending its involvement as soon as the experimental machine had been completed. Most importantly, authority was given to the War Office to place an initial order for 50 machines if the trials should prove a success; and to raise a force of 75 officers and 750 other ranks to man them.

The meeting also charged Swinton with coming up with a name for the new weapon of war. The reasoning was that if surprise was to be a key feature of its impact, names like 'landships', 'land cruisers' and 'armoured machine gun destroyers' were likely to give the game away. Swinton sat down that Christmas Eve night with his colleague Walter Dally Jones to write up the minutes of the meeting. They threw some names around, still thinking perhaps of the original design of Little Willie, the box on tracks. The ideas the two men came up with suggest that neither could have looked forward to a post-war career in advertising. 'Container' was soon rejected. So was 'receptacle'. 'Reservoir' had appeal, thankfully only briefly. The same went for 'cistern'. In the end, they settled on 'tank', rightly thinking a monosyllable more likely to catch on. Their report that night was the first to refer to the tanks by the name with which the world would soon be familiar.

More than a year of war had passed, with months of almost imaginably high losses on the Western Front. In a war of artillery bombardments, the killing was scarcely less heavy on the German side. The German machine-guns had done particularly cruel business against British infantry assaults. Yet the army had been almost as reluctant to recognise the potency of the machine-gun as they were to encourage the tanks.

In the meantime, there were changes at the top. Sir John French resigned as Commander-in-Chief and was replaced by Douglas Haig. Haig soon heard about the tank project, and sent Hugh Elles, a member of his staff at General Headquarters (GHQ), to poke his nose into a few offices in London and brief him on progress.

Baker

On 6 November, at the end of another day on the range and an instruction session for the reserves, Baker and his comrades heard the news for which they had been waiting from pretty much the moment they enlisted: a Battalion Order notified them that they would leave for France on 13 November – Friday 13th. A frantic final week of preparation began at once, broken only by a parade for review by Queen Mary, for which the whole division turned out on Salisbury Plain. 'A fine spectacle and a glorious day,' Baker wrote. 'Left at 7am returned at 3pm. Nothing to eat, which wasn't so glorious. Queen was in a car and drove along each line.'

The same day, they handed in their bedding, and would sleep fully-clothed on boards for the last few nights before they sailed. The machine-gun and transport sections went a day later than the others, on the 14th. 'Night before, everyone on the rush to get things absolutely right for the morning. Our kit with rifle weighs 70lbs in all. We have to march 1½ miles to Ludgershall station. Train leaves at 6 o'clock.'

The entries of the next few days show that as with most operations of this scale, not everything went according to plan, and that the quality a soldier often needed above all others was patient stoicism:

> Nov 14 Left camp at 5am. Docks at 9am. All day in a shed – no smoking, no moving, filed up gangway at 4pm. Goodbye England!
>
> Nov 15 8pm Still in Southampton Water near Lee-on-Solent. All private food eaten 24 hours ago, only bully and biscuits to eat. We keep making tea to soften the biscuits which are exactly like dog biscuits.
>
> Nov 16 pm Still anchored off Lee-on-Solent. Sending letter by tugs that come alongside now and again. Service without books this am.
>
> Nov 17 Still at Lee.
>
> Nov 18 Back at Southampton.

The gunners finally set foot on French soil nearly a week after setting off from Ludgershall. Now followed another 23 hours of travelling by train in order to meet up with the rest of the battalion, about 15 miles from the frontline. 'In horse boxes (30 men). Very, very cold. Bully and biscuits. Snowing all the time. Marched 7 miles – good sleeping quarters in barn on dry straw. Lillers (8 miles behind front line).'

At the end of this gruelling journey, Albert Baker was about to have his first taste of life in the trenches. Everything had been leading up to this. He would be in France for the next three months. Understandably, but very frustratingly for anyone wanting to know what this experience was like for him, this is the period during which Tablet entries are fewest, and carry least detail. He recorded his movements from place to place, but little of how his days were passed, what action he saw and how he responded. We have enough other accounts of what life was like in the trenches to be able to imagine some of it. But each soldier had his own story. We will not speculate about Albert Baker's, nor the many reasons he might have decided not to share more, and will report only those details that he left behind in the Tablet.

> Nov 26 We have all had two spells in the trenches, 24 hours and 48 hours, and in the meantime have been shelled up and down the line. First time in trenches – tuition. Short spell. Casualties 3k 3w for Battn.
>
> Dec 5 In trenches taking over part of line alone. 2 days in, 2 days in reserve (dugouts) with ½ mile trench, mud and water. Festubert. 10 days.
>
> Dec 14 Out of line.
>
> Dec 25 Village billets for 2 days. Then to Béthune.
>
> MG Xmas Dinner – 14. Menu enclosed. Also Xmas card from Colonel's wife. BTHMGX
>
> Jan 16 In trenches 12 days – 4 to go.
>
> Jan 21 In trenches – out tomorrow with eggs at Estaminet in A. Move back to Bethune in a few days.
>
> Jan 26 Out for 4 days (23–27) of front line in reserve trenches. 27th is Kaiser's birthday and expect a good strafe when we get back tomorrow night.
>
> Feb 16 Sent as instructor to Bde in G School but can't stick it more than 3 or 4 weeks. Bn 5/6 miles away. Terrible time in last lot of the trenches, rained all the time.
>
> Feb 2 Bn to reserve tomorrow (4 miles from very large town). Leave possible. Lox and several others managed it last week. Going back for commission! Strong rumour.

We can at least deduce from this spare commentary exactly where he was on Christmas Day. The mysterious reference 'BTHMGX' was part of a code Baker had devised to keep Miriam apprised of his whereabouts without falling foul of the censor. He had explained it to her in a note in November. Each letter related to the one following in the alphabet – so BTHMGX became CUINHY, probably meaning Cuinchy, a village east of Béthune, and close to the frontline between the British forces and the Germans. It had been in British hands since December 1914 and remained so until 1918. During the course of the war it was almost completely reduced to rubble by German artillery. The position of the frontline barely moved during that period. The code, and the references to Béthune, suggest that this is where Baker and his comrades had their first taste of trench warfare from the end of 1915 until around February 1916. Although they were in the frontline of trenches for only short stretches, a combination of German fire and wet weather made for a dismal experience.

Swinton

By late January 1916, HMLS *Centipede*, or Big Willie, was ready to show its paces. At 28 tons it was much larger than the 16-ton Little Willie. Both were transported with great secrecy from Lincoln to Hatfield Park north of London, where an assault course had been prepared across Lord Salisbury's private golf course – with his permission.

A dry run went well, and the official trial was set for 2 February. The viewing party was impressive. Lord Kitchener was there, as was Arthur Balfour, who had succeeded Churchill at the Admiralty. Lloyd George, the Minister of Munitions, and Reginald McKenna, Chancellor of the Exchequer, were in the gathering. So, too, was General Sir William Robertson, Chief of the Imperial General Staff and a number of other senior army officers. Swinton could have been forgiven his nerves. He knew that first impressions were critical.

'It was a striking scene when the signal was given,' Swinton recalled. 'A species of gigantic cubist steel slug slid out of its lair and proceeded to rear its grey bulk over the bright yellow clay of the enemy parapet. Intense was the anxiety of its sponsors. But it went through its performance perfectly. On this occasion it crossed a trench nine feet wide and more than fulfilled the conditions.'

The politicians were hugely enthusiastic. But Kitchener, who had arrived early for a personal demonstration, was notably more sceptical, dismissing the tank as 'a pretty mechanical toy, but without serious military value'. Not without justification, he thought the machines were too slow, and offered too inviting a target to the enemy.

Swinton was disappointed. Kitchener was the man he had most wanted to convince. But the opinions that mattered even more were those of GHQ in France. Haig's emissary, Elles, was there. So was his trusted Deputy Chief of General Staff, General Richard Butler. And Butler for one liked what he saw. In fact, he had only one question: 'how soon can we have them?' A few days later, the demonstration was repeated for the benefit of the King, who also expressed great enthusiasm.

Eustace d'Eyncourt, chair of the original Landships Committee at the Admiralty, summed up the general air of enthusiasm and optimism after the success of the trial. 'The machine was complete in almost every detail and fulfils all the requirements finally given me by the War Office,' he reported to Churchill, who had maintained a keen interest in the tanks even though he was no longer closely involved in their evolution.

> The official tests of trenches etc were nothing to it, and finally we showed them how it could cross a 9ft gap after climbing a 4′ 6″ high perpendicular parapet. Wire entanglements it goes through like a rhinoceros through a field of corn. It carries two 6-pounder guns in sponsons (a *naval* touch) and about 300 rounds; also smaller machine guns, and is proof against machine-gun fire. It can be conveyed by rail (the sponsons and guns take off, making it lighter) and be ready for action very quickly. The King came and was greatly struck by its performance, as was everyone else; in fact they were all astonished.

News was now awaited from France as to whether or not the army were equally smitten with *Centipede* – or 'Mother' as it was now called. While he was waiting, Swinton expanded his paper of three months earlier and produced the first serious study of the way tanks might be employed on the battlefield. Its 15–20 pages were in hindsight, remarkably prescient, even if they were fated to be largely ignored for more than 18 months.

Swinton was at pains to emphasise that the tanks would be at their most effective when used in cooperation with the infantry. They would break through barbed wire and machine-gun defences and allow the foot soldiers to pour through the gaps without suffering the hideous losses that were a feature of any offensive on the Western Front.

'The tanks cannot win battles by themselves,' he wrote. 'They are purely auxiliary to the infantry and are intended to sweep away the obstructions that have hitherto stopped the advance of our infantry beyond the German first line. They are designed for the express purpose of assisting attacking infantry by crossing the defences, breaking the obstacles and of disposing of the machine guns. The tank is primarily a machine gun destroyer which can be employed as an auxiliary to an infantry assault.'

The section of his paper most egregiously ignored in the months to come was that headed 'Limitations to Progress'. After a general overview of the tanks and their capabilities, Swinton was candid about their shortcomings. 'It is certain that rivers or canals of a depth of water much over 1 foot, having a muddy bed, or having banks of over 3 feet in height steeper than a slope of 1/1, cannot be crossed until a crossing with ramps and hard bottom has been prepared. The ordinary small bridges in the hostile zone, even if not destroyed, will not carry these machines.

Woods and closely planted orchards also form an absolute obstacle to their movement. Though the tanks can cross soft soil and muddy ground they will travel better in dry weather.'

There were further warnings under the heading, 'Vulnerability'. The tanks would be destroyed by a direct hit by any kind of howitzer shell. They would probably be put out of action by all except the most glancing hits of high explosive shell fire, or shell fired by any form of high-velocity, small-calibre Quick-Firing gun, of the sort the Germans were believed to have deployed in their defensive positions.

Another note of caution was also destined to be ignored. Swinton emphasised the advantage of surprise, but also stressed that once this card was played, it could not be played again to the same effect. 'It follows therefore that these machines *should not be used in driblets*, but that the fact of their existence should be kept as secret as possible until the whole are ready to be launched, together with the infantry assault, in one great combined operation.' The italics are his.

Although these cautionary points were well made, the tone of the paper as a whole was positive and analytical, looking at every aspect of the way the tanks might be deployed as part of a wider, combined military strategy. It was the first detailed discussion of tank tactics, and its arguments were more than vindicated by subsequent events – even if that vindication was some time in coming. Hugh Elles would later write: 'it is remarkable that one of the first official papers on the tactical use of tanks, written by General Swinton, should have been almost literally translated into action on August 8, 1918.'

On 11 February 1916, word came from France: the army wanted the tanks. Haig had written to the War Office to tell them so. 'The officers who represented me at the trials lead me to the conclusion that these "Tanks" can be usefully employed in offensive operations by the force under my command. It is understood that thirty to forty would be available in May. I recommend this number should be ordered at once... and would be glad to be informed what number might be supplied by the middle of July.'

Swinton thought 40 too few and successfully suggested increasing the figure to 100. Albert Stern had been seconded to the Ministry of Munitions to organise supply, and had already started contacting manufacturers in anticipation of a green light. Foster's were given a contract, but they could not handle the work alone, and another was granted to the Metropolitan Carriage, Wagon and Finance Company of Wednesbury in the West Midlands. Lloyd George, as Minister, signed the paper authorising the construction of the 100 tanks.

Things were moving, and moving quickly. A tank had been designed, built and tested and was about to go into production. As to the question of creating an organisation to man the tanks and take them into battle, however, nothing had been done. Swinton was the obvious person to create the necessary infrastructure. He was given the job of setting up the new Tank Detachment at home. But creating a specialist body of several hundred men from nothing, and finding somewhere to base them, would be no easy task.

Another man with a highly colourful name now enters the story. Christopher

D'Arcy Bloomfield Saltern Baker-Carr was, like Swinton, a veteran of the Boer War, retiring from the army in 1906 to follow a career in farming. When war came in 1914, he and many others like him were desperate to return to the colours. Though only 36, he found all doors closed to him, so he volunteered as a civilian driver in France, transporting senior officers around the front. This provided him with useful contacts and a clear view of the progress of the fighting.

Like Swinton, Baker-Carr had seen the potential of the machine-gun in the Boer War, and its use in the Russo-Japanese War. He saw how vital it could be to the domination of the battlefield, especially as a defensive weapon. A single machine-gun could hold up a battalion, and wreak terrible carnage. The Germans saw this very clearly. The British did not.

Baker-Carr was of an independent cast of thought, with a healthy lack of reverence for established authority, and outright contempt for what he called 'the Military Mind'. He saw the leadership of the British Army as actively resistant to new ideas and change, a group of middle-aged cavalry officers, bluff and inflexible, still fighting the last war or the one before that. They still believed in the bayonet, and were baffled and suspicious about the way the technical age was beginning to transform the face of warfare. The machine-gun was one of the biggest new factors, and the British did not have any of them to speak of. To Baker-Carr's enduring frustration, no one could see it that this was a problem. In fact, what few machine-guns the army had were generally regarded as a nuisance.

'Until the beginning of the Great War, the subject of machine-guns, for some reason, had never been taken seriously in the British Army in spite of the lessons, which might have been learnt from the Russo-Japanese War,' Baker-Carr wrote in his autobiography after the war. 'It is safe to say that the German Army, alone of continental armies, was the one in which the possibilities of the weapon were fully appreciated. I encountered widespread resistance when striving to secure the recognition of the machine-gun as one of the most important weapons of the foot soldier.'

At the start of the war, there were fewer than 400 machine-guns in the entire British Army. Not only did the Germans have many more – around 12,000 – but they had also established a hand-picked and trained elite force to operate them. They would repel many British and French attacks over the next four years, inflicting grievous losses as they did so. Many of the Tommies who went over the top were cut down before they managed to advance more than a few yards into No-Man's-Land. Even as the soldiers fell in their thousands, scythed down by vicious and withering German machine-gun fire, the British were slow to change their attacking strategies, and slower still to develop an effective machine-gun capability of their own.

While still a civilian driver, Baker-Carr was given an unexpected opportunity to advance his arguments during a chance conversation with General Capper, chief engineer of the Third Army. Remembering that Baker-Carr had once been an instructor at the School of Musketry in Hythe, Capper suggested he hand in his driving gloves and train some machine-gunners instead. Baker-Carr suggested that his brief should spread across the whole army, not just Capper's division. He got his authority, and began working on what would become the Machine Gun School.

He soon ran into the sort of resistance with which Swinton was wearily familiar. Even after the School had doubled and then trebled in size and trained tens of thousands of machine-gunners, he still encountered indifference or outright hostility higher up the chain. When he suggested increasing the number of guns per battalion from a niggardly two to a still modest four, he was rebuffed. He was nothing daunted. His success in circumventing official scepticism owed much to the fact that he was not a regular soldier. He took risks and cut corners that would have ended the careers of others.

'It was only later that the High Command, by hard and bitter experience, was forced to realise that no other weapon of itself was capable of completely holding up an attack,' Baker-Carr lamented. 'Artillery barrages might inflict heavy casualties on the attacking forces, but they did not annihilate them in the same way as machine-guns did on a hundred different occasions.' Thousands of British soldiers perished in the face of what Wilfred Owen called 'the stuttering rifle's rapid rattle' before this lesson was learned. In a typical assault on a German trench, half the men in the leading company would be killed by machine-gunners, with three quarters of their officers.

Eventually, pressure in the newspapers and from the frontline began to tell. Baker-Carr got his four guns per battalion and promptly asked for eight. Another rebuff. But now he was working on the idea of a special force, with its own command, and with knowledge of how the guns were most effectively used in battle. He proposed nothing less than the formation of a Machine Gun Corps. Its personnel would be 'selected men, whose training would be complete and uniform and whose employment in battle would not be at the whim of a commanding officer, enthusiastic perhaps but hopelessly inexperienced in the first principles of machine-gun tactics.'

Again, he was met with opposition, but once he had the opportunity to put the idea directly to Lord Kitchener, Secretary of State for War, he was able to win him round. Kitchener decreed that he should have the 40,000 men he wanted, and the Machine Gun Corps came officially into existence in October 1915. It was based at Belton House near Grantham in Lincolnshire.

The new corps quickly merged with the Motor Machine Gun Service (MMGS), founded at the start of the war, when the action was still fluid. Once stalemate descended on the battlefield, the impact of guns mounted on motorcycle sidecars had diminished. The central training base of the MMGS at Bisley in Surrey would become the first home for the tank men. Several officers from the MMGS were recruited by Swinton for his Tank Detachment.

Baker-Carr and Swinton knew each other well, and had much in common. They shared an intense frustration at the closed minds of those in charge of conducting the greatest war in history. Their individual methods of operation were very different. Swinton was an insider, well-connected and skilled in the workings of Whitehall and the military. He worked the system and knew which buttons to press and when. Baker-Carr was a maverick, what we would now call an outlier. He lay outside the establishment and achieved results by circumventing procedure and by risk-taking, understanding to within a millimetre just how far he could push and still get away with it.

Both men had foreseen the defensive power of the machine-gun in future conflicts, and fulminated against the apparent British willingness to tolerate a calamitous level of slaughter rather than accepting the fact. Baker-Carr had fought that battle almost single-handedly as he struggled to set up his Machine Gun School and then bring about the creation of a separate Corps. He was strongly supportive of Swinton, who had embarked on a similar journey with the tanks, again in the face of official resistance. From now on, Baker-Carr would have a substantial involvement in the future of the tanks, first absorbing the early tank recruits into his Machine Gun Corps, later leading a tank brigade in battle.

Swinton trawled widely in his search for recruits. Each tank would have a crew of eight, led by a junior officer. Orders had been placed for 100 machines. He needed around 1,000 men and 150 officers just to crew them, with massive engineering and maintenance support as well. The men of the Motor Machine Gun Service already at Bisley, all of them with mechanical and engineering experience, gave him a head start. There were a number of officers and about 700 partly-trained other ranks ready to be transferred to the emerging tank section.

But it was not enough, and a public recruitment campaign was impossible because of the need for secrecy. Even the title 'Tank Detachment' was short-lived, in spite of the fact that no one at this stage knew what a tank was. Swinton's command was now called Machine Gun Corps (Motors).

The search for crews was conducted in part in *Motor Cycle* magazine through a weekly recruiting call for men who could drive 'light cars'. The editor personally interviewed many of the applicants – an unorthodox role for a journalist. The War Office circulated a notice marked 'Strictly Secret and Confidential' that asked for volunteers for 'an exceedingly dangerous and hazardous duty of a secret nature'. Around 300 men were sufficiently intrigued to respond, and Swinton found 30 of his officers in this way.

Baker and Swinton

The army had grown so rapidly since September 1914, and so many men had fallen in battle, that there was a general shortage of officers. To make good the deficit, Officer Cadet Units (OCU) were set up across the country in February 1916 as a means for those in the ranks to qualify for a commission. These units also offered a potentially fertile recruiting ground for Swinton.

There was an OCU based at Balliol College, Oxford, and one of the first to pass through its doors was Albert George Baker of the Royal Fusiliers. The 21st (Service) Battalion was being disbanded on its return from France, and Baker was one of 100 of its members accepted for officer training on the course at Oxford. They arrived home from France at the end of more than four months in the field, and were at Balliol within a week. 'We form No 6 Battn,' he recorded. 'All stripes are off. We just wear a broad green band around our caps. Uniforms to come later, so they say.' A further requirement was revealed to help prepare them for a career as an officer: 'we've been requested to grow a moustache!'

The four-and-a-half-month course upon which Baker and his fellow trainees embarked in early 1916 was a miniature version of that offered at Sandhurst, the main training academy for officers. It included physical fitness, bayonet and musketry work and drill. More up-to-date field skills such as tactical work, bombs, gas, and map reading were backed up by classes in military law and administration. The recruits were also coached in the social skills necessary for them to survive nights in the officers' mess. Baker described it as 'a very thorough course', with a strong incentive to succeed: 'if we don't pass, we go back to the trenches and our old rank.' There were benefits too: 'Food in College Hall – marvellous. College beer and baths galore and playing fields.' Balliol might have been less enthusiastic about its guests, many of whom had very recently been living under canvas or in trenches in France. Two days after the trainees arrived, the college rooms had to be deloused.

Baker shared a room with three others from the Royal Fusiliers, including his best friend Ted Loxley. The trainees, he reported, were all sergeants and full corporals. 'They have now taken our uniforms away, we look proper mutts, not even a belt.'

Swinton made a rapid tour of some of the Officer Cadet Units in early April as part of his recruitment drive. He began at Chelsea Barracks, where he selected for commission about 30 cadets of the type required, men with a degree of mechanical knowledge. Then it was off to Oxford. 'I drove down that afternoon, and next morning chose about 50 more cadets with similar qualifications. We then went on to Cambridge, where we made a "bag" of about the same size.'

On 12 April 1916, Swinton interviewed Bert Baker and nine other officer cadets in Oxford for a command in the Machine Gun Corps (Motors). 'It's for MGs with motor driving knowledge,' Baker wrote before the interview. 'Hope we get through.'

Baker did get through as one of the Oxford 'bag'. It cannot have been a difficult decision for Swinton. Baker had been in the army for 18 months, seen service in the trenches, and was not only trained as a machine-gunner, but had also been deputed to instruct others – he had spent his last month in France as a sergeant instructor at a divisional machine-gun school. He and his fellows were exactly the stuff that the tank recruitment team were looking for. In fact, they wanted them so badly that their officer training was cut short. Baker's record of service shows that his last day of training was 15 April – only three days after his interview, and barely a quarter of the way through the course. After a break for Easter, he would be off to Bisley. On 28 April he reported: 'Commissioned to MMGC. London to buy outfit and report to Bisley in one week.' He would be a second lieutenant in the new tank detachment. And with his fast track elevation to officer class, the two strands of our story come together. From now on, Bert Baker's wartime fortunes and those of the tank would run along parallel lines.

5
CRAWLING TOADS

If you see a nightmare shape
Like what sets your mouth agape
When the DTs with your optics plays a prank
And it crawls along the ground
With a rumbling sort of sound
You can bet a bloomin' pound
It's a Tank
(Anon)

As the new recruits poured into Bisley, full of excitement and enthusiasm about their role as pioneers of a new secret weapon, Swinton's problems reversed themselves. After Mother had passed her test, he had secured a commitment to the tanks but had no men to crew them. Now he had the men, but the tanks had yet to arrive. And he was still fiddling with the specifications. He had originally conceived the tanks as machine-gun destroyers, and the 6pdr guns supplied by the Navy would serve this purpose admirably. As well as their effectiveness at short range, the flash and detonation they produced would have a demoralising effect on the enemy. But Swinton was concerned that the tanks would be vulnerable to a rush of men attacking them at close quarters. As he rather brutally put it: 'some more wholesale close-range man-killing weapon was requisite'. There was a more practical problem too: the Navy had promised 100 of the 6pdrs – only enough for 50 tanks. Twice that number were now on order. Swinton solved both issues by partnering each tank armed with 6pdrs with a 'consort' tank equipped only with machine-guns, capable of firing 1,200 bullets a minute from each side and offering protection to its companion. These would be designated 'female', while those with the 6pdrs would be 'male'. Swinton asked for 100 females to match the 100 males already in production. He had to settle for 75 of each.

It would be some while before Mother's offspring – the Mark I tanks – would start to arrive. In the meantime, the men at Bisley had to be occupied somehow, and their natural and lively curiosity about the nature of their task had somehow to be held in check. They could surmise a certain amount from the preponderance of machine-gunners among their number, and the reference to driving abilities on what little recruiting material had passed the secrecy requirements. But that was as far as it went. Within a week of arriving at Bisley at the beginning of May 1916, Baker's entry in his Tablet probably summed up pretty much everything any of them knew about the enterprise in which they were engaged: 'We are not to have much leave, because ours is a secret job,' he wrote. 'To be a surprise for the Germans. An entirely new form of car to be used – also guns.' They were already in training on the Hotchkiss and Vickers machine-guns. The word 'tank' had yet to enter their vocabulary. With a touch of satire, they nicknamed the mystery machines 'hush-hushes'.

To add to the sense of mystery and uncertainty, the organisation of the men and the names of their units changed with bewildering speed. On his arrival at Bisley with four of his fellows from 21st Company of the Royal Fusiliers, Baker was put in L Company, Armoured Car Section, Motor Machine Gun Corps. Since 'Tank Detachment' had already been abandoned as a name because it gave too much away, 'Armoured Car Section' hardly represented an improvement. The point was taken. A few days after his arrival Baker reported: 'Hear our name is to be changed to Heavy Section, Machine Gun Corps.' Later, that would become the Heavy Branch. By the end of the month he was in B Company, Third Battalion of the Heavy Section. Less than a fortnight after that, he was in F Company. By now there were six companies at Bisley, A–F. Although they did not yet know it, each company would be allotted 25 of the tanks under construction. There would be four sections per company, each with three male and three female tanks, and one spare.

Swinton was very pleased with the results of his recruitment, especially the quality of the other ranks. 'The unit was fortunate in being filled with men of a remarkably high class. All those transferred to it were of superior education, having motor or mechanical engineering experience.' The recruits were also united by the appeal of being part of something new and exciting. A Sergeant Littledale probably spoke for most of them when he wrote: 'The spirit of adventure called us to the tanks. The call for volunteers found us ready, and when the word of acceptance came, our hearts beat quickly and our hopes were high.'

They were impatient to get going. But things were moving slowly, and Swinton sensed a growing feeling of frustration. There was soon a degree of low-level grumbling bordering on resentment. Those who had signed up for something called the Armoured Car Section were being put through strenuous courses of fitness and machine-gunnery, but weeks were going by with not a car in sight, armoured or otherwise.

Swinton addressed a parade of the whole Heavy Section, and told them the real purpose of their work would very soon be revealed to them. But he decided the time had come to level more fully with his officers. After lunch one Sunday in late May, he assembled them in an orchard near the camp, and told them what they wanted to hear. 'After a warning as to the secrecy of what I was about to say, I explained the whole scheme and object of the Tank, and read them my printed memorandum.' This was the document he had drawn up three months earlier, as a first effort at discussing how the tanks might operate in battle. Swinton emphasised that first and foremost, the tanks were designed to assist the infantry. Some former infantrymen – Bert Baker one of them – were among those smoking their pipes under the cherry trees and listening to his presentation. Swinton thought they would be a receptive audience: 'The stress I laid on the fact that the Heavy Section was being created to save the lives of the infantry naturally aroused special interest among those who, as infantry, had already experienced the enemy machine guns.'

Intensive machine-gun training continued – Baker reported one stint of four consecutive days firing on the range. But Bisley was essentially a rifle range, and there was a problem with practicing with the 6pdrs there. The Royal Navy came to the rescue again. Having provided the guns, they now provided training and target practice at HMS *Excellent*, the shore-based home of the Naval Gunnery School, located on Whale Island in Portsmouth Harbour.

Baker was put in charge of one of the groups sent down to Portsmouth. 'Am down to take a party of 30 men to Whale Island for a gunnery course,' he recorded on 15 July. 'Leave on Sunday at 2pm for about a week. I'm to live in naval barracks and use the big naval mess. HMS *Excellent* it's called.'

He was to enjoy the naval life as much, if not more, than that of the army. 'Now finished Monday's work,' he wrote at the end of the first day. 'It's a wonderful place. I'm in love with everything belonging to the Navy. Wish I'd joined the Navy.'

The rest of the week was just as enjoyable: 'We were out on a gunboat shooting at towed targets today down the Solent, off the town of Yarmouth (IoW). Very deaf from barking of the guns. Good fun, several sick.' The next day there was more of the same: 'Firing in the gunboat. Beautiful weather. Saw submarines, airships, planes and warships by the score.' Shooting across the water was not the ideal preparation for the conditions the tanks would meet on land, but it did familiarise the men with the performance and handling of the guns.

Bisley had still yet to see a tank, and in spite of the chafing of his men Swinton was happy to keep it that way. The area was far too close to a number of towns for his liking, all full of inquisitive eyes that could jeopardise the secret. Lurid stories and rumours about an extensive German spy network had abounded even before war broke out. In fact, only a handful of spies were arrested in England during the war, most of them untrained amateurs who had betrayed themselves by their own ineptitude. But Swinton could be excused his anxieties, and his desire for a more remote training ground. If the Germans were to get an inkling of the nature of the tanks, much of the impact of their first appearance would be lost. On a practical level, there also remained the issue that there was no artillery range near Bisley. To practice the skills learned at Whale Island, the men had to travel as far as Salisbury Plain. A remote location was needed, where the crews would be able to practice with real tanks and without interruption. Two days after returning from Portsmouth, Baker and the Heavy Section were on the move again. This time they were heading for just such a location – an idyllic stretch of countryside in Norfolk.

The Elveden area, just outside Thetford, was part of the Iveagh estate and was nicknamed 'the Land of the Shoots'. This was nothing to do with the army – the estate offered some of the finest game shooting in the country, and the King was a frequent visitor during the season. Its 15 square miles of arable, heathland and woods and its remoteness also made it an ideal choice as the first purpose-built training ground for tanks. Lord Iveagh agreed reluctantly to loan it to the army for this purpose, and work began to turn his shoots into a passable imitation of a modern battlefield.

When it came to preserving secrecy, no stone was left unturned. Those living on the estate were summarily evicted, and the site was sealed off, with screens erected where the land ran alongside the main road, now the A11. The site was patrolled around the clock by 450 members of the Royal Defence Corps, with 100 sentries on duty at any one time. All the locals were told was that the site was called the 'Elveden Explosives Area', and that they must draw their curtains and look the other way if they heard any unusual activity outside. This was because the first tanks arrived at Barnham, the railway station nearest to the camp, and then had to be driven to the camp itself by road under the cover of heavy tarpaulins. Later a spur was built to enable them to be brought directly into the camp by rail.

By the time Baker and his companions arrived at the end of July 1916, the first production tanks were already there, and they were afforded their first glimpse of the new weapon. They too remained sworn to secrecy, and Baker's Tablet gave nothing away. He recorded a visit from the King, who had continued to take a keen interest in the tanks after seeing the test at Hatfield Park. 'The King came to see us yesterday and saw our cars at work,' he recorded, within a day or two of his arrival. 'Wish I could write more about them.'

Getting to Elveden had involved an arduous journey. 'We started early [from Bisley] and marched three miles to the station. Then across London, then from Thetford. The men were very done up – in full kit and new to army life. Several collapsed on the last lap. The weather was broiling, and meals very scrappy.' But Baker was enchanted with his new surroundings. 'This place really is charming,' he reported on arrival. 'Elveden – just in the edge of a grand pine wood and miles from a village even.'

The first days were busy, but there was time to do a little exploring too. 'Have been digging a cellar for food today, and many jobs in taking over new camp,' he wrote the day after arriving. 'Four of us went into Thetford in a lorry this evening to try to buy or borrow four push bikes – no petrol available, or very little. Hired two boats and explored the River Thet. Full of weeds. DT has given up rowing, and I'm writing a letter in the bottom of boat. Strange coincidence: the boat is called *Miriam*!'

A couple of days later, he and two others, including his friend DT, went by bicycle to the village of Brandon. 'A very fine road through pine woods. Brandon is on the banks of the Ouse, a dear little village. Had an excellent tea in the "fishing" hotel and boated in the evening. Then to White Hart Inn and dined off cold rabbit pie. We had bottles of wine to celebrate DT's promotion to full Lieutenant.'

He was given leave to return to East Dulwich for the weekend, and then it was back to the rural idyll. 'Got my gun today,' he said on his return. 'Going rabbiting tomorrow – thousands of them.' A few days later: 'Got four rabbits and a partridge this evening.'

It wasn't all boat trips and rabbit pie. The first tanks would soon be heading to France, and the time for training was at a premium. There were still not many machines at Elveden by this stage, and a large number of men were yet to familiarise themselves with them. Some crews would set off for France with barely an hour or two of training in an actual tank.

A huge mock battleground had now been created across Lord Iveagh's beloved shoots. There were replica trenches, for which Swinton had had to indent for a million sandbags, and miles of barbed wire. 'The model battlefield was over one and a half miles in width,' he wrote. 'In depth it included the British support and front lines, No Man's Land, the German first, support, second and third lines. It was as complete a copy of the real thing as time, experience, labour and money could make it. It comprised breastworks, wire entanglements, abatis [tree trunks placed at an angle with sharpened tops facing the enemy], shell craters, communication trenches, dugouts, machine-gun emplacements and nests, magazines, grenade stores, in fact every sort of work which, according to the latest information, might be met with in the defensive zone. The various posts behind the enemy front line were marked by notices in German, and the men were instructed in their meaning.'

A week before Baker's arrival, a mock battle had been staged over this assault course involving 25 tanks. Once again, a party of VIPs was there to see it from a raised platform, among them Lloyd George, now War Minister as well as Minister of Munitions. The exercise was a success, and was repeated on a smaller scale a few days later for the benefit of the King – the visit reported by Baker. 'The trial definitely showed that the tanks could surmount all the battlefields of the Western Front,' wrote Swinton. 'For the designers and constructors of the new engines of war, it was a day of triumph.' One can forgive them their feelings of satisfaction at the culmination of what Hugh Elles would later describe as 'a remarkable effort of persistent and courageous faith, of determination to succeed in the face of lukewarmness and even scepticism, of the overcoming of many practical difficulties'. Elles singled out the 'clearness of vision' displayed not only by Swinton, but by Stern and d'Eyncourt as well.

Haig was impatient to have the tanks in France. He had hoped to get them in June, for the offensive that became the Battle of the Somme, but Swinton told him this was impossible. He promised Haig the first consignment in August, which from his point of view was still a very tight schedule. But the battle was not going well, and there was no possibility of further delay. Practice and training time were much too short, but the first tanks were ready for shipment to France in the middle of the month as promised. The new rail siding was used to load 13 tanks of C Company onto a train, with a second train carrying their sponsons, extra guns and other spares. The company's 12 remaining tanks followed a few days later. They were loaded on board ships at Avonmouth Docks, while the crews sailed from Southampton, and were reunited with their machines in Le Havre. Within a few days, the whole company had arrived at Yvrench, near Abbeville, where a training centre was being established. A little over six months after Mother had rumbled through her paces at Hatfield Park, the tanks were going to war.

Swinton had not had long to savour his 'day of triumph'. He was a worried man, for a number of reasons. The first 150 tanks would soon be completed, and if more were to be required, an order must be submitted to the manufacturers as soon as possible. But GHQ wanted to see how the machines fared before they committed to ordering more. Swinton was further appalled to hear that Haig apparently intended to throw the tanks into action at the first opportunity, without waiting for the whole force to be assembled. He had strongly cautioned against precisely this. The tanks should on no account be used in driblets, he had argued – and he thought Haig had agreed. Haig had certainly appeared to be on message.

With Sir Henry Rawlinson, commander of the Fourth Army, Haig went to Yvrench to watch five tanks take part in an exercise, which he described as 'quite encouraging', adding 'we need to clear our ideas as to the tactical handling of these machines'. Later, he made it clear that he did not intend to employ the tanks in small numbers. Tellingly though, he gave himself legroom by adding '... unless and until I am convinced that the advantages to be gained by doing so are great enough to outweigh the disadvantages of making known to the enemy the existence of these new engines of war'. By now, the state of the battle was forcing Haig to reassess where that balance lay. Swinton could do nothing but watch and wait, and worry.

The tank known variously as Big Willie, *Centipede*, and Mother, was now officially called the Mark I. The machines arriving in France were based on the wooden model Swinton had first seen on his visit to Lincoln. The Mark I weighed 28 tons and was powered by a 6-cylinder engine from Daimler of Coventry. Wilson's distinctive rhomboid shape was a feature of this and all future First World War tanks. It was designed to move over flat ground at 3–4 mph, or up to 120 yards a minute, along chain tracks each 90 feet long. Speed was reduced to 30–40 yards a minute when it was crossing trenches, and to a very slow crawl when travelling in the dark. It could crush all sorts of barbed wire defences, as per Swinton's original objective. It could traverse a trench more than 11 feet wide, surmount obstacles of up to 5 feet and climb at an angle of up to 1 in 2. Its armour was 12mm thick, making it vulnerable to armour-piercing bullets.

The tank had a crew of eight: a commander, who was a junior officer; a driver, four gunners and two gearsmen. The officer sat to the left in the front, operating the brakes, the driver to the right. The gearsmen were at the back, one to each track. In each sponson sat two gunners.

A feature of the Mark I – abandoned in later models – was a tail assembly, a sort of cart with two large-diameter wheels, which was pulled behind the tank and was able to move like a rudder and help steer the vehicle over uneven ground. It also added stability and length when the tank was crossing a trench. It was not essential – the tank could steer without it and the driver could lift the whole mechanism clear of the ground if required. In practice, the tail wheels caused endless difficulties and became an obvious target for enemy gunners, and it was soon concluded that they were more trouble than they were worth.

Mark I Tank
Number made 150 (75 male, 75 female)
Weight 28 tons (m) 27 tons (f)
Length 32ft/10m (including tail)

Width 13ft 6in/4m
Height 8ft/2.4m
Crew 8
Engine Daimler/Knight 6-cylinder sleeve valve, 16-litre 105hp
Fuel capacity 50 gallons/227 litres
Fuel consumption 2mpg
Max speed 3.7mph/6kmh
Trench crossing 11ft 6in/3.5m
Armament
Male 2 x Hotchkiss 6pdr (57mm) 40-calibre quick-firing
Maximum range 7,500yds/6,850m
3 x 7.62mm Hotchkiss air-cooled machine-guns
Female 4 x Vickers .303in machine-guns
Ammunition
Male 332 6pdr rounds; 6,272 machine-gun rounds
Female 24,000 machine-gun rounds.

For the following description of the operation of the machine, I have drawn heavily on the Haynes *Owners' Workshop Manual* by the tank expert David Fletcher. The manual relates to the Mark IV model, but the process was substantially the same on the Mark I.

Nothing about the movement of the tanks was easy. Even the business of starting the engine involved the coordinated efforts of most of the crew. The driver, sitting next to the commander in one of the two forward seats, began by activating the ignition by means of a switch located behind him. He opened the throttle slightly and raised a lever at his side to engage the starting handle drive with the crankshaft. Up to four men now began to crank the starting handle clockwise until the engine fired. From this point, the noise inside the cabin meant that all subsequent operations were conducted using sign language.

The engine was allowed to run for a few minutes to warm up. When the tank was ready to move, the driver depressed the clutch and engaged first gear in the primary gearbox, while at his signal, the two gearsmen in the back also selected first gear in their respective gearboxes. When the clutch was released, the tank began to edge forward – although such was the din and vibration that the driver or commander might have to peer out of their visors to reassure themselves that it was actually moving.

It wasn't long before the temperature inside shot past 100 degrees, and exhaust fumes began to leak into the cabin The crew were now deafened, nearly blinded, roasting hot and half-suffocated with the fumes. The machine had reached its standard running condition. This would be the atmosphere in which they would have to operate for hours at a stretch.

So much for moving forward – or backwards, if reverse gear was engaged. Changing course, or 'swinging' the tank, could be achieved in one of a number of ways, all of them cumbersome in the extreme. The commander, sitting on the driver's left, had access to a pair of brake levers, one for each track. By hauling on one of them he could effect a gentle turn in that direction. To swing further, the *Tank Driver's Handbook* recommended the use of the secondary gears in differing ratios. In order to complete this procedure, the tank had first to be brought to a halt. One of the secondary gears was put into 'high' mode and the other one into 'low'. With the tracks now moving at different speeds, the tank would begin to turn. In practice, this method put huge pressure on the transmission and was not much favoured by the crews.

The method of swinging most commonly employed was to stop the tank, and then instruct one of the gearsmen to select neutral and the other to select first gear. The brake was applied to the neutral track to stop it moving, and the tank was turned within its own length by the other track as it continued to rotate. About 5 feet of track, or eight links, were in contact with the ground at any one time, to improve ease of turning. The shorter the length of track in contact with the ground, the less the resistance when the tank began to turn.

This laborious procedure had to be repeated for each manoeuvre. Given that the tanks could barely travel at walking pace when going straight ahead on a firm surface, any journey was agonisingly slow. Throw in some variables such as boggy conditions, and insofar as their heads were clear enough to think at all, the crews must have felt appallingly vulnerable as they lumbered painfully forward. Speed and agility were not among their strengths. These manoeuvres could take many minutes to complete, during which time the tank offered a static and very tempting target.

The sheer physical demands were astonishing. The heavy 6pdrs were swung round on their swivels only by the straining sinews of the gunners. Firing them accurately on the move was impossible. Vibrations from the tracks were transmitted through the body of the tank, making it problematic for any of the crew even to locate the target, let alone focus on it.

There was nothing remotely appealing about life inside the tank. The design and construction of Mother, on which the Mark I's were based, had been done at breakneck speed by comparison with conventional process. The comfort of the crew had not figured as a priority. Ventilation was poor, suspension non-existent. Every movement over uneven ground jarred the bones of a crew already shaken by the vibrations of the engine. If they threw out a hand to steady themselves, it was likely to come into contact with a blisteringly hot pipe. Within a few minutes of starting, the temperature rocketed to up to 120 degrees, and the cabin filled with steam from the cooling system, and with a ghastly brew of smells – burning oil, petrol and exhaust fumes, sulphur and cordite from the ammunition.

Even the simple act of getting in and out of the machine was something of a performance. There were two tiny doors in the sponsons, a small aperture in the rear and a manhole cover on the roof – not a recommended means of exit when under fire. Daniel Hickey was a section commander who served with the tanks in France. In his memoir *Rolling into Action* he described some of the difficulties: 'It was no easy matter to get in and out of these steel boxes. The doorway was only two feet by four feet. In a male tank one entered in a more or less upright position, for the door was vertical. But the door to the female tank was placed horizontally so that the only way to get in was to lever oneself in on one's stomach.'

Once inside, only the officer and driver of a male tank were able to sit down. Everyone else had to stand, or more accurately stoop or squat. In the females, the gunners were also able to sit, on saddles attached to the machine-gun mountings. Almost the entire interior space of the tank was taken up by the engine. Each crew member was issued with two gas helmets, one pair of goggles and a leather cap to shield his head from contact with the hull.

'The officer and driver occupied two raised seats in the nose of the tanks and the rest of the crew was confined to two narrow gangways,' Hickey recalled. 'These gangways were one foot wide and eight feet long, and ran the whole length of the tank on either side of the engine and machinery. It was impossible to stand upright, for the height of the roof at the gangways was only about five feet. The 100hp petrol engine reached almost to the roof; but there was a small platform behind it covering the machinery. Over this platform was the starting handle, which it required four men to turn. Between the officer and the gearsman on one side and between the driver and the other gearsman on the other side were the gunners, two in each gangway.'

There were plenty of demands on what little spare space there was. Another early tank man, Basil Henriques, provided an inventory of the equipment issued to each member of the crew: 'Two gas helmets, one pair of goggles, service cap, anti-bruise helmet, field dressings, first aid dressing, revolver, haversack, iron rations. There are eight people in a tank and as soon as they get in they naturally take off all these things, which lie about the floor... .'

Not forgetting essential supplies for the whole crew: 'Sixteen loaves, thirty tins of food, cheese, sugar, tea, milk, one spare drum of engine oil and one of gear oil, two small drums of grease, three water cans and two boxes of revolver ammunition, four spare Vickers barrels, one spare Vickers gun, a spare barrel for the Hotchkiss and two wire cutters and three signal flags.' Every time they crashed over another jarring obstacle all these items flew out of their storage spaces and littered the floor of the tank.

These were minor inconveniences. The tanks were essentially death traps. The engine was in the centre of the hull, exhaust fumes expelled imperfectly through the roof. The heat inside was intense, and the noise deafening. Because the petrol reached the engine by gravity, the fuel tanks had to be raised. When the nose of the tank went down to cross an obstacle, the fuel supply was cut off until it came up again. On the Mark Is, two 25-gallon tanks were located in the front of the hull on either side of the cab. If either was hit, the officer and driver would certainly be burned alive, and probably everyone else too, given how long it would take to escape. It was not a place for the claustrophobic. If entering the tank required such a series of contortions, one can only imagine the scene if a crew of eight needed to evacuate the machine in a hurry. Among the losses sustained by the tank crews during the war, death by burning was by far the most common.

There were other obstacles to surmount. It was almost pitch-black inside, and visibility outside was practically zero, since any aperture in the hull would represent a point of weakness and a target for enemy fire. When the front shutters were closed, the commander had to peer through reflectors and sight holes, or try his luck with a small periscope. As Hickey put it, with a degree of understatement: 'one could see very little of what was going on outside'. A compass was used to establish position, assuming there was enough light by which to read it. There were small holes in the side, big enough to fire a handgun through or release a carrier pigeon. If they too were closed, the gunners were reduced to squinting through three tiny holes only a millimetre wide.

Because it was so hot inside, the crews would often wear shorts, and remove the brown leather helmets they were given to protect their heads as they were flung this way and that. There were no peaks on the headgear – the men needed to be able to press their faces directly against the miniscule viewing holes. They tended not to bother with the highly uncomfortable chain mail masks that hung over their faces to deflect the 'splash' of flying metal splinters dislodged on the inside when the tank came under fire from the outside.

In battle, the crews might have to spend many hours inside the tanks in these conditions. After the war, a major in the Royal Army Medical Corps compiled a report on the effects of being in a tank. Impetigo-like skin rashes were common, caused by exposure to inferior brands of petrol and oil. Oppressive fumes caused burning of the nose and throat and smarting of the eyes. Carbon monoxide poisoning led to, in sequence, 'headache, giddiness, palpitation, vomiting, unconsciousness, collapse and convulsions'. Before passing out, the crew suffered 'mental confusion'.

It was not surprising that the tanks made an immediate and indelible impression on the crews when they at last came face to face with them, and set off for a first excursion across the training area. Bert Baker did not recount the experience of his maiden voyage, but Sergeant Littledale did. 'There is not one of us who will ever forget his first ride,' he wrote. Littledale continued:

> The crawling in at the sides, the discovery that the height did not permit a man of medium stature to stand erect, the sudden starting of the engine, the roar of it all when the throttle opened, the jolt forward and the sliding through the mud that followed until at last we came to the 'jump' which had been prepared. Then came the downward motion, which suddenly threw us off our feet and caused us to stretch, thrusting a hand towards the nearest object – usually, at first, a hot pipe through which the water from the cylinder jackets flowed to the radiator. So, down and down and down, the throttle almost closed, the engine just ticking over, until at last the bottom was reached, and as the power was turned full on, the tank raised herself to the incline like a ship rising on a wave, and we were all jolted the other way, only to clutch again frantically for things which were hot and burned, until at last with a swing over the top, we gained level ground.

The shock and pain and fear of the experience then gave way to feelings of exhilaration, even a sense of destiny. 'There came to us a thrill of happiness in that we were to sail over stranger seas than man had ever crossed, and set out on a great adventure.'

The full impact of some of the difficulties involved in operating a tank would not become clear until exposed on the battlefield – a rendezvous that was drawing ever nearer. Training at Elveden concentrated only on the basic operation of the machines – how to steer and manoeuvre them, how to seek out and destroy enemy machine-gun positions. There was no time for anything else. The tanks went to France never having practiced firing at a target while on the move. There was neither theory nor practice about how best to work in combination with the infantry. Various methods of communication between the tanks and infantry, and with each other, had been tried and all found wanting. In the end, the favoured form of communication was a low-tech one – carrier pigeons, two to a tank.

In lieu of tactical training, a sort of crib sheet, a survival guide to the battlefield, was drawn up to convey in the most basic terms the essentials of working in a tank:

> Remember your orders
> Shoot quick
> Shoot low. A miss which throws dust in the enemy's eyes is better than one which whistles in his ear
> Shoot cunning
> Shoot the enemy while they are rubbing their eyes.
> Economise ammunition and don't kill a man three times
> Remember that trenches are curly and dugouts deep – look round the corners
> Watch the progress of the fight and your neighbouring tanks
> Watch your infantry whom you are helping
> Remember the position of your own line
> Smell out the enemy's machine guns and other small guns and kill them with your 6 pdrs
> You will not see them for they will be cunningly hidden
> You must ferret out where they are, judging by the following signs:
> Sound
> Dust
> Smoke
> A shadow in a parapet
> A hole in a wall, haystack, rubbish heap, wood stack, pile of bricks
> They will usually be placed to fire slantways across the front and shoot along wire
> One 6 pdr shell that hits the loophole of a MG emplacement will do it in
>
> Use the 6 pdr with care: shoot to hit and not to make a noise
> Never have any gun, even when unloaded, pointing at your own infantry,

or a 6 pdr pointed at another tank
It is the unloaded gun that kills the fool's friends

Never mind the heat
Never mind the noise
Never mind the dust
Think of your pals in the infantry
Thank God you are bullet-proof and can help the infantry who are not
Have your mask always handy.

This document was aptly summarised by Norman Dillon of the Heavy Branch: 'The only tactic was to get into your tank and drive towards the enemy. The infantry, with any luck, would follow you.'

Once in France, the tanks had to establish a base and infrastructure and organise their various support mechanisms. As ever, they were starting from scratch. While training continued at Yvrench, a headquarters was established first in a single hut in the village of Beauquesne, and later in a dilapidated chateau at Bermicourt, 30 miles north-east of Abbeville. From there, the operation spread in various directions as more men and tanks arrived, and the level of support they required increased. Within a few weeks, the men were quartered in eight or nine villages around Bermicourt. A large Central Workshop that would issue, maintain and repair the tanks was created at Érin-sur-Tournoise, a couple of miles away, where there was a railway connection. Érin would eventually become a sort of industrial estate, covering acres of workshops and store sheds, miles of railway sidings and a vast volume of equipment. Later, there would be a gunnery school at Merlimont, on the coast just south of Le Touquet, and a practice area for driving over broken ground at Wailly, a ruined village outside Arras.

The tanks now found themselves treated like some sort of circus act, required to put on performances twice a day for crowds of visiting officers, British and French, all eager to get a glimpse of the new gadget. Basil Henriques found himself part of the show when sent up to an area known as the Loop, a few miles behind the frontline. The countryside reminded him of Hampstead Heath. 'When we got there we found Brigade had received orders that the tanks were to perform daily 9–10 and 2–3, and every officer within a large radius and an enormous number of the staff came to inspect the tanks – we were an object of interest to everyone. This did not help in one's work.'

It certainly didn't. Not only did these displays risk spilling the secret, they also put the crews under undue pressure and imposed a huge strain on the ever-fallible tanks themselves. Swinton, who paid a brief visit at the end of August, was not amused to see his babies looked upon as 'a new kind of toy'. Discussions about how they might be deployed also caused him serious misgivings. The demonstrations were raising expectations perilously high: 'There was an air of amused tolerance or contemptuous scepticism towards the New Arm, in some a tendency to place too much reliance on the influence of a few tanks to make up for the recent disappointment of the offensive. There seemed to be little inclination to make allowance for the imperfections of a brand-new weapon or for the difficulties of those who were handling it in strange surroundings after very little practice.'

The daily performances meant there was little scope to catch up on the training that had been skimped at Elveden. Indeed, D Company reached its assembly point in France only two days before it went into action. 'We did a show before General Joffre and the commander in chief, and the greater proportion of the staff were there,' said Henriques. 'But that did not give us confidence, for we did not know our tank and we did not know the capabilities of the tank.'

The inexperience of the men was unnerving. Henriques lamented this lack of preparation. 'We had no training with the infantry, even at home, and the infantry with whom we were to fight had never heard of us until they actually saw us in battle. We had never driven in England with our flaps closed, so that we had never used the periscope, and we had only driven with a clear view on perfectly level ground.'

Christopher Baker-Carr was also concerned. 'Most of the officers and crews had been suddenly pitchforked from the calm, almost academic, atmosphere of a training camp in England into the ear-splitting, nerve-racking tornado of the front line.' The young tank commanders, most of them inexperienced junior officers, did not understand operational orders, and the generals who would be deploying them had next to no appreciation of the capabilities or limitations of the tanks.

Clough Williams-Ellis, an early tank man, identified an even more fundamental problem. The men in charge of the Heavy Section had little knowledge of the nature of warfare in the age of the trench and the machine-gun. As a result, they were unable to give their men any meaningful sense of what they were headed towards. 'This was where the training of the first tank crews fell short,' wrote Williams-Ellis after the war. 'Their teachers had a rather hazy mental picture of the actuality of battle. They did not squarely face the essential question upon whose answer all specific preparation depends: the question, that is, *what is it going to be like?* Thus, though they did teach most of the essentials, they left out half a dozen subjects of which an accurate knowledge was ever afterwards held to be absolutely essential.'

Williams-Ellis said that with time so short, they had to prioritise training, and came to their decisions largely by guesswork. 'Would physical fitness or map reading prove more important when the day came? Signalling or esprit de corps? Visual training or revolver drill? There was no time for everything.' Every member of the crew had to have a working knowledge of the duties of his comrades, so great was the risk of casualties. Beyond that, the key thing was to build up the ability to work as a team, 'each with his special work as a brakesman, gearsman, driver or gunner, but each still part of an organic whole.'

When the first tanks arrived at the newly-established training ground at Yvrench, the problems persisted. 'Most of the men and many of the officers had not been to France before,' said Clough Williams-Ellis. 'There were no staff or instructors, the ranges were too short and the conditions for battle practice quite unlike those which prevailed on the Somme. But it had to suffice. The tanks were wanted at once.'

The place Haig wanted them in such a hurry was far from ideal as a proving ground. The Battle of the Somme was being fought along a front four miles wide and 20 long. In more than two months of fighting, millions of shells had rained down, leaving a pulverised landscape described by the writer John Buchan as being like 'a decaying suburb'. By the time the tanks entered this shattered terrain, about three million shells had fallen on it. Craters and splintered trees made it all but impassable when it was dry: when it was wet the whole turned into a churning morass of mud that enveloped anyone and anything foolhardy enough to attempt to move across it. This was no place for tanks. Hugh Elles, the man Haig had sent to London to find out about the new weapon, had remained closely involved, and was aghast at the idea of deploying them here. 'The Somme ground when dry was like aerated soft sand, and when wet a quagmire, conditions which simply appalled the tank officers to whom I showed them.'

But the advance was faltering. The casualty rates were appalling – nearly 20,000 British dead on the opening day, and a million dead and wounded on both sides by the time the fighting came to an end in mid-November. Early gains had not been built upon, and Haig was desperate for forward momentum. He decided to throw his tanks into an attack by the infantry on a line of four villages that stood in the way of the strategically-important city of Bapaume.

Of the 60 tanks that had so far arrived from England, 49 were serviceable and they would all be deployed. They would work in subsections of two or three, and attack specific strongpoints along the way. Haig was taking a big gamble: the going was bad after two and a half months of artillery shelling and ground fighting; the tanks would be fighting in what Swinton would no doubt have referred to as driblets, such that their impact would be diminished; and the element of surprise would be sacrificed once and for all. The arguments about the wisdom of Haig's decision remain unresolved to this day.

The tanks moved up into their positions on the evening of 14 September 1916. Of the original 49, only 32 made it to the starting line. Some fell into a dugout and were completely submerged. Others either broke down or became ditched in the muddy shell holes. The crews would find that it was harder to keep their tanks running than it was to engage the Germans. But at first light the following morning, male tank 765, crew D1, under the command of Captain Harold Mortimore, rumbled forward to lead the offensive. In doing so, it ushered in a new age of land warfare. There should have been two other tanks with him, but they had been delayed. It was an early indicator of what was to come.

Only the tanks allocated to the 25th Corps enjoyed any kind of success in this first tank battle, known as Flers-Courcelette after two of the villages that were among the objectives of the attack. The orders were to attack all strongpoints east and west of Flers, and to help the infantry take the neighbouring village of Guedecourt and the sunken road to the west of it. More machines broke down or became ditched as the attack went on, but there were two small successes. Most famously, a tank made it into the main street in Flers and accompanied the infantry as they rounded up German prisoners. This episode was spotted by a Royal Flying Corps observer, who sent back the message: 'A tank is walking up the High Street in Flers, with the British Army cheering behind it.' Another tank got into Guedecourt and did considerable damage before being disabled.

These were solitary achievements. Overall, results had been mixed, to say the least. Nine of the original tanks proved highly effective and another nine were useful in mopping up operations. None of the other 32 had made it to the starting line.

One highly gratifying aspect of the action, however, was the effect that the sight of the tanks had had on the defenders. As Douglas Browne put it: 'in almost every case where a tank succeeded in reaching its objective, the mere sight of it was enough. The enemy fled or surrendered on the spot.'

Most of the infantry and their commanders, however, were profoundly unimpressed – as they had expected to be. But the man whose opinion mattered most, Sir Douglas Haig, was notably enthusiastic. 'Some of the tanks have done marvels,' he wrote in his diary. When Haig saw Swinton that evening, he declared himself satisfied with their efforts. The tanks had not achieved all that had been hoped for, he said, but had saved many lives and fully justified themselves. He told Swinton he wanted five times as many.

In fact, he wanted even more than that. He sent his deputy, Butler, to London to demand 1,000 machines, to be delivered by the beginning of March 1917. For all their lack of reliability and penetration, the tanks had passed their test, at least as far as Haig was concerned. Butler was less enthusiastic, but he dutifully reported his chief's requirements and drew up plans for the necessary expansion of the Heavy Section. Its strength would increase to 12,000 men, to be organised in a number of brigades.

Butler was also doing some political manoeuvring. There was to be a change of command for the tanks in France, with Haig insisting on the appointment of 40-year-old Hugh Elles. It was not a popular choice, not least because Elles was so junior, only a colonel. But Butler made it happen.

At home, a general would be appointed to the overall command of the enlarged Heavy Section in England. Once again, Swinton looked like the obvious choice. But he soon heard on the grapevine that he was being passed over. That left him without a role. He was, in effect, being sacked, and he returned to his job at the secretariat of the War Cabinet. He claimed later that he had never been given a satisfactory explanation for his removal. Perhaps it was a sign of the bitterness he must have felt that his personal account of the history of the tanks came to an end at this point, a full 12 months before they began to make their most impactful contribution to the war effort. His constant pushing and cajoling of a sceptical and largely hostile War Office and GHQ, and his open exploitation of his political contacts at the highest level, had probably made him more than a few enemies in the senior ranks. Years later he told the official historian that his 'intrusions' arguing for the tanks, and his 'cavalry spirit' had been resented from the start. Now it was payback time. What Baker-Carr contemptuously referred to as 'the Military Mind' had exacted its revenge.

News of Haig's demand for 1,000 tanks would have been met with some surprise and not a little resentment among his senior officers. A sober military assessment of their first day in action would at the very least reserve judgement on the performance of the tanks. They had shown undoubted potential, performing well in conditions that were not ideal, but too many of them had suffered mechanical failure or become bogged down. So too had the offensive as a whole. The operation had been a failure: the infantry had failed to advance to Bapaume. Those who had been sceptical about the tanks from the start were not slow to apportion much of the blame to them. Haig seemed to be their only cheerleader.

He soon had public opinion on his side. The commander-in-chief's official despatch of the action around Flers, referred almost as an aside to 'a new type of heavy armoured car, which has proved of considerable utility'. A single sentence, but it was enough to send every journalistic antenna in Fleet Street oscillating wildly. The newspapers fell on the story like a pack of ravening wolves. As Williams-Ellis put it: 'they set to ransack their dictionaries for octosyllables in which to describe the new all-British destroyer of Germans'.

Reporting of the debut of the tanks bordered on the hysterical. The secret was out at last, and the tanks were an overnight sensation. 'New Forts on Wheels Make Huns Run Like Rabbits' was one headline. Some correspondents had been in on the secret for a while, but been forbidden from publishing anything. Now the shackles were off, and they did not hold back.

Philip Gibbs, one of five official war reporters, who wrote for the *Daily Telegraph* and the *Chronicle*, produced a sensational account of 'the wonderful part played by the tanks' in the Somme 'victory'.

> The new 'Tank' device – picturesquely compared to a prehistoric toad or to the primeval ichthyosaurus – accomplished feats which, if they had not been witnessed by the cheering soldiers, would almost surpass belief. For instance:
>
> It 'leant' against a broken wall until it fell and then crawled over the debris
> It went irresistibly through High Wood, the trees smashing like matchsticks before it
> It went up to machine gun emplacements, crushed the gun under its ribs, and passed on, spitting death at the demoralised Germans
> It 'stamped' down a dugout as though it were a wasps' nest
> It 'sat on' heaps of ruins and fired down a village street
> It went right through the old German trenches
> It put a battery and a half of guns out of action near Flers, according to Reuter's correspondent, who calls the Tank 'a Land Dreadnought'.

Haig's communiqué had contained none of these inflated claims. Gibbs' report gave the strong and highly misleading impression that the exploits of a single tank had been replicated triumphantly across the battlefield.

Gibbs was not the only one to give his imagination free rein in the absence of further hard information about the 'tank device'. Hall Caine, the most popular and celebrated novelist of the day, was one of the first into print. He had been drafted into a secret propaganda team and wrote frequently for the *New York Times*, with the aim of encouraging America to join the war. Under the heading 'England's New Juggernaut Car', Caine really let himself go, in a style that owed more to the novelist in him than the reporter:

> What is this new and terrible weapon of war? For weeks past I have been hearing whispers of a new arm, which, shortly to be launched on the battlefields, would drive everything before it. News of it was a secret not to be revealed until the day it came into action. Nobody was to know where or how it was made or yet what it was.
>
> It was impossible not to be stirred by the mystery that surrounded the new arm, and by the confident faith of those who knew of its irresistible power. It was a gigantic car, a colossal Juggernaut, a moving arsenal of unimaginable driving force. Nothing could stand before it.
>
> It would pass over trenches like flat ground; climb out of the beds of rivers and walk over houses as over ant-hills. In the inferno of its interior, the men who worked it, nearly nude, would be safe from any force known to military science except that of the unconquerable monster they controlled. I am told that the power of this new Juggernaut is such that if it rolled up Broadway (which God forbid) and were directed at the *New York Times* building (which also God forbid) it would bring it down and roll out at the other side almost as rapidly as I tell the tale. I am also told that if we had 3,000 of the new Juggernauts they would end the war in a month. It sounds like a dream. Some will surely say it sounds like madness, but few or none will be so sceptical of this tremendous story as not, at least, to hope for the sake of humanity and the future peace of the world that, please God, it may be true.

Here is part of another correspondent's enthusiastic – and speculative – analysis of Haig's despatch, published in September 1916:

> In the Army, it has been whispered for some days past that a development of the ordinary armoured car had successfully passed the experimental stage, and was likely to be employed during the next phase of the great offensive. Little was known of the actual construction of the new vehicles. Those who had seen them referred to them mysteriously as 'tanks', while the soldiers who had helped handle them named them humorously 'Willies'.
>
> It was evident from the nature of the country over which any armoured car would be obliged to operate – a desolate, shell-torn, roadless and

> trench-intersected wilderness – that no vehicle mounted upon ordinary wheels could hope to surmount the innumerable obstacles to its progress. It was obvious also, that to be of any practical utility, an armoured car must be invulnerable to rifle and machine gun fire, shell splinter and indeed anything less formidable than a direct hit from a heavy projectile.
>
> Sir Douglas Haig's message makes it clear that the problem must have been successfully solved. Otherwise the 'new type of heavy armoured car' would hardly have 'proved of considerable utility'. Of the precise quality of their utility we are told nothing. Whether it lay in the efficiency of their armament, or in their success in crushing down such impediments to an infantry advance of barbed wire can only be conjectured. The gratifying fact seems to be that the inventors have not hesitated boldly to tread unbeaten paths, and to have sought, in this war of machinery, to give practical shape to ideas which, had they been conceived by imaginative novelists, would have been regarded as fantastical. When the secrecy which rightly surrounds the construction of this our most recent addition to our fighting machines can be lifted, we may perhaps be enabled to imagine the feelings of the German infantry in their shell-battered trenches when, in the uncertain light of dawn they saw advancing upon them an array of unearthly monsters, cased in steel, spitting fire and crawling laboriously but ceaselessly over trench, barbed wire and shell crater.

He did not have to imagine the feelings of the Germans for long. The official German press condemned the use of 'these cruel and barbarous weapons'.

Here is another typical contemporary report, picking up on Haig's reference to the tanks:

> The plain man asked obvious questions with eager curiosity. What are these travelling engines, and what the nature and degree of their utility? Do they attack as battering rams or as gun carriers, or both? Are we to conceive them as a sort of ironclad van or land-monitor, ploughing ponderously onward through hedges of wire, over holes, over trenches to the bewilderment and affright of the Hun? The private soldier seems to regard the new 'war-car' as a tank-like or rather coffin-like object more apt to spread death than receive it.
>
> The French Press says more on the subject than our own. We hear from Paris of steel monsters with ram-like fronts cutting entanglements as though they were giant lawnmowers and barbed wire were grass, and shoving through everything with unmoved stolidity like true British machines. The new fighting engines, we assume, could not have been of considerable utility unless they had been capable of driving at a machine gun with no more respect than if it had been a hosepipe; but how these 'land-monitors' managed to elude or defy the enemy's artillery as they forged ahead is a thing we shall doubtless know in good time.

It is evident that few if any of these accounts were based on first-hand experience of what a tank even looked like. One correspondent who could claim actually to have seen one tied himself into all sorts of knots trying to describe what kind of creature it was. Like so many, he didn't know whether to laugh at it or be terrified by it:

> What animal are they really like? Candour compels one to reply that they are not like any animal, except insofar as they are even less like anything else on earth. If you must have some particular animal to compare them with, they perhaps resemble in general contour a toad more than anything else – a toad rather elongated towards its hinder end.
>
> In size the thing is – well, large. Not to be too exact, it is bigger than an ordinary motor car and smaller than a labourer's cottage. In these circumstances it can hardly be expected to move fast, and the deliberateness of its advance coupled with the fact that it has no visible wheels or legs, gives to it a perfectly ridiculous solemnity. When one sees the unspeakable things moving, with their great blunt noses thrust in the air before them, limbless and wheelless, going with a movement as smooth as that of a snake, but majestic and deliberate as a giant tortoise, it is such a mixture of pantomime and pure horror as no nightmare ever equalled.

Nowhere were these reports more enthusiastically devoured than at Elveden, where training was still continuing apace. These and other articles were cut out and collected into a scrapbook by Bert Baker, and remain among his papers at The Tank Museum at Bovington. Perhaps this was the only source of hard information filtering through into the camp, but Baker for one was ready to accept that the operations had been a triumph. He was also very happy that the secret was finally out, and he too could talk freely about the tanks.

'The papers are full of the wonderful tanks!' he wrote to Miriam on 20 September. 'That's us. We have heard details of what they have done in France and are very pleased with ourselves. It's been a wonderful secret. I've known since Bisley, of course. We first saw them at Elveden. Like great toads crawling over the ground. Shall never forget the first morning I saw them.'

Next day he reported: 'The news from France has caused things to hum – another Coy went out today and we take their place three miles away in Central Training Ground.' With all of England buzzing with the stories of the tanks, those that were still serviceable after the Flers attack were preparing to go into action again. After a single encounter with the enemy and the terrain, there were now fewer than 20 of them in working order. It put the excitable press coverage and the order for 1,000 tanks into some sort of perspective.

Some of the tanks were now ordered to join an attack on Thiepval about three miles west of the site of the earlier operation, while the rest were directed to have another crack at Gueudecourt. Once again, fortunes were mixed. Of the eight tanks heading for Thiepval, two were quickly knocked out and the others all got stuck.

At Gueudecourt, there was better luck. The infantry had been held up at a mile-long stretch of the Gird Trench, which was well wired and strongly defended by the Germans. A single female tank was called up and moved along the trench firing its machine-guns. The infantry followed up and secured some strongpoints. The official report of the 25th Corps stated: 'No difficulty was experienced. The enemy surrendered freely as the tank moved down the trench. They were unable to escape owing to our holding the trench at the southern end. The infantry then advanced to their final objective, when the tank rendered very valuable assistance. The tank finally ran short of petrol south-east of Gueudecourt. In the capture of the Gird trench, eight officers and 362 other ranks were made prisoners and a great many Germans were killed. Our casualties only amounted to five. Nearly 1,500 yards of trench were captured in less than an hour. What would have proved a very difficult operation, involving probably heavy losses, was taken with greatest ease entirely owing to the assistance rendered by the tank.' The village itself fell the following day.

This was a tremendous endorsement. The officer commanding the tank, Second Lieutenant Charles Storey, was awarded the DSO, a first medal for the tank men. Haig noted on the citation: 'I consider this to be the best tank performance up to date'. In truth, that was not saying a great deal. The exceptional activity of this one machine served to highlight that it was just that – the exception. In the two operations to date, most of the tanks had failed to get close enough to the action to take any part in it at all.

Back in Elveden, the camp was emptying out. It was B Company's turn to head for France, leaving only E and F still there. In the meantime, there was still plenty to do. 'Lots of new "Willies", very busy breaking them in,' said Baker. 'We're very bucked by what our other boys have done in France.'

Bad weather meant that Baker's last days in Elveden would be grim. As winter began to set in, he must have looked back longingly on those long summer evenings in boats or country pubs. 'Very wet and cold in camp – we want huts. Lox and I bought a large lamp and Beatrix stove to improve our tent.' That was on 10 October. Baker reminded himself to buy a British Warm for the winter – a type of military greatcoat that had just been developed for officers. They had been told they would soon be moving to a place called Wool in Dorset, but nothing was definite. 'Still here,' Baker wrote on 2 November. 'Cold as North Pole under canvas.' His habitual good cheer was about to be tested even further. 'Camp blown away, or down, this w/end,' he recorded on 7 November. 'The parts not blown down are flooded out. We packed up once for Wool and it was cancelled. On Saturday night both the mess marquee and the Orderly Room marquee blew down. We got some up and on Sunday at 7am went into the area driving "Willies". Returned at 2pm and found all the lot blown down again. Our mess was beyond repair, glass and crockery broken. We went to Brandon for supper and spent the night in our clothes, rain coming in through all the tents. Yesterday we lived out in the open air, packed ready to move and the order to cancel came along! The rain stopped and we dried things a bit, but didn't undress. Going to Wool in the morning, definite.' Next day: 'Still here, going tomorrow,' and go they finally did, heading for the new headquarters of the tanks, Bovington Camp, near the small town of Wool in Dorset.

Ten days later, the tanks in France made their final appearance of the year, south of the river Ancre. The weather was very bad and the ground sodden. Once again, the conditions were completely unsuitable for tanks. Three were sent out to support an infantry advance, but all were ditched. Two more on a similar mission nearby met the same fate. A final foray by three more tanks the next day saw one hit by a shell and the other two ditched. Even so, they were able to bring their 6pdrs and machine-guns to bear on a strongpoint from which 400 Germans surrendered.

As the year ended, the tanks were withdrawn to the Central Workshops at Érin for repairs. There was enough evidence now to draw some conclusions, based on how they had fared in the heat of battle. One thoughtful observer was Sir Henry Rawlinson, commander of the Fourth Army.

'The tanks in certain circumstances rendered very valuable service, but they failed to have that effect on the fighting, which many of their strongest advocates expected. They laboured under great difficulties. The officers and men who were driving them had not been under fire before; they had had great difficulty in maintaining their direction, owing to their limited vision; and their very low speed over ground torn by shells was a very serious handicap... until they have more engine power, can maintain a speed of 4mph over really bad ground and until the personnel has had more experience, they will not be of much value to an infantry assault.'

It was a fair assessment of the performance of the tanks, but cut little ice with those who had been most closely involved with their development. Sir Henry was not stating anything that they had not themselves been saying repeatedly from the start. In their view, the tanks had not had a fair trial because they had been used in abominable conditions and in ways that severely reduced their potential impact.

One of the tacticians with whom Elles had surrounded himself at Bermicourt was J.F.C. Fuller, whose angular features had earned him the nickname 'Boney'. Fuller was another of the unconventional characters who found themselves drawn to the tanks. An infantry officer, he shared with Swinton and Baker-Carr a cordial dislike of the closed minds and received opinions of his seniors at GHQ. He became a key strategist, and earned a reputation in the years after the war as a highly authoritative military thinker, whose ideas would even influence Hitler's war machine. Fuller now summed up what the lessons were as far as the champions of the tanks were concerned:

– the machine in principle was sound, though needed some mechanical improvements
– it had been made for good going and fine weather, and had been used

on 'a pudding of mud'
– the need for secrecy meant commanders had little feel for tactics in the field
– there had not been time to train the crews properly
– the success of any tank operation depended on good reconnaissance
– better communications were needed
– the tanks needed their own supply organisations
– the tanks drew fire away from the infantry, so having as great an encouraging effect on our own troops as they have a demoralising one on the enemy's.

Again, it was a fair verdict. Swinton agreed with it, and was scathing of the decision to throw the tanks into the fray without more careful consideration. 'The debut of the tanks was an error of judgement by reason of the gulf which lay between the utmost that could have been achieved then, and what might have been gained by waiting. We threw away a surprise. We discounted a possible great coup in the future for the slender prospect of a small immediate gain.'

Henriques, from his perspective as a tank commander, took the same view. He again lamented the toll taken by the requirement that the tanks put on a twice-daily show, almost as a form of entertainment. 'If only we had a little more sleep and a little less showing off, what a marvellous story this Somme battle might have been,' he wrote. 'As it was, this precious secret was out, and our own infantry hated us.'

If there was an 'error of judgement', it was Haig's. The commander-in-chief's actions and reputation have been appraised and reappraised by successive generations of historians for more than a century. In the immediate aftermath of the war, as a slew of memoirs was published, the chief had his defenders. He had thrown away the key advantage of surprise, but the secret could not have been kept forever. The tanks had been demonstrated in England, and as we have seen, had become something of a fairground attraction on their arrival in France. How much the Germans had known about the phenomenon coming their way was not clear, but they had certainly known something. Their intelligence networks had picked up rumours of some sort of armoured land cruiser being developed by the British, and their gunners had been issued with armour-piercing bullets at various points along the line. Perhaps Haig felt that the cat would be out of the bag long before he could assemble the large force recommended by Swinton, and decided to make a virtue of necessity. His pressing need to inject momentum into the Somme battle and staunch the shocking level of losses might have made the decision rather easier.

The performance of the tanks in their brief and inconclusive interventions provided evidence to bolster the arguments of sceptics and supporters alike. For the critics, they had proved slow and unreliable and maddeningly prone to breaking down or floundering in the mud. The Germans had seen them now, and, their initial terror overcome, were already working out ways to neutralise them. Flers was a flash in the pan. The Gird Trench was a one-off. Swinton was a fantasist. The tanks would never unlock the stalemate of the last two years.

Those who believed in the tanks could hardly argue with much of this. But they could, and did, contend that in adverse conditions the tanks had shown enough to suggest that they could be game-changers if lessons were learned. Christopher Baker-Carr, who is about to re-enter our story, had taken a close interest in the tanks from the start, the more so since they had been absorbed into his Machine Gun Corps. He produced a report on the early appearances of the tank in battle. His paper emphasised the effect the tanks had had on German morale, and was clear that the main cause of their comparative failure was a lack of organisation and proper preparations, in particular the absence of reconnaissance work. Better intelligence might have resulted in a decision to hold the tanks back until the ground was firmer. These were problems that could be solved.

Baker-Carr shared the disappointment that the tanks had not done as well as had been hoped, but concluded: 'I felt quite convinced that the moderate success, if closely analysed, demonstrated that there was nothing inherently wrong and that given more reliable and less complicated machines, the tank under favourable conditions and with suitable organisation would prove to be of inestimable assistance in breaking the deadlock on the Western Front.'

With the fighting at an end for the winter, there was an opportunity to absorb the lessons of 1916 before this assessment would be put to the test. At least the next batch of officers and crews would undergo more rigorous training and preparation before being sent to France. Albert Baker and his fellows were in for a busy few months at Bovington Camp.

Portrait of Bert Baker by R.A. Newell.

Village life in 19th century Kirdford: the forge ...

... and the village school.

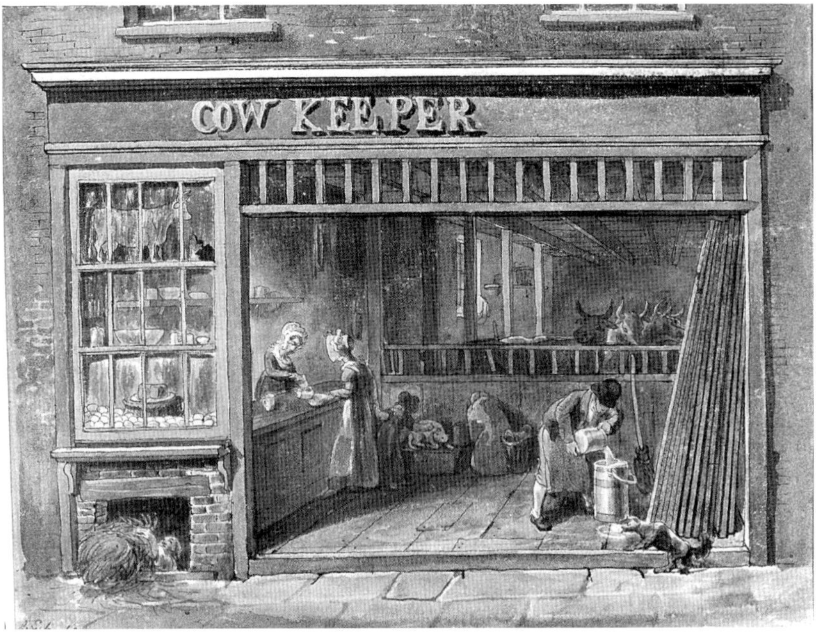

An early urban dairy in London, c.1825, with the cows at the back of the shop and the customer counter at the front.

A typical late Victorian urban dairy, located between residential houses. This is Hine's Dairy, East Dulwich, c.1900, about half a mile from the Baker dairy.

No 75 Pellatt Road as it is today - now two flats,
but with the original shop front still visible.

The interior of a Mark IV tank showing the commander's seat with backrest removed. Directly ahead are the two steering brake levers and to the right the primary two-speed and reverse gear lever.

Bert Baker (in mannequin form) with his five grandchildren at the opening of the 'Tank Men' exhibition at The Tank Museum, 2016.

The Graincourt Gun on display at The Tank Museum.

Lordship Lane, East Dulwich, c.1900.

Pellatt Road in the 1890s, at about the time George Baker started his business.
The site of the dairy is tantalisingly hidden from view just beyond the awning on the right.

The only known photograph of the whole Baker family, taken in about 1905.
From left: George, Cis, Reg, Winnie, Bert, Len, Lily, Emma.

Bert, Cis, Reg and friends on a day trip, June 1906.
Bert is standing in the middle of the first group ...

... and second from left, back row, in the second.

The main street in Cuinchy, France, in 1915. Bert was stationed here at Christmas 1915 during his period in the trenches with the Fusiliers.

Flanders mud.

The first tank: 'Little Willie'.

One of the first tanks to go into action: a Mark I heading for the Somme battlefield, 1916.

'Big Willie', or 'Mother', going through its paces during trials in early 1916.

Drawing by D.G. Browne of the crossing of the Steenbeck on the way to the Cockcroft, August 1917.
Browne commanded a tank in the action, and later wrote a classic account of the early days of the tanks.

THE DAILY MIRROR, Wednesday, November 22, 1916.

FIRST PICTURES OF THE TANKS IN ACTION

The Daily Mirror

CERTIFIED CIRCULATION LARGER THAN THAT OF ANY OTHER DAILY PICTURE PAPER

No. 4,082. Registered at the G.P.O. as a Newspaper. WEDNESDAY, NOVEMBER 22, 1916 One Halfpenny.

"HUSH, HUSH"—A TANK GOES "GALUMPHANT" INTO ACTION ON THE WESTERN FRONT.

At last! To-day we are able to publish the first photograph of one of his Majesty's land ships, which have been making such successful cruises on the sea of mud on the Somme. They are the first to be published in any British newspaper, and two others will be found on pages 6 and 7. This "juggernaut," this "Diplodocus," to give it but two of the hundred and one names which have been conferred upon it, was seen "galumphing" into action, its progress being best described in the immortal language of Lewis Carroll. The tanks have been at Flers—one "led" the men down the High-street—and many of the important battles of the great "push" in France. Before them barbed wire becomes as limp as macaroni, while they mow down trees and pass casually over trenches, dealing out death as they go.—(Exclusive to *The Daily Mirror*.)

The *Daily Mirror* scoops its rivals with the first photograph of a tank.

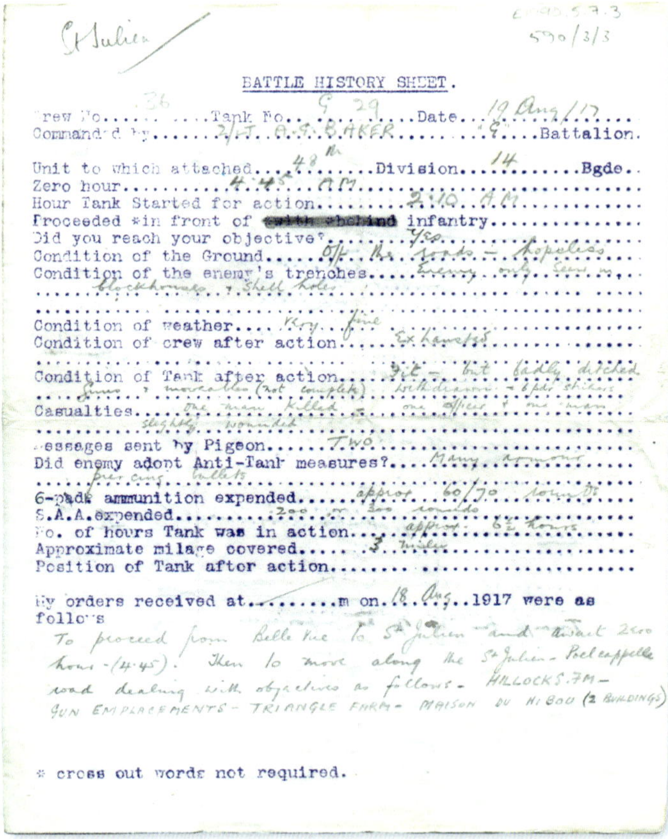

St Julien

590/3/3

BATTLE HISTORY SHEET.

Crew No........36.....Tank No......G 29.....Date.....19 Aug/17.....
Commanded by.....2/Lt. A. G. BAKER.........."G"....Battalion.

Unit to which attached.....48th.....Division.....14.....Bgde..
Zero hour.....4.45 AM.....
Hour Tank Started for action.....2.10 A.M.....
Proceeded *in front of [redacted] infantry.....
Did you reach your objective?.....Yes.....
Condition of the Ground.....Off the roads – hopeless.....
Condition of the enemy's trenches.....Enemy only seen in blockhouses & shell holes.....

Condition of weather.....Very fine.....
Condition of crew after action.....Exhausted.....

Condition of Tank after action.....Fit – but badly ditched. Guns & moveables (not complete) withdrawn – 6pdr strikers.....
Casualties.....One man killed – one officer & one man slightly wounded.....

Messages sent by Pigeon.....TWO.....
Did enemy adopt Anti-Tank measures?.....Many armour piercing bullets.....

6-pdr ammunition expended.....approx 60/70 rounds.....
S.A.A. expended.....200 or 300 rounds.....
No. of hours Tank was in action.....approx 6½ hours.....
Approximate milage covered.....3 miles.....
Position of Tank after action.....

My orders received at..........m on 18 Aug..1917 were as follows
To proceed from Belle Vue to St Julien and await 2400 hours (4.45). Then to move along the St Julien – Poelcappelle road dealing with objectives as follows – HILLOCKS FM – GUN EMPLACEMENTS – TRIANGLE FARM – MAISON DU HIBOU (2 BUILDINGS)

* cross out words not required.

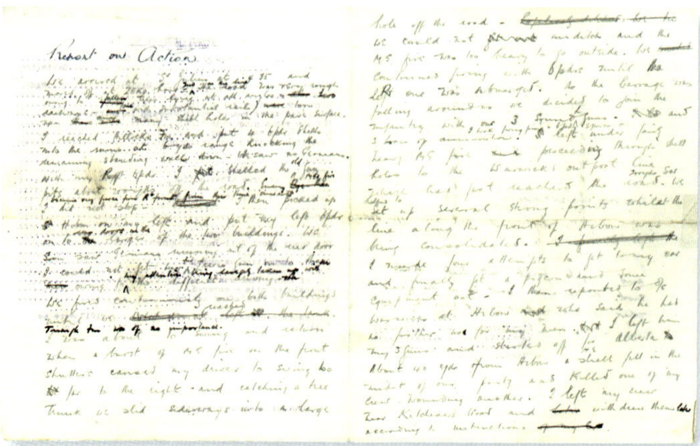

Report on Action

Bert Baker's completed Battle History Sheet from the Cockcroft, and his handwritten account of the action.

Willard's tank still ditched in the Steenbeck after the Cockcroft action.

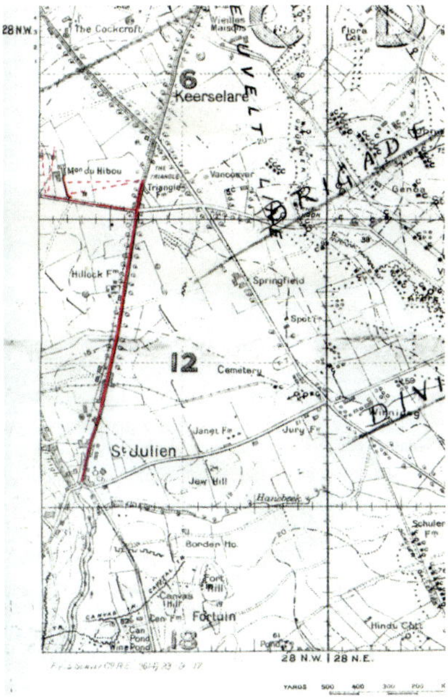

Part of the map issued to Bert Baker showing the area of the Cockcroft action. He later added the red line showing the progress of *Gorgonzola I*.

Gorgonzola photographed in 1920, still ditched by the roadside outside Maison du Hibou.

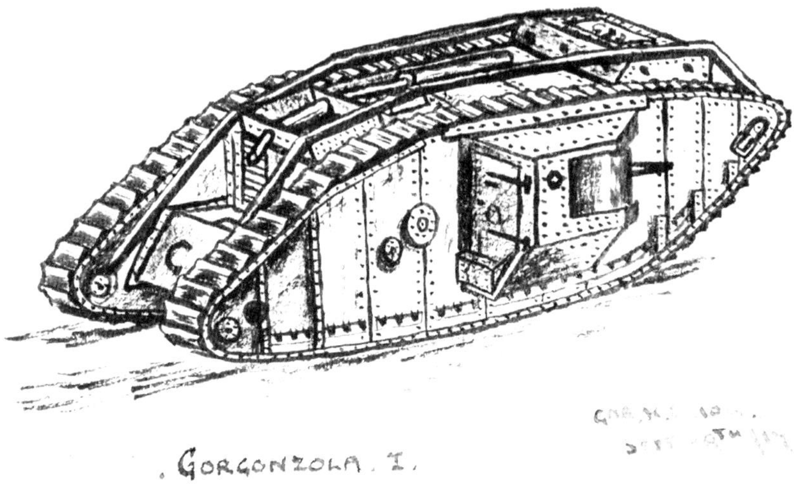

A sketch of Baker's tank *Gorgonzola*, dated 29 September 1917 and signed by Gunner Prior, presumably one of the crew. He must have drawn it from memory – the tank was ditched outside St Julien by this time.

Head-on view of a Mark IV male tank.

Sponson of a male tank showing the 6pdr gun.

Tank tackling barbed wire.

Tank ditched in the mud.

6
GALUMPHANT!

In No Man's Land one early morn at sixty in the shade
From out the British lines there came the famous Tank Brigade
The Huns began to strafe 'em, couldn't make it out at all
Especially when the tanks began the Caterpillar crawl
And the tanks went on, and they strolled along with an independent air
And their guns began to blare, and the Huns began to swear
For they pulled the trees up by the roots,
and they made the Huns look like galoots
Did the tanks that broke the ranks out in Picardy.
(from *The Tanks That Broke the Ranks* by Castling and Carlton)

The instant love affair between the public and the tanks, fuelled by journalistic hyperbole, showed no sign of cooling. No matter how modest their actual achievements in France, tank mania took hold in earnest. There were poems, popular songs, a new dance – the Tanko – and clockwork toys. When a tank took up residence in Trafalgar Square, as part of a drive to raise money to build more, it attracted £13 million in war bonds, the equivalent of five or six times as much today.

National newspapers were engaged in a highly competitive race to be the first to print a picture of an actual tank. That race was won on 22 November 1916 by the *Daily Mirror*, with an exclusive front-page picture and a headline that borrowed from Lewis Carroll's poem Jabberwocky: 'HUSH HUSH – A TANK GOES GALUMPHANT INTO ACTION ON THE WESTERN FRONT'. The accompanying text was breathlessly excited:

> At last! Today we are able to publish the first photograph of one of His Majesty's landships, which have been making such successful cruises on the sea of mud on the Somme. They are the first to be published in any British newspaper, and two others will be found on pages 6 and 7. This 'juggernaut', this 'Diplodocus' to give it but two of the hundred and one names which have been conferred upon it, was seen 'galumphing' into action, its progress being best described in the immortal language of Lewis Carroll. The tanks have been at Flers – one 'led' the men down the High Street – and many of the important battles of the great 'push' in France. Before them, barbed wire becomes as limp as macaroni, while they mow down trees and pass casually over trenches, dealing out death as they go.

Juggernaut and Diplodocus were not words heard very often in Bovington or around Bermicourt. To their crews, the machines were 'willies', 'cars', or 'buses'. But these names were far too prosaic to satisfy the gentlemen of the press. They strove to outdo each other in their descriptions of the tanks, which found themselves characterised variously as Land Dreadnoughts, Giant Toads, Motor Monsters, Touring Forts, Travelling Turrets, Whales, Slugs and Boojums – this last another nod to Lewis Carroll. The writing may have been overdone, but the newspapers had certainly understood that the tanks represented a game-changing moment in military history.

With war correspondents now operating in France, it became possible to do some real reporting on the ground, rather than relying on dry official communiqués and their own imaginations. One of the most comprehensive early accounts was filed by the *Daily Express* special correspondent Percival Phillips. The prose, in his front-page report of September 1916, was no less purple than that of the *Mirror*:

> I listened today to the stories of some of the young men who took the tanks into action on Friday, Saturday and yesterday. They were told in an open field, where a group of battle-scarred cars were resting after their labours. You might have thought that the heroes of these fantastic exploits were talking about commonplace everyday incidents, instead of a new kind of warfare hitherto undreamed of. They had tilted at German trenches, heard the furious rattle of machine gun bullets against their armour, been shaken by bombs and even battered by shells while ramming dugouts and mowing down Bavarians, but the dry recital of their nightmare experiences did not even hint that they had accomplished anything out of the ordinary.

Phillips went on to record a number of eyewitness accounts of some of the early experiences of the tank crews. The theme throughout was one of quiet heroism. It can be seen again in this account by another war reporter, Malcolm Ross, also the result of an interview with a tank commander:

> I have had just had a talk with the captain of the tank that crawled into Flers. He was calmly, after his adventure, writing up his diary in the bowels of his own pet saurian monster, and seemed to have enjoyed his perilous and exciting escapade. In some places, the Boche when he saw their oncoming ran like men possessed. But the machine laid many a running Boche low that day. The skin of this great saurian had been splashed with German bullets that had bounced off it like hail from an iron roof. Some bullets had only scraped its paint away.
>
> The Germans had spotted the tanks coming up towards our lines the day before, either from their observation balloons or their aeroplanes. But they apparently regarded them simply as a new type of armoured car, and the first Boche that saw them in the early dawn crawling forward over tremendous obstacles must have rubbed his eyes in wonder. Nothing like them had ever before been seen in war.

The *Manchester Guardian* published a riveting first-hand account by a young Australian soldier who had been wounded in one of the first actions. This particular individual apparently had something of a reputation for embroidering a story, so it needs taking with a pinch of salt. But his description, told in staccato fashion, did capture both the intensity and grim humour of the experience:

> Out for first time. Strange sensation. Worse than being in a submarine. At first unable to see anything, but imagined a lot. Bullets began to rain.
>
> Got a peep at frightened Huns. They tried to bolt like scared rabbits but were shot down before getting to their burrows. Machine guns brought forward. Started vicious rattle on our 'hide'. Not the least impression was made. Shells began to burst. We moved on and overtook some more frightened Huns. Cut their ranks to ribbons with our fire.
>
> They ran like men possessed. Officer tried to rally them. They awaited our coming for a while. As soon as our guns began to spit at them, they were off once more. Infantry rounded them up and survivors surrendered. Very curious about us. Stood open-mouthed and wide-eyed watching, but weren't much the wiser.
>
> Experience was not altogether pleasant at first. Tank sickness is as bad as seasickness until you get used to it.
>
> Tuesday – Off for another cruise. Peppering began at once. Silly blighters thought they could rush the tank like they would a fort. Dashed up from all sides. We fired at them point-blank. Devilish plucky chaps some of them, for all their madness. The survivors had another try. We spat at them venomously. Most of them went down.
>
> The blessed old tub gave a sudden jerk ... A tremendous thud. The whole outfit seemed done for. Nearly jumped out of my skin. Looked at each other and wondered what it was. Still a roof over our heads, thank God.
>
> It was only another Hun trench. Our 'spitting devils' opened fire and swept the trench clear of the enemy right and left. Some Huns tried the rushing dodge. Their rushing days are over.

Another powerful and more authentic-sounding piece was produced by a machine-gunner who took his readers right into the heart of the action, and into the heads of those riding a tank into battle:

> Our Tanks have made their debut, and what a startling debut it was. Heavens, what a warm day's work! I can speak of it, for I was there.
>
> We were in the front line with our tanks in little groups of crews under the command of an officer. The enormous silhouette of ours amid the ruins of Pozières – where it had been quartered waiting to be brought up to the line of fire – called up in the moonlight the idea of some fantastic monster of prehistoric times. It looked like a tortoise with a hump. There

were Tommies from London and Northumberland, Scotsmen, Canadians and New Zealanders – who were presently to march into the firing line with us – staring at my machine with curiosity and respect.

But the hour is approaching. Dawn will soon be here. I smoke my last pipe because, once inside the tank, farewell to any other chance of smoking! My good old pipe, though it may be really and truly my last one! I gaze at the enormous machine whose engines are already beginning to groan terribly; it seems like a gigantic tomb. How will it behave if a large shell falls on top of it? I fear it would be the end of everything – both of us and the steel beast itself. After all it is war; we must wait till we see what happens. Here comes our officer. There is a quick rally and a short address. He reminds us of our respective roles and of what Sir Douglas Haig expects both of us and of the tanks, and compliments us on our courage and our cool-headedness. A manhole is opened in the side of the Tank and one by one we enter the interior, like cats going in through a hole in the door.

The whole crew climbs on board this fortress on wheels. I install myself in the narrow space, by the side of my machine gun, whose muzzle is pointing outside the steel-plate sides of the tank, and fix my eye to the loophole. 'How hot it is' says my neighbour. 'It will be worse in an hour!' Through my loophole I can just see a strip of sky which looks light to me, although the day has not yet fully dawned. In front of me I see undulating fields which have been ploughed up by guns of every calibre.

There is a crater to the left of the wood which, according to the reports of our airmen, the Germans have converted into a fortress. This is the objective of the Tank on our left. At the right of the wood there is a redoubt described to us as extraordinarily powerful: walls of interminable barbed wire chevaux de frise, a formidable entanglement of all sorts of vile contrivances. A real 'nest' of vile beasts! This is to be our job. By Jove, how stifling it is! Suddenly the glare of a rocket lights up the sky, followed by ten, twenty, thirty others. A sharp whistle sounds strangely in our prison. The hour has really come: we are to start.

My heart is beating violently – I do not know why. One needs to have 'sea-legs' to avoid knocking oneself against the sides of this carcass of steel, which is now waddling along ungracefully over ruts and uneven places. I take hold of the metallic handle of a case of machine gun ammunition. The motor system of our Tank is gripping the soil, sticking to it, gliding and dragging itself along like a centipede. We move inwards, while the enthusiastic cheers of our infantry reach our ears, in spite of the fearful din. As we advance, the earth everywhere around our track is ploughed up and thrown aside. But Heavens, how stifling it is and how infernally far away the wood seems to be!

There is a sound like hailstones beating against the window panes of a moving train. The German guns have opened fire on us. But in faith they

> are wasted shots. They have as much effect on our machine as pellets of bread against a wall.
>
> Our Tank advances steadily and inexorably. A ditch: we clear it; an incline: we scale it; a heap of rubbish from a demolished house – we pass over it. And then we come to the first barbed-wire entanglements. Our Tank does not even make an effort: everything breaks, everything is crushed, everything is torn up. Splinters of wood jump on all sides of us, the chevaux de frise are beaten down. I have the sensation of being in the interior of a gigantic iron wedge which is cutting through something like butter.
>
> As for us, we fire without ceasing, hand on gun and eye glued to the loophole pierced in the steel, with the sweat pouring down our foreheads.
>
> The Germans are in the greatest disorder. They throw themselves flat on their stomachs, they raise their arms to heaven, some of them try to run away. A whistle in the Tank sounds and it stops. Then wild cheers come faintly to my ears, and I soon see the dear old uniforms of our boys who are taking possession of the 'nest' and gathering up everything living which remains.

This appears to be an account of one element of the Bapaume action, and an unusually successful one. It gives a powerful idea of what it was like inside a tank under fire – and how little the early crews knew what to expect once they rolled into action. The reference to Canadian, Australian and New Zealand soldiers is a reminder that the British forces contained many soldiers from across the British Empire.

The most fanciful description of the new wonder weapon appeared in another newspaper, and was not, one assumes, intended to be taken entirely literally: 'Tanks can run along like a spider; they can climb over a row of houses quite easily. They can jump like a champion hurdle racer and could clear a ten-foot wall with grace. They can bark like ten thousand wolves. They chew up barbed wire and turn it into ammunition as they go along. There are only two things the tank cannot do: they cannot fly and they cannot make poached eggs on toast.'

The crews in France took a largely jaundiced view of the tank hysteria at home, because they knew that little of substance had actually been accomplished, and that tougher tests lay ahead. Clough Williams-Ellis said the newspaper coverage actually cast a pall of gloom over the Corps, because it exposed them to a degree of derision from the rest of the army. 'They had been unmercifully twitted by unfeeling gunmen and infantrymen who knew the real facts.'

At Bovington, those pouring into the new camp were happy enough to bask in the reflected glory, and wonder when their turn would come. There were the inevitable musical chairs as new battalions were formed. Under the latest reorganisation, the four companies of tanks now in France would be converted into four battalions. A further five battalions would be raised in England, with the existing E and F companies as their core. Each battalion would be sub-divided into three companies, and three battalions would comprise a brigade. Later there would be further expansion. There was a determination to learn the lessons of the last few months, and prepare the crews as thoroughly as possible for the spring 1917 offensives in which they could expect to take part.

The camp at Bovington sat in 1,300 acres of heathland, and had been used by the army as a training area for infantry since 1899. Discipline was notably stiffer than at Elveden, where German prisoners of war were already restoring Lord Iveagh's estate to its pre-tank tranquillity. There was a feeling that the regime at Elveden had been rather slack, and it was clear that Swinton's successors intended to remedy that. 'Very strict CO at head, and 3 or 4 Majors,' commented Baker. 'Everything done in proper forms.' He was one of an ever-growing body of junior officers as the new battalions were assembled. 'Each have a large squad of recruits to drill. Nearly hoarse after two days of it. Small squads of recruits everywhere, being taught L & R turn! Lots of new officers keep arriving – 60 today alone.' He was, as ever, happy to be in the thick of the action, and ambitious to get on. 'Still sorting things out,' he wrote at the end of November. 'I want to go for dental treatment but am afraid to be away. You must look out for yourself when they are handing out new jobs.'

The weather became very bad. 'Several night ops in fog, sleet and mud galore. No British Warms yet.' For once, he sounded less than enamoured of his surroundings: 'Have lost our cubicle,' he wrote early in the New Year. 'About 90 of us now in a dreadful draughty hut in NE corner of camp. Lox and Tommy Morgan still with me. The language is terrible, all work no leave, better off in France. There are infantry huts where there is a much smaller proportion of officers, consequently not enough cubicles for us all. The sergeants are better off than we junior officers.'

But still, he considered that things were 'shaping well'. In the new battalion structure, he had been allocated to 20 Company of G Battalion. 'We shall be a very fine branch of the service – another "Flying Corps" soon. Special uniforms to be issued soon. 106 officers in mess now – Battn mess of G Bn.' As well as all the drilling, which would sharpen up the tank men and instil in them the necessity for obedience, smartness and teamwork, there were continuous courses and exercises. Separate schools were set up in tank driving and maintenance; tank gunnery; tank reconnaissance; tank signalling (by lamp, flag, semaphore and carrier pigeon); bombing; camouflage; use of revolver; response to gas attack and use of compass. Baker's service record shows that one after the other in early 1917, he took courses in bombing, tank driving mechanisms, gas defence and signalling. Once he had acquired the skills himself, he passed them on to others. 'Bovington Camp was really a military academy,' said Daniel Hickey. 'With this difference: that the officers were not only students, but lecturers as well, for they had to instruct the men.'

Slowly but surely, the commanders and their crews began to find their way about the strange beasts. Familiarity did not breed contempt: they remained in awe of the monsters, even as they struggled to exert control over them. An officer who was training at Bovington at the time left an evocative account of the sight of the tanks returning to camp after a day's training on the heath: 'It was a most impressive and fearsome sight. Over the brow of the hill, dimly outlined against the dusk, loomed a herd of strange toad-like monsters. The noise of the whirring engines and the weird flap-flap-flap of the tracks, like the padding of gigantic webbed feet, filled the air. The vast snouts went up and up, and then suddenly dipped down abruptly as the creatures made for home. They made one shiver: they were so repulsive, so inhuman, so full of menace. Even though there was no danger, one felt fear creeping through one's veins. The impulse was to turn and run for dear life, but instead one stood there rooted with horror and admiration.'

Inside the tanks, the crews were learning the hard way as they were tossed and buffeted about. They went through the sort of rigorous manoeuvres for which there had not been time at Elveden. Some of these exercises would have been terrifying even in the relative safety of a training ground. The driver would be instructed to climb an almost perpendicular rise, then stall the engine and restart it by sliding back down in reverse gear. The tanks would follow assault courses of sharp bends, steep inclines, sunken roads and sudden drops. Perhaps the greatest test of nerve was the 'swallow dive' – mounting a steep rise, balancing precariously on the top and then plunging down the other side, the driver throttling down as soon as he felt the machine begin to topple. The officer at Bovington described one such operation in gripping detail:

> Slowly the tank went forward, inch by inch it crept over the top of the incline. Suddenly the nose of the tank tilted forward, and the huge machine went down and down and down. He had the sensation of dropping gently through space. The throttle was almost closed, the engine ticking over: without warning the tank plunged violently downwards and with a terrific bump the snout struck the ground. The tank, for a second, practically stood on end. One of the gearsmen in the rear, taken unawares, was hurled clean out of the sponson door. The others clung wildly to anything within reach, their feet sliding and scraping over the steel floor. Grease drums, oil cans and stray tools shot forwards in a clattering mass, landing on the driver's back and spraying him with oil. The driver himself was at such an angle that he looked straight into the earth a couple of feet in front of his face. But the throttle was now opened out full and as the engine raced, the caterpillar tracks gripped firmly, and foot by foot the tanks crawled up to the top of the crater. Then, slightly shaken but triumphant, the driver got out to watch the next tank go over.

As duty officer, or 'orderly dog' on occasion, various random tasks fell to Baker. One such day was 11 January 1917. 'Orderly dog today, it happens to be Thursday and guest night in the mess. I have to sit at top table with the CO and guests, and when the CO proposes the health of the King, I have to rise on my hind legs with a glass of port and say "Gentlemen, the King!" The port goes round clockwise from the CO, everyone in strict turn.'

Someone had the bright idea of supplementing the training with an address from one of the few people who had any practical experience of going into action in a tank. Lieutenant Basil Henriques had been in one of the first companies to go to France from Elveden, and was now at Bovington. In early March he gave a lecture to his fellow officers, setting out what he had seen and what he had learned.

It is probable that Bert Baker missed this address, because he was engaged in large-scale night operations in the week it took place, and there is no mention of it in the Tablet. 'Very big night ops,' he recorded in his notes for this particular week. 'Drove the new buses across country without lights. Very exciting with such a large number. No mishaps – over hedges, ditches, trees, craters etc, just as they come.'

This level of practice was far removed from the experience Henriques had had the previous year. We have already heard some of his complaints about the lack of preparation, and the distracting requirement to put on daily demonstrations of tank work for gawping officers. The closely-typed script of his Bovington lecture, with many handwritten revisions, is held in The Tank Museum. Over a talk of about an hour, he set out with devastating candour just how ill-prepared the tanks and their crews had been the previous August. He was later to write of the terror of his first foray into action, a fear that had stayed with him long afterwards. He must have decided that now was not the time to share this particular memory with those who were preparing to follow in his footsteps. But that was where his self-restraint came to an end. While dispassionate and factual, his account amounted to a shuddering reality check for his listeners. If they had felt any complacency about their new careers, he would surely have jolted them out of it.

Henriques began on a positive note, praising the calibre of those who had joined the Heavy Section as men of more than ordinary intelligence, most of whom knew their way around an engine and enjoyed fixing it if it went wrong. They were also thoroughly at home with the Vickers machine-guns. He felt it was a great advantage that the tank commanders had trained their own crews: 'Not only did we feel a terrific pride in our Company and section, but also as a tank crew against other crews. There was always healthy competition, and this competition carried us right out to France. We were able to tell the men, whom we got to know thoroughly, that <u>our</u> tank was going to go through at all cost. We were able to get that spirit into them because of the training which we tank commanders had been able to give the crews ourselves. We knew our men thoroughly.'

He felt this was critical. 'I want to make a special point of this. It is absolutely essential to know the character and psychology of your men. Although we are in a machine, yet the action of individuals in a machine can never be mechanical, and unless you know your men and know them well enough to judge how they are likely to act under certain circumstances, you are likely to be let down in action. Very few of our men had been in action before.'

Henriques went on to catalogue in telling detail the training they had received before leaving Elveden – or, more accurately, the lack of it. The first Company to go out had been under tremendous pressure, because the tanks did not arrive until the last minute and there was no time for much of what was in the supposed syllabus. Henriques and his crew suffered more than most, because their tank developed engine trouble the day it arrived, and they worked as a crew only once before leaving.

There had been no instruction in map reading. This was a bad miss. 'It is as essential for the men to be good map readers as it is for the officers. When orders come through at the last minute, you have to scribble a map and explain it to your crew in a short time. It makes it very much easier for you if your crew has been trained in map reading.'

There had been no practice in reconnaissance, which had soon come to be regarded as imperative. There had been no instruction in the use of a compass, or practice with one. There had been no guidance in understanding orders. 'When you work with a division, you get very long orders, and you need to discover what concerns you and what does not. Unless you have practice in this, you find it difficult to grasp them right away. We had no knowledge of the dissemination of available information.' Henriques said: 'We did not know what information we needed or where to look for it.'

Inexorably, he pressed on. There had been no signalling training. There had been a single day of revolver practice, a single day of shooting on the range. They had been issued with goggles and gas helmets but when the men had a gas drill, they had not known how to put them on. They had been issued with new guns, many of which had not been test-fired before they went into action.

He was not done yet. They had had no practice in driving with the flaps closed and using the periscope. 'We had never driven over unknown courses. We never went over a course that we had not been over step by step carefully beforehand. Perhaps the most important point of all was that we had only once fired from a moving tank. A man may be able to fire well when stationary, but unless he has had practice at picking up targets on the move he will find his firing will not be of much use when he gets into action.'

Finally, they had not had enough physical training, and not enough discipline had been instilled in the men by their commanders.

The net effect of all this was that they had boarded the ship for France heavy with misgivings about what lay ahead, and full of apprehension – the reverse of what their situation required. 'You need to go out feeling confident in your machine and yourselves and certain you will make a success of it. It was impossible for us to go out feeling absolutely confident when we had never worked together in a tank, had never once driven over unknown ground and only once fired from a moving tank – and bearing in mind the other parts of our training that we were forced to leave out.'

He ended this part of his talk with a withering reflection on the quality of the leadership at Elveden. 'The day before the second half of our company went out, we were inspected by the colonel. He must have known that there was this lack of confidence in the men, as it was obvious that we had not had sufficient training. It would have made a terrific difference if the colonel had given to us one of those inspiring messages, telling us that we were going out to make history. Instead of that the Commanding Officer merely asked a few men if they had their identification cards.' This, Henriques noted wryly, 'was not encouraging'.

Safe to say that by now his audience was hanging on his every word. They at least were getting a much better preparation than Henriques and his fellows had had. But what about conditions when they actually reached France? Henriques now moved on to describe these.

On the day after arriving at a position a few miles behind the frontline, the section commander and tank officers, Henriques among them, had gone for a bike ride. 'Our general idea was to get some knowledge of the country in which we were to operate, but this is where we failed – in our knowledge of reconnaissance. We did not know what to look for or where to look for it, and so we could only look on it as an enjoyable bicycle run into extremely interesting country. We gained no experience that day which would be useful to us in action.'

Soon afterwards had come the arrival of spare parts, most of them completely superfluous. 'A great many things were given to us which we did not want, and some which we did not know how to use. But we were glad at any rate that the tank would be supplied with a track spanner. Before, we had shared one with 7–8 others.'

Henriques went on to describe to the officers his experience of going into battle, and the lessons he had learned:

> The points I would like to bring out to you from the actual fighting are these: it is almost impossible for the tank commander to see the target of the gunners on the left or right. He cannot control their fire and if he wants to draw their attention as I did on one occasion, he cannot make himself heard. My NCO was then at the gears and all that I could do was to hit the man on the shoulder with my stick. Shout as you will, you cannot make your order heard by the crew.
>
> It was tremendously difficult to keep direction. We had no compass – the one with us was useless – and I discovered that the steering gear was not working properly. If the tank commander has such an extremely limited control over the fire of his men, through their not being able to hear his orders, and as he is not able to see their targets, it is absolutely essential to train as much as possible the initiative of the men. They must be able to act quickly on their own.

His engagement with the enemy had been chaotic and exceptionally perilous.

> I found the Boche in front of his line in shell holes and they were simply potting me the whole time as I had to look through the flaps. They succeeded in laying my driver out, hitting him over the eyes. As you know there are two flaps, a large and a small one. I did not know that the small one was in two pieces, and it was extremely unpleasant to find that this was split in

two and one piece was hanging by a thread. Consequently, a good deal of machine gun fire got through into the tank. I thought that this loose flap was going to fall off, and if it had then most of the crew would have been done for.

When we finally reached the German lines, bullets came through the left sponson. I have not yet been able to discover whether it was a faulty sponson or armour-piercing bullets. But it had a bad morale effect, and I did not know how far it was going and how many of the men it would lay out. In addition to the bullets running through, I had the fear that the flap would break off. I could not open the big flap without opening the little one. One of the periscopes was broken and the officer's periscope could not be used because of the broken flap. Two of my guns were put out of action, because in one case the muzzle attachment had been blown off and the other had a No 3 stoppage (a very bad one) which he did not seem to be able to remedy. Thus, we had no guns on the left side and I had to decide what to do. There was in my mind also the risk of being captured. The inability to see and guide my tank made me practically helpless in the shell holes.

I decided under the circumstances that I had better withdraw, and it is a big question whether I ought not to have remained longer. The tank laid out one machine gun for certain, probably two, and according to reports from the crew we had about 40 Boches.'

Little wonder that he would later recall the sheer terror and helplessness he felt in these circumstances. A sense of isolation also came across clearly – it had felt as though the tank was all alone on the battlefield, with no means of communicating with anyone, properly controlling its direction, or being able to see its targets – even being able to see where it was going. It was clear that months later, Henriques was still agonising about whether he had done the right thing in withdrawing when he did: 'The work of a tank commander is absolutely one of initiative and personal responsibility,' he concluded. 'It can only be compared with that of a man in the RFC. There is no one to ask, and if you do not know your work yourself you cannot possibly get along. When you come out of action there is a tremendous amount of speculation as to the things you might have done.'

One imagines you could have heard a pin drop when Henriques came to the end of his lecture. This was not the stuff they had been reading about in the newspapers. There was nothing remotely glamorous in the remorselessly candid and frankly terrifying narrative Henriques had put before them, giving them for the first time an authentic account of the grim reality of life in a tank. The prospects for a tank commander and his men would have felt nasty, brutish and short. The officers must have trooped out in a sober mood, seeing their immediate future in a new and unwelcome perspective. They would be in France themselves in only a few weeks' time.

Henriques would no doubt have been pleased to know that the current crop was at least picking up some knowledge of reconnaissance work. 'Several big reconnaissance schemes,' Baker reported. 'I always enjoy them, spying out the country and working out attacks, map-making etc.' The mood in the camp was lifted when the first of Haig's promised fleet of 1,000 tanks began to roll in at the beginning of April. They were three months late, manufacturing having been hampered by a lack of manpower and raw materials. But their arrival was welcomed by everyone except the local inhabitants, who were less than thrilled with their new and exceptionally noisy neighbours. They had already complained about the din of the practice firing with the 6pdrs and machine-guns, and it had been shifted to the coast at Lulworth. Now, as the new tanks began to appear at Wool station on their way to Bovington, they did not appreciate being instructed – as the locals at Elveden had been – to draw their curtains and avert their gaze. There was still a strong desire to keep the tanks away from the view of the outside world. 'Courses galore,' reported Baker. 'Everyone happy because there's plenty to do. Should like to say what we are doing, but everyone is warned about letting information get around.'

Part of the desire for continuing secrecy might have been because the arrivals were new models. The Mark I tanks that had featured in the actions of 1916 had been swiftly followed by later versions. The originals had been thrown together at great speed, an entirely new form of weapon progressing from drawing board to battlefield within a matter of months. As soon as the Mark I was in production, Tritton and Wilson were at work on its successors, attempting to correct some of the most glaring design deficiencies of their first effort.

The Mark I was swiftly followed by the Mark II. With Haig having demanded 1,000 tanks, working models were needed on which to train the crews. The Mark II tanks were intended to fulfil this purpose; an interim order was placed for 50 of them, and the first were at Bovington by the end of 1916.

The Mark II kept the same basic shape as its predecessor, although the steering tail wheels were now abandoned. A new form of cover was added on the top, which allowed for slightly better visibility and another possible means of escape. There were changes to the configuration of the sponsons and guns, and the fuel supply. It was decided to replace the Vickers and Hotchkiss machine-guns with Lewis guns – a change that proved deeply unpopular and was later reversed. As they were intended for training rather than frontline action, the Mark II's were made with milder steel, rather than the thicker boilerplate that was used on the combat tanks. Even so, some of them did find themselves in France before many months had elapsed, because of delays in production. Another order was placed for Mark IIIs, which incorporated only minor changes in design. These, too, were intended for training and were lightly armoured. There is no record of any of the Mark IIIs having been used in the fighting.

By October 1916, Tritton and Wilson were working on the Mark IV, which would become the standard fighting machine throughout 1917 and well into the following year. Eventually, 1,200 of them would be built. Some, including those of G Battalion, were still in use at the end of the war, even though by then they had themselves been superseded by the Mark V.

The Mark IV represented a real step forward. It had the same basic outline as the Mark I, and the same armaments. But the new design incorporated a host of improvements, which would surely have been popular with the veterans of the Mark Is. It was made easier to get in and out of the machines. The petrol tanks were moved outside and to the rear, considerably improving the survival chances of the occupants if they were hit. Rather than being dependent on gravity, the feed was now pressurised. The fuel tanks were bigger too, to give the tanks a greater range. A two-speed and reverse gearbox enabled the driver to engage first and second gear without other assistance – a big advance. Engine noise was reduced by an improved silencer, and engine cooling improved.

A particularly useful new feature, given the inhospitable terrain in which the tanks had been obliged to operate, was the unditching gear devised to help them free themselves when bogged down. This consisted of a wooden beam, 4 to 5 metres long, carried on the top of the machine. In early experiments, railway sleepers were used. In the event of ditching, the beam was fastened widthways across the tracks by clips and chains, and the tracks were engaged. As they went round, the beam was dragged under the machine, and provided a purchase that enabled the tank to climb out of the obstacle. If it sounds straightforward, it would not have felt that way to the two crew members obliged to leave the tank and fix the chains to the tracks – not an easy job at the best of times, particularly unpleasant when performed under fire. Once the tank was freed, they had to go out there again and disconnect the beam. In the endless mud of the Western Front, this procedure might have to be repeated at regular intervals.

Another innovation designed to improve traction was the 'spud', occasionally employed on earlier models, now fully incorporated. Spuds were metal extensions attached to the tracks at intervals to help with grip on soft or broken ground. The part of the spud that came into contact with the ground was a spade shape, digging into the surface like a claw to improve traction. The spuds had a tendency to snag on barbed wire or foul the unditching beam, and they had to be removed again if the tank had the luxury of travelling on a paved road, which simply flattened them. Browne said his tank carried 44 spuds, which with the unditching beam, might have added as much as two tons to the overall weight of the machine.

Mark IV Tank
Number made1,220 (420 male, 595 female, 205 tenders to carry supplies)
Weight 28 tons
Length 26ft 5in/8m
Width 13ft 6in/4m
Crew 8
Engine Daimler/Knight sleeve valve, 16-litre 105hp
Fuel capacity 70 gallons/318 litres
Fuel consumption 2mpg

Max speed 3.7mph/5.6kmh
Trench crossing 10ft
Armament
Male 2 x Hotchkiss 6pdr (57mm) 40-calibre quick-firing
Maximum range 7,500yds/6,900m
3 x Lewis .303in air-cooled machine-guns
Female 5 x Lewis .303in air-cooled machine-guns (In some later Mark IVs the Lewis guns were replaced by Hotchkiss .303in guns.)
Ammunition
Male 332 6pdr rounds; 5,460 machine-gun rounds
Female 13,000 machine-gun rounds.

February had given way to March, but the weather was still bitter. Living conditions at Bovington, however, had improved. 'Now have one cubicle between two officers,' Baker wrote. 'Much more comfortable than open huts. Terrific ice and snow – still very cold. Had to spend £4 on a compass, also mess tin 12/6 and w bottle 10/-. Before we go abroad we get three months' field allowance in advance, £12.' He added: 'We go to France at the end of March.' The compass survived, and is in the possession of The Tank Museum.

The end of March came and went with no movement overseas. 'Had several days at Lulworth firing 6-pounders,' Baker reported in early April. 'Very good fun, lovely coast and some fine sea views. Fed at local pub each night – no proper mess available.' The following week, there was another course: 'Just finished a signalling course, first day – lasts for 8 days. Exam at end – want another first class.' His ambition was undimmed – he was determined to get first class pass marks in all the courses.

There was now a definite sense in the camp that the move to France would not be long delayed. The men started making preparations. Baker had bought himself an Enfield motorcycle soon after arriving at Bovington, and now he drove it over to Emsworth near Portsmouth for safe keeping at the home of his Aunt Ellen, his mother's younger sister. His uncle and aunt kept him company on the way back as far as Portsmouth. 'Aunt Nell very upset.' He later sent all his camp kit to Emsworth for storage.

The last days at Bovington were taken up with farewell dinners at various messes and a farewell concert by the battalion. He managed to get up to Chellaston to see Miriam, and joined a party on a trip to London, where they all met up at the Long Bar at the Trocadero. Then it was down to business. On 23 May 1917, he reported: 'Everything packed for "off". DT came over to say goodbye this evening and we shall be several days on our way. Loading tanks at Wool camp.' A couple of days later, they were on the boat to France.

While the newly-formed English battalions were making their final preparations at Bovington, those already in France were taking part in their first action of 1917. But for the delays in supply, they might have been involved sooner. As it was, the force that was assembled to support an attack on Arras was a makeshift one. The new Mark IVs did not arrive until after it had started, and the force of 60 tanks comprised those Mark Is that had not been left in the mud of the Somme the previous year and 26 of the new Mark IIs that had been designed for training only and were not considered by their commanders to be suitable for anything other than that. 'It was a desperate move,' wrote the distinguished tank historian David Fletcher. 'At close range, they were even vulnerable to machine-gun fire. But there was no alternative.' On 8 April, the day Baker and his fellows were enjoying practicing with their 6pdrs at Lulworth, this ragtag force moved forward.

The Battle of Arras was essentially a diversionary action, designed to tie up German resources while the French launched a much larger offensive 50 miles further south. At first, the gains made by the infantry were sensational by the standards of the Western Front, with the Canadian capture of Vimy Ridge the highlight. But the usual pattern of events quickly asserted itself. The advances of the first day were not built upon. As always, the Germans defended stoutly and counter-attacked fiercely, and it was not long before another stalemate developed. The British gains were made at great cost in terms of casualties.

They were also made with little or no help from the tanks. Nothing had been learned from the Somme in terms of their deployment. Once again, they were split up into Swinton's hated 'driblets' and once again they sallied forth into swampland. As a result, the outcome was depressingly reminiscent of the year before. Many of the tanks were wallowing helplessly in the bog long before they reached their starting positions. Across terrain that was now like a sponge after heavy rain and a snowstorm, they bellied one by one, and in most cases resisted the frantic attempts of their crews to dislodge them from the sucking mud. Six of them all but disappeared into a bog that had not been properly reconnoitred. Tank traps and flooded ditches suggested the Germans had not been idle during the winter in calculating how to counter the threat of the tanks. During the Battle of Arras, they also discovered that the tanks were vulnerable to armour-piercing bullets, knowledge on which they were quick to act. As in the previous year's campaign, where tanks were able to join the battle they made a valuable contribution. But once again these bright spots were the exception rather than the rule.

An attack on the fortified village of Bullecourt, where the tanks were supposed to be supporting Australian soldiers, was a case in point. The tanks arrived late, and the few that made it through either broke down or were destroyed by enemy fire. In the snowy landscape, they presented large and inviting targets. The Australians, who suffered grievous losses as the attack faltered, were incensed at the lack of support they received from the tanks, and put the failure down to the 'windiness' of the officers commanding them. When a second attack was ordered on Bullecourt a couple of weeks later, the Australians refused to have anything to do with the tanks. The second assault was another costly failure, and the tanks again failed to make any sort of contribution. In the south, the French offensive was also going disastrously badly.

None of this shook Haig's faith in the tanks. His response to the Bullecourt fiasco was to ask for a huge increase in the establishment of the Heavy Branch, that would have the effect of almost doubling its size. His rationale seems to have been a growing conviction that the more tanks that were deployed, the fewer would be the casualties among the infantry. With losses of literally thousands of men a day, this was a powerful consideration. Perhaps it also helps explain Haig's willingness to deploy the tanks in conditions in which they could not possibly prosper.

Few shared his view that the tanks were part of the solution. The belief was taking ever-stronger hold that the tanks were much more trouble than they were worth, and were soaking up vital raw materials that might be better employed elsewhere. 'They were still regarded as a 'stunt' rather than as an established and permanent auxiliary arm,' Baker-Carr wrote. 'Their hold on existence was still precarious. In the struggle for priority of manufacture, they ranked far down the list of precedence, even below that of motor lorries. The High Command remained obsessed with artillery and the production of guns and shells. Any failure now by the tanks might lead to their immediate disappearance.'

Suspicion and outright hostility notwithstanding, the new Mark IVs, and their new fully-trained crews would soon be arriving from England. Perhaps that might signal a change in fortunes. Among the arrivals, as the Battle of Arras limped to an inconclusive end, were Bert Baker and the officers and crews of G Battalion. They were now part of the 1st Tank Brigade, under none other than Christopher Baker-Carr. The man who had started the war driving officers around the front in civilian vehicles was now back in the ranks at the head of a brigade. He later celebrated the journey in the title of his book, *From Chauffeur to Brigadier*.

Baker-Carr was more than happy with his new charges, and G in particular. 'G Battalion proved to be one of the very best in the whole Tank Corps,' he wrote later. 'In spite of various readjustments, rendered necessary from time to time as the corps was doubled and redoubled in strength, G Battalion remained as an integral part of the 1st Brigade until the ceasefire was blown, and no commander was ever better served.'

As G Battalion settled into life in France, the next phase of the campaign was beginning. To try to make good the failures of the French advance, the action now headed back north, again with the intention of diverting German defences. The object now was to capture their naval bases on the Belgian coast. This would be achieved by two attacks to the north-west of Lille: one on Messines, whose commanding heights gave the Germans a useful vantage point to observe British positions towards Ypres, a few miles further north; and the second, and bigger attack, on Ypres itself. In the Messines action, the tanks would be represented by the 2nd Brigade, with 72 tanks working with four corps of infantry. Nearly all these tanks were the new Mark IVs, going into action for the first time.

The battle lasted a week, and as a preliminary to the imminent attack on Ypres, it was successful. Messines Ridge was captured, as the Mark IVs made their combat debut. The Germans suffered heavy casualties and the loss of the Ridge had a demoralising effect on them. It was not a tank battle as such, but well over half the tanks reached their objectives and provided useful support for the infantry. A much greater role was proposed for them at Ypres. All three brigades would support the Fifth Army operations, which would begin on the last day in July. For the first time, G Battalion would be seeing action on the frontline.

Life had been pleasant enough for the men of G since their arrival in Le Havre at the end of May. The trip had put Baker in mind of his previous journey along the same route, on his way to the trenches. 'A very nice trip across. I slept most of the way. Much better than my first trip up the line with the Fusiliers.'

After resting for three days, the battalion had travelled by train to Wavrin, about 20 miles west of Arras. The men were billeted in surrounding villages. 'Safely reached Wavrin, near St Pol. Arrived at 8am after 14-hour train journey. Nearly the same route as with the Fusiliers, but very different conditions! Nice country around, reminds me of S Derbyshire. I can hear the cuckoo (not in French). The mess is two sheds and kitchen. We are billeted in companies – 26 officers in our mess. 3 miles from St Pol.'

It was a cosy billet. 'Nicely settled in – wouldn't mind staying for the rest of the war in this place. Just a faint rumble of guns in the front line and lots of lorries and planes going to and fro, otherwise very peaceful. The food has changed a little – a sprinkling of French on our table. Lots of German prisoners working on the roads all the way up from the base.'

The weather was hot – too hot. 'Heat and dust terrific. Just had a 3-mile wander round the camp and in a state of collapse. We're allowed to wear drill shorts – very comfortable.' He sent an order for the delivery of 200 cigarettes a week for two months. 'Can't get good cigs here.' There was also a morale-boosting message from the commander-in-chief. 'A very very tremendously important general addressed the officers this am. Also gave us a message from Earl Haig, saying the Germans will collapse at any moment. If we can keep at 'em, we can finish them before next winter.'

The tanks were now putting in valuable groundwork for what lay ahead. 'Moving each day in own buses. Very busy preparing for big show – in few days? Beginning to know my crew really well, very pleased with them.' A couple of days after the end of the fighting at Messines, the battalion were at the Central Workshops at Érin for engine instruction. On 11 July, 36 Mark IV tanks were issued to G Battalion at Érin.

By now the tank crews had copied their counterparts in the artillery and Royal Flying Corps and started giving their machines names, which were painted on to the hull. The names had to begin with the letter of the battalion to which the tank belonged, but other than that, anything not considered too vulgar was acceptable. Baker christened his tank *Gorgonzola*. He came to regret the name, but felt it would be bad luck to change it. My father always believed that he chose the name as a reminder of his youthful career in the dairy, although it seems unlikely that much home-made Gorgonzola ever issued from the doors of 75 Pellatt Road.

The tanks were put on trains and taken to Oosthoek Wood, four miles outside of Ypres. G Battalion's narrative history recorded: 'All officers were busy with the reconnaissance of the ground to the east of the Yser Canal, and all crews with the preparation of the tanks for an attack on the enemy's positions along the Steenbeck Line. Sections marched daily to the woods at Oosthoek, which were shelled periodically and bombed every night from the air; and officers went nightly in pairs to study, in the gas-poisoned precincts of the canal, the enemy's artillery treatment of the available crossings.' One lesson at least of the Somme had been taken to heart. The tank commanders spent hours walking the terrain and poring over aerial photographs and maps of the area.

Other lessons remained stubbornly unlearned. It would have been clear from this preparatory work that, once again, the tanks were being sent into conditions in which their chances of success would be nil. Ypres was 25 miles from the Belgian coast, but centuries before it had been an inland port. Swathes of land had been reclaimed from the sea for agricultural use, but were kept workable only by an elaborate network of water courses, drains, dikes and ditches criss-crossing the landscape. Local farmers had a legal responsibility to maintain the system, and were fined if they did not do so. Even so, the water levels were never more than a few inches below the surface of the ground.

All this intricate husbandry had gone out of the window in the autumn of 1914. The system of maintenance came to a halt as Ypres and its environs repeatedly became the centre of some of the heaviest fighting of the war. Millions of shells landed on the land, pulverising it out of all recognition – or 'crumping' it, to use a word coined to describe both the artillery barrages and their results. The whole area had been returned to virtual swampland, pitted with craters. The prodigious rainfall that was a regular feature of the fighting on the Western Front did the rest. Acres of land were reduced to a thick soup, impassable on foot and way beyond the capabilities of a tank or any other form of land transport.

On the face of it, things were headed in the right direction for the tanks. Four days before the battle, a Royal Warrant had announced the creation of the Tank Corps. The Heavy Branch was no more. A pay scale was established. 'Tank mechanists', with the rank of private, would receive 2 shillings and tuppence per day. Lieutenants like Bert Baker would be on 9s 6d per day – about £35 in today's money. By now he was also earning an extra 2s 6d field allowance. A captain was paid 13s 6d per day with a field allowance of 3s. Like the machine-gunners before them, the tanks had formally been recognised as an independent entity, a separate arm. The new corps had been given more tanks. Messines had gone well. The weather in July had been fine, and on the surface at least, the ground was firm.

But the weather had not fully dried out all the craters left by the crump of numberless artillery shells. Baker-Carr, whose brigade would be heavily committed to the battle ahead, flew over the site, and found a landscape that was far from hospitable. 'Everywhere it was churned up by shellfire and had the semblance of a face badly pitted by smallpox. All the craters were half-filled with water, and it looked as if there was as much water as land. Many square miles of land consisted merely of a thin crust of soil below which lay a bottomless sea of mud and water.' His conclusion: 'No more unsuitable spot could have been discovered.' Not for nothing has the site been dubbed the world's worst battlefield.

Elles and Fuller were only too aware of the potential catastrophe that would ensue when the tanks advanced over such ground; but they were powerless to do anything about it. It would have appeared perverse for them to insist that the tanks be withdrawn from the forthcoming offensive because the ground was not good enough. No one wanted to hear that the crust would simply give way when 30 tons of tank passed over it. Even with his status as commander of the new Tank Corps, Elles did not have sufficient clout to modify or overturn the decision. Politically, it would have been unwise to try. But he and Fuller knew that from a tank perspective, the enterprise was folly. Elles thought his masters had gone 'stark staring mad'.

The tanks badly needed a public relations success, and it was becoming evident that the forthcoming offensive was not going to provide it. Rather the opposite. But the die was cast. The date of the Big Push, which would become known as the Third Battle of Ypres, was looming ever nearer. Baker's diary entries, which betrayed no sign of the apprehension and anguish of his superior officers, fell off significantly at this point. No doubt he had a thousand and one more important things to do. He recorded little of the battle, which was launched on 31 July 1917.

A couple of days earlier, the 19th and 21st Companies of the 1st Brigade had moved their 24 tanks up from Oosthoek to a position christened Frascati Farm, just over a mile from the frontline. The tanks of the 20th Company, of which Baker was a member, were held in reserve a little further back at Fantasia Farm. The move was accomplished over successive nights, each of the three companies requiring their own train. They were anxious not to attract the attention of the enemy, but it was difficult to move quietly in the woods at the dead of night. The tanks of the 21st Company were the first to arrive, among them that commanded by Douglas Browne: 'Parking tanks (especially Mark IVs) among timber at night is always a noisy and trying operation, resembling in sound and destructiveness the gambols of a herd of inebriated elephants. The tank driver, unaided, can see nothing whatever, and has to be guided by the flashings of an electric torch, with which refinements of signalling are difficult and generally misunderstood.' One by one, the companies finally got themselves into position.

On the night of the 30th they moved closer still, to within 500 yards of the front. At 3.50am on the morning of 31 July, the tanks of the 19th and 21st Companies went forward with the infantry under the cover of an artillery barrage. At the worst possible moment, the weather broke, and heavy rain began to fall at about 8.00am with the now-familiar and wearily predictable outcome: soft ground broken up by artillery fire rapidly turned into a mudbath. At once, the tanks ran into their customary problems. Those that did not ditch or succumb to mechanical failures were disabled by direct hits. Without much help from the tanks, the attack resulted in the capture of the line of the River Steenbeck and the village of St Julien just outside Ypres.

The disabled tanks were abandoned. A few weeks later, Daniel Hickey of H Battalion came across them and described the scene: 'We saw what had happened to tanks when they had gone off the causeway into the swamp below. They had sunk in the marsh and been knocked out by direct hits from a light gun in a concrete pill box as they had crept too slowly forward. There lay anything up to a dozen tanks – derelicts with huge holes blown in them, and their tracks smashed to pieces.'

Hickey's account is a reminder that while the arguments continued about the wisdom of deploying the tanks in conditions euphemistically termed 'unfavourable', real and terrible human consequences of the decision to do so could be seen everywhere in the Flanders mud. No sober account of a military action can do justice to what it was actually like to be in the middle of it. At the distance of 100 years, it is all too easy to become inured to the staggering levels of slaughter, and the awful reality that lay behind the raw statistics. Perhaps the closest we can get to an understanding of the horrors of this action is through an anonymous account, written by an engineering officer sent forward during the fighting at Ypres to see what could be done to salvage a tangle of immobilised tanks.

'As I neared the derelict tanks the scene became truly appalling. Wounded men lay drowned in the mud, others were stumbling and falling through exhaustion, others crawled and rested themselves up against the dead to raise themselves a little above the slush. On reaching the tanks, I found men had crawled to them for what shelter they could afford. The nearest tank was a female. Her sponson doors were open; out of these protruded four pairs of legs. Men had sought refuge in this machine. The dead and dying lay in a jumbled heap inside.'

Rain now set in with a vengeance, and barely let up for a fortnight. Fuller recalled that he knew by the third day that 'the battle was over as far as the tanks were concerned.' Elles respectfully suggested to the Fifth Army that his tanks be saved for a later attempt 'under more favourable conditions and on more favourable ground', but his appeal went unheeded. From London, d'Eyncourt wrote politely to Haig in the same terms. The commander's reply accepted that conditions were 'unfavourable' for tanks, but that he had decided that 'on the whole, it is advisable to make use of them'.

The only point one can take with clarity from this rather airy statement was that the plan was not about to change. On 13 August, the tanks of the 20th Company, including Baker's *Gorgonzola*, began to move up to positions behind the frontline, preparatory to supporting an infantry attack on the 16th on the road between St Julien and Langemarck. But the tracks could not get a grip on the boggy ground. After two nights of struggling forward, ditching and unditching and towing each other out of the mud, it became clear that only the four leading tanks had any prospect of reaching the line in time to take part in the attack. These four ploughed valiantly on, but one by one they too had to submit to the impossibility of the ground. The attack began without the support of a single tank.

After a year of disappointments, it was a new low. Even the official history of G Battalion headed the description of this experience, 'A Failure'. Once again, the defenders of the tanks would protest that they had been deployed recklessly, without regard to the conditions or their acknowledged vulnerabilities. In early September, Elles was permitted to withdraw four of his eight battalions from the battle. The others held on until the fighting ground to a halt in November, still plagued by mud and unable to make any significant contribution to proceedings.

Douglas Browne of G Battalion still sounded angry about it when he came to write his account of the battle after the war. 'From the first introduction of tanks in the field, the conditions with which they had to contend had gone from bad to worse. Ypres was the climax. The tanks were sent by scores and then hundreds, to drown ineffectually in a morass, and the very existence of the corps was imperilled by this misusage. The whole country was waterlogged... our own bombardment finished the work of ruin, pulverised the ground beyond repair, destroyed what drainage there was and brought water welling up within shell-holes as fast as they were formed.' Hickey had felt the same when he had come across the graveyard of the tanks. He found the loss of life and machinery infuriating. 'When correctly used they would, I felt sure, prove their real worth. It was obvious that tanks could not satisfactorily be used in the Salient and it seemed contrary to common sense to persist in such unnecessary waste. It struck me that if the Tank Corps was to be scrapped, putting it to work under impossible conditions such as these was a certain way of doing it.'

Swinton could not have expressed it better. Nor could Elles or Fuller, who had watched in anguish as the inevitable drama unfolded. But they were impotent. After a year of bitter experience, the gulf between the men who had designed, built and operated the machines, and the generals who deployed them in the field, had never been greater.

7
'MY BUS DID SPLENDID WORK'

It sailed along at the break of day
And smashed all things that got in its way
While Tommy looked on and shouted 'hooray'
The Day we used the Tanks

We were all surprised as it dashed along
Just like a Dreadnought, big and strong
So Tommy just whispered 'oui, oui, tray bong'
The Day we used the Tanks

It went for Fritz with a headlong dive
To stop its career poor Fritz did strive
But it didn't leave many poor Boches alive
The Day we used the Tanks
(Private Tommy Bannister *in the Daily Express,* 1916)

The whole tank project was now in serious trouble. Their dismal showing of mid-August, when not a single tank had managed to reach the action, seemed to sum up the experience of the previous months. Much had been hoped and expected of the new weapon. But by any measure, the tanks had been a disappointment. Since their debut on the Somme almost a year earlier, through the Ancre, Arras and now the Third Battle of Ypres, the new machines of war had signally failed to impress. They had proved themselves remarkably prone to mechanical breakdown. Those that had made it into action had spent most of their time ditching and unditching in the endless mud. They had failed to break through the enemy lines by crushing barbed wire and machine-gun posts – supposedly their principal strengths. Far from protecting the infantry and saving lives, they had developed a tendency actually to attract enemy fire, such that the soldiers were reluctant to come anywhere near them. And because their progress was so slow and ponderous, they had shown themselves to be worryingly vulnerable to attack. What few successes there had been had come from individual tanks in particular circumstances. The triumph of a tank galumphant, leading cheering troops down the main street of Flers, was becoming an increasingly distant memory.

In vain did the champions of the new arm protest that none of these deployments had allowed the tanks to demonstrate what they were capable of. Rather the opposite: the conditions in which they had been sent out to fight were precisely those that Swinton and others had warned from the start would render them useless. They could not be expected to wallow through water-filled craters and gaping shell-holes in which their tracks could gain no grip. The tanks had in effect been set up to fail, and they had duly obliged. Even the few commanders in the field who saw their potential did not seem interested in the first principles of how best to deploy them. They were desperate for results, and they threw into the fray whatever resources came to hand. They actively ignored all the advice they had been given since the time Swinton had cautioned against the use of tanks in driblets.

Worst of all in the eyes of those who had laboured to give birth to the tank was that one of its key advantages – that of surprise – had been almost wilfully squandered. The Germans had never seen anything like the tanks. Many were completely unnerved when first confronted with them, and either surrendered at once or ran away as fast as they could. Their terrifying appearance was a trump card, but it could be played only once. The element of shock and surprise could never be repeated to the same degree as in the first fateful encounter. But the advantage had been thoughtlessly tossed away in the unforgiving morass of the Somme. The Germans already showed signs of understanding how to neutralise these fearsome new weapons.

A more tolerant perspective came from an unexpected source: Hugh Elles, the commander of the Tank Corps. Writing in the immediate aftermath of the war, he supported Haig's view that even if the tanks had not been used to their best advantage, something was better than nothing. 'The employment of Tanks in Flanders has often been criticised, without intelligent appreciation of the fact that had they not fought in Flanders, they would probably have fought nowhere. Better, therefore, that they should fight and pull less than half their weight, and still save lives, than that they should stand idle while tremendous issues were at stake.' There was surely an element of hindsight about this assessment: at the time, as we have seen, Elles had felt as frustrated and angered as anyone by some of the early deployments.

The tanks had never had many friends. Now they had next to none. A general sense of scepticism prevailed, and even those who acknowledged their occasional successes thought it unlikely they would ever have a decisive influence on the battlefield. The view was that the money and resources being poured into producing hundreds more such white elephants would be much better diverted to making ever greater numbers of artillery shells.

Perhaps the nadir came with an analysis from General Gough's Fifth Army Headquarters, based on assessments from the infantry on the performance of the tanks to date. With its grim logic, it made for gloomy reading: '1 – Tanks are unable to negotiate bad ground. 2 – The ground on a battlefield will always be bad. 3 – Therefore the tanks are no good on a battlefield.'

The tank men had never sought to conceal the first of these points – that tanks could not operate on very soft going. Their frustration lay in the fact that even with this knowledge, that was exactly what they had been asked to do, with disastrous consequences. Now they were being blamed for it. In his memoir, *A Company of Tanks*, William Watson recalled: 'In the Third Battle of Ypres the reputation of the Tank Corps was almost destroyed.

We must have left behind two or three hundred derelict tanks sinking by degrees into the mud.'

Those two or three hundred reminders of the tank's deficiencies were a serious embarrassment. For some they offered tangible evidence that sticking with the project was a waste of time. 'Tank Corps Headquarters heard it all,' reported Williams-Ellis. 'They knew well enough that in well-informed but irresponsible London circles, the remark "I hear the tanks are going to be abolished" was a common one. They were not even frightening the enemy any more.' The comments of Lieutenant Norman Dillon demonstrated that these frustrations had percolated through to the tank crews as well. 'There was a very strong feeling among all the tank units that we'd made a world beater and it was being frittered away.' Hickey, too, thought the tanks were being made a scapegoat: 'The rumours went round that the tanks were to be scrapped because they had been such a failure in the Ypres Salient. I could not see that such a drastic step was necessary – after all, every branch of the service had its limitations. It was as impossible for the Flying Corps to go up and reconnoitre in a thunderstorm as it was for tanks to go out and work in a swamp. Within their limits, both services could do good work, but exceed their limits and disaster was as inevitable in the one case as in the other.'

His commanding officer was equally gloomy. 'Already it was being stated in high quarters that tanks were no good,' wrote Baker-Carr. 'The general feeling was decidedly hostile, and there was apparently no-one, except a few people in the fighting line, who had a good word to say for us.'

Even Elles was worried that one more straw would break the camel's back. The tanks had already had to endure so many early crises. 'Any one of them, unless cured, would have caused a permanent disappearance of the arm,' he wrote later. They seemed to have reached the end of the road.

Winston Churchill, one of the few steadfast friends that the tanks could muster, told Albert Stern, the Director of Mechanical Warfare, that the War Office were ready to wash their hands of the tanks. Their view, he said, was that 'there had been a total failure of design, and the money spent on tanks wasted. Their belief in mechanical warfare is so low that they propose to give it up entirely.'

It was beginning to look as though the days of the tank were numbered. 'It was probably the greatest crisis in the history of the tanks, and without doubt the very existence of the weapon trembled on the brink of destruction,' Baker-Carr recalled. But he felt they could not afford to concede defeat. To do so would be to lose the argument once and for all. 'It seemed almost certain to my mind that if we retired from the contest and said that it was impossible, owing to the unfavourable conditions, to take any further part in the fighting, the disappearance of the tanks, probably for ever, was inevitable.'

Baker-Carr determined to roll the dice. The advance north-east of Ypres had foundered for more than a fortnight before a row of strongly fortified German gun emplacements, built on the sites of abandoned farms. They presented a formidable obstacle. 'Like most of these little fortresses, they had been extremely skilfully placed,' wrote Williams-Ellis. 'An unwary advance would be trapped in their wire just within convenient range of their machine-guns. They were almost impossible targets for heavy guns, and as they were built of reinforced concrete at least three feet thick, the ordinary high explosive shell thrown by a field gun had no effect on them.' The only way to take them was through a full-frontal infantry attack. But the price would be immense: it was estimated such an attack might cost the lives of 600 men, perhaps as many as a thousand. Even so, such an attack was actively being planned at that moment.

Baker-Carr saw an opportunity, and went to see General Sir Ivor Maxse – one of the few commanders who was sympathetic towards the tanks. Baker-Carr persuaded Maxse that the German forts might be taken at a fraction of the cost in casualties if he and his tanks were given their heads.

The German positions were in a line of several hundred yards stretching north and east from the bombed-out and abandoned village of St Julien, about five miles outside Ypres. Between the British and German lines was the River Steenbeek. Behind the most forward German defences – the fortified emplacements – was the road between St Julien and the next village, Langemarck-Poelcappelle. Beyond the road lay their secondary line of defence. Baker-Carr's plan was to get the tanks across the Steenbeek and into St Julien. From there they would be able to use the firm surfaces of the road to pass between the two lines of defence, attacking the fortresses from the rear – at their weakest points – from relatively short range. Once they had succeeded in clearing out the enemy, they would give the supporting infantry the signal to move in and occupy the positions.

It was a daring plan and fraught with difficulty and danger – perhaps more than Baker-Carr appreciated as he laid the scheme before Maxse. It would differ from previous tank actions in a number of important details. Surprise would be key – there would be no artillery barrage to warn the Germans that an attack was imminent. Instead, the artillery would be asked to lay down smoke to blind the enemy to the approaching tanks. Once in St Julien, the tanks would be operating on a road – a luxury denied them in their previous deployments.

Maxse took Baker-Carr to explain the plan to his divisional commanders. They listened to him in what he described as 'contemptuous silence'. But Maxse liked the scheme and told them to cooperate, and to provide the necessary infantry support. Baker-Carr returned from the meeting to start preparing for the operation.

A body of 12 tanks would be required, a composite force to be selected from across the three companies of G Battalion. Douglas Browne, who would command one of the tanks, regarded the selection of G as a notable mark of favour. They had been in action only a few days earlier, and had far from a full complement of machines. But insofar as any tank men had managed to establish a positive reputation, it was the crews of G Battalion. All the commanders would come from G. One of those selected with Browne was Second Lieutenant Albert Baker. His close friend Tommy Morgan was another.

Movements recorded in the Tablet offer little detail as to Baker's activities in the days since the beginning of the Third Battle of Ypres and his part in the abortive efforts to support the infantry. On Sunday 4 August, he reported attending a church parade and that everywhere was ankle deep in mud: 'everything we have is wet'. The following week he was 'up and down the line again. Very busy. Very little sleep.' The week after that, 20 Company had been ordered up to the Langemarck–St Julien front to support the infantry. The tanks had struggled in terrain that was little short of a swamp, and spent most of the time unditching themselves or lending a tow to ditched comrades. As we have seen, only four tanks made any progress, but they could not complete the journey either, and had to withdraw. It seems that Baker's tank was one of these four, and therefore one of the few serviceable enough to be part of what Maxse called 'Baker-Carr's battle'. A letter from Baker to Miriam confirms that as soon as he had returned from the abortive efforts to reach the front, he was told to prepare himself and his crew for another mission. 'Had a hectic week and very tired,' he noted on 17 August. 'PS: just ordered to prepare for another stunt, so must get some of the lost sleep.'

The exhausted Baker was one of several officers from G Battalion who had been told to fill their tanks with petrol, oil and ammunition and be ready to move again at 6 o'clock the same evening. Under cover of darkness, they were to move the tanks up to Oosthoek Wood, ready to attack the German forts in the early hours of 19 August. Baker and his fellow commanders and their crews could have been forgiven for not sharing Browne's satisfaction at the compliment G Battalion was being paid in being entrusted with this mission. A few hours of dreamless sleep undisturbed by the crump of artillery fire would have been appreciated a great deal more.

After a frantic afternoon of preparation, a long and tedious journey lay ahead to the ruins of a farm called Bellevue – a name that had become less and less appropriate as the battle around Ypres raged once again. There they would lay up, before moving on the following night to the wood near St Julien. Even before their little convoy set off, their strength had been reduced. One of the tanks intended to be part of the operation had never had much prospect of joining it; not only did it have mechanical troubles, it was also half sunk in mud from the earlier operation. That left a taskforce of 11 tanks, of which two were male and the rest female. The line-up looked bottom-heavy from the beginning: if they succeeded in getting round the back of the German positions, where the concrete was less thick, it was the 6pdr Hotchkiss guns of the male tanks that were likely to do the most damage. But nine of the 11 would be armed only with machine-guns.

The party made good headway along the road until it ran into the nightly ammunition trains taking supplies up to the forward battery positions and returning empty. Most of the haulage was done by mules. The mule trains covered the whole width of the road, and the tanks had to keep stopping for several minutes at a time to let them pass. They had no option but to be patient, not daring to leave the road for fear of becoming ditched. Even though most of the crews walked outside the tanks, it was an exhausting journey. On a good day it might have taken less than an hour to cover the distance, which was only a mile and a half. With all the congestion, it was two in the morning by the time they turned wearily into Bellevue, eight hours after setting out. The crews parked the tanks behind a hedge and covered them with camouflage. Then they made themselves some cocoa, washed it down with a tot of rum, and tried to grab some sleep amid the roar and the flashes of the field batteries hurling their projectiles into the darkness.

During the following day, Baker and the other officers were briefed by Major Ralph Broome, commander of the composite company from G Battalion. Broome ran through the latest iteration of the plan. The original idea had been to head for targets along a triangle of roads. It had now been modified, and would concentrate on just one side of the triangle, the road between St Julien and Langemarck–Poelcapelle. Baker also met the infantry commander whose men would be following him at a distance of around 250 yards. Close cooperation between tanks and infantry would be critical to the success of the mission.

The modified plan still left several formidable targets to be overcome. The largest of them, the Cockcroft, would give its name to the entire operation. It was the furthest along the road, about a mile from St Julien. It would be attacked by two tanks from 19 Company, a male tank commanded by Lieutenant Willard and a female under Second Lieutenant Coutts. The other male tank, G29, *Gorgonzola*, was Baker's. With his friend Tommy Morgan, a fellow Second Lieutenant from 20 Company, he was to head for two buildings called Maison du Hibou – sometimes referred to as Mont du Hibou, and freely translated by Baker as 'Owl Hill'. Though smaller than the Cockcroft, which garrisoned 100 German soldiers, Maison du Hibou was just as heavily fortified, and contained another 60 troops. The other targets were smaller again, though still well defended. Kane and Close, also of 20 Company, would attack Triangle Farm. Claughton and Browne of 21 Company were deputed to deal with Hillock Farm and a line of gun pits on the far side of the rod. Each pair of tanks was to be accompanied by a platoon of infantry, ready to move in and consolidate once the tanks had made the breakthrough. Chaddock, in the ninth tank, was to follow the others as a 'mopper-up', providing back-up wherever it might be needed. The two other machines were held in reserve at Bellevue.

The day was spent going over these orders, liaising with the infantry and grabbing what rest they could. Even in their state of weariness, it must have been hard to sleep. The operation seemed straightforward enough on paper: the tanks were to sneak round behind the back of the enemy blockhouses and, with the help of the infantry, flush them out. But there were plenty of things that could go wrong, and any one of them could scupper the entire mission. Baker and the others would not have been human if their minds had not strayed at least for a while to some of the potential pitfalls.

The key to their success would be the extent to which they could creep up on the German positions undetected. That meant a slow descent from the wood to the Steenbeck, keeping engine noise to a minimum and hoping alert German sentries would not detect any noise or faint sparks in the darkness. This would be in some ways the most hazardous part of the mission. If the Germans got wind of the approaching tanks, the chances of success were all but gone. This was acknowledged by Colonel Edward Hankey, the commander of G Battalion, in his report of the operation written two days later. 'It seemed a big gamble as to whether the tanks would be heard approaching the Steenbeck... and getting into position at the Starting Point by Zero Hour, as the enemy were within 400 yards of the Starting Point.' It is not known whether the crews themselves were made fully aware of the 'big gamble' they would be taking. Diversionary fire had been arranged to distract the Germans and an aircraft from the Royal Flying Corps would carry out a series of noisy low-level swoops in the two hours before Zero Hour.

While striving not to alert the Germans, the tanks would have to drop down in darkness to the banks of the Steenbeck, ford it successfully, and then climb the steep bank on the other side to reach the village. In normal times, the Steenbeck was hardly worthy of being called a river along this stretch, being only a few feet wide. But the effects of months of shelling had widened and deepened it considerably, and it was now less a river and more a large bog. There was no guarantee that the tanks would get across it without difficulty. To help them find their way in the dark and then cross the river, preparatory work had been done to lay guide tapes along the route for the tanks to follow, and for the bed of the river to be bolstered with closely-bound bundles of brushwood to provide a firm footing for the tracks.

Once in St Julien, with dawn breaking, they would be reliant on the smoke barrage to disguise their movements from both sides of the road – the target blockhouses on their left and the secondary German lines on their right. The smoke barrage would last for two hours, reducing their chances of being spotted, but also rendering them near blind as they made their way along the road to the targets. If the smoke rose in the wrong place or lifted suddenly, the slow-moving tanks would provide easy pickings for armour-piercing shells.

The next unknown was the state of the ground they would be expected to negotiate. So far, the story of the tanks had been their helplessness in the deep sucking mud of the Flanders battlefields. Once in St Julien, they would have the luxury of being on a road. But they could not be sure what sort of condition it would be in, how wide it was, or how passable – or exactly what lay on either side of it. Whatever its state, they dare not leave it: any tank that left the road would immediately become ditched.

All these obstacles would have to be overcome before they even reached their targets. The German positions holding up the British advance were heavily fortified and strongly defended – in the case of the Cockcroft and Maison du Hibou, Baker's target, formidably so, each housing dozens of German soldiers. In some places, the concrete was eight feet thick. They had already demonstrated their capacity to offer stern resistance. Some of the tank men had their doubts about how much reliance they could place on the timely support of the infantry even if they managed to do their own jobs successfully. Coutts of 19 Company had spent some time in conference with the 33rd Brigade, who were to follow him and Willard to the Cockcroft. He returned feeling less than confident about how well the partnership would work. His misgivings would be fully justified.

Taken together, these considerations were unlikely to be conducive to peace of mind as the hours ticked by. No doubt the men did not discuss what was running through their heads, but kept their thoughts to themselves. Instead, the crews of the nine designated tanks spent a fitful day keeping themselves occupied – examining maps and photographs, checking and rechecking guns and engines and fitting the 'spuds' – the steel plates bolted on to the tracks at intervals to improve grip. Finally, after a meal of bully beef, cocoa and rum, they settled down for a couple of hours of sleep. They were to be formed up and ready to set off at 1.00am. That would give them nearly four hours to make it across the river and into St Julien in time for the start of the smoke barrage at Zero Hour: 4.45am. It was only a mile and half, but the journey would have to proceed at little more than a crawl to keep the engine noise to a minimum. Smoking was forbidden for those walking outside in case the glowing tips of the cigarettes were detected. There was never any question of lighting up inside, in an atmosphere thick with petrol fumes.

At 1.00am the nine tanks formed up on the road to begin the slow descent to the Steenbeck. Willard was in the lead tank, G4, *Gloucester,* followed by Coutts in G43, *Gordon.* They had the furthest to travel up the road to reach The Cockcroft. Behind them, Baker took his place in G29 *Gorgonzola,* bound for Maison du Hibou with Morgan in G32, *Gargoyle.* Then came Kane and Close in G31, *Galatea* and G28, *Geisha.* Claughton followed in G52 *Guiseley,* and Browne in G47, *Gitane.* Chaddock brought up the rear in G44, *Glengarry.*

The first setback was not long in coming. Gases from the exhaust of Willard in G4, the lead tank, were finding their way into the cabin, threatening to asphyxiate the crew. A quick fix was put in place, and the column set off again, now beginning the gentle descent to the river. But G4 was soon in trouble again, and as he was now in an exposed position, Willard could not risk any further adjustments to try to repair the exhaust. He carried on with all doors and hatches open, pulling over to let Coutts take the lead on the approach to the river.

Coutts, Baker, Morgan and Kane made their way gingerly across the river, relying on the grip afforded by the brushwood. But not everyone made it. The unfortunate Willard got stuck, while Kane, fifth in line in G31, misjudged the position of the bundles – which had now disappeared below the water under the weight of the leading tanks – and was soon irretrievably ditched as well. Fortunately, there was room for the remaining tanks to squeeze past. But there were now just seven machines negotiating the steep slope that led from the Steenbeck to St Julien. Willard was eventually able to follow, but too late to take any part in the action. Ill-luck continued to dog him, because his tank got stuck again, for good this time, on its return to the Steenbeck.

Coutts, now leading the convoy, made good time and waited in the village for the others to catch up. But the loss of Willard was potentially a grievous blow to the success of the mission. His was one of only two male tanks, and Coutts was unlikely to make much of an impression on the defences of the Cockcroft on his own, armed only with machine-guns. The other male tank, G29, commanded by Baker, was committed to Maison du Hibou. There does not appear to have been any discussion about changing the plan, and redirecting Baker to the Cockcroft. Perhaps communication was not possible. Perhaps there was a thought that he might go on to the Cockcroft after knocking out Maison du Hibou. Perhaps it was felt that if he went first to the Cockcroft, the defenders at Maison du Hibou might be waiting for him on his return. Whatever the reason, the valiant Coutts was left to tackle the Cockcroft on his own.

The last of the seven tanks reached the ruined village of St Julien on the stroke of Zero Hour. As they did, the smoke shells and the shrapnel barrage began, and the far end of the village was enveloped in dense white smoke. The tanks set off on the road to Langemarck-Poelcapelle.

At first, the going was good. Although St Julien had been all but obliterated in the previous few weeks, the rubble that littered the road proved no obstacle to the tanks. Once out of the village however, they were met with a very different proposition. As in so many French towns, the road, or pavé, on the outskirts of St Julien was bordered by an avenue of trees, with deep ditches behind them on either side. If they were not to be ditched, the tanks must stay on the road. This was easier said than done. While much of the surface was relatively undamaged, there were still large holes in places and the going was slippery.

Trees presented a much more formidable obstacle. Many of them had been brought down by the bombardment, and lay across the road at all angles. The tanks had no choice but to attempt to surmount them, an operation requiring huge skill and nerve on the part of their drivers. Their field of vision was severely restricted at the best of times, but now they were in the middle of a smoke barrage. Climbing a fallen tree was one thing, a matter of judging the angle of approach and hoping the trunk would not shift under the weight of the tank. Controlling the descent was quite another, and the risk of being thrown off the narrow road into the ditch was very great. There was also the highly unpleasant sensation for the crew of the shattering crash at the point of descent, which threw them off balance and sent the contents of the tanks flying in all directions. The fact that all seven tanks negotiated these hazards in such extreme circumstances reflects the greatest credit on the competence of their drivers.

The targets nearest St Julien were the German gun pits to the right of the approaching tanks. The first five tanks passed them under cover of smoke, Baker later reporting that he had fired his 6pdrs at them as he went by. He did the same at Hillock Farm on his left about 50 yards further on, knocking down some walls. The gun pits were then engaged in earnest by Claughton and Browne bringing up the rear of the convoy. At first they could see nothing in the smoke, but when it cleared momentarily, the gunners spotted a row of high mounds about 150 yards from the road and began firing on them. The fire was returned, but not for long. The gun pits were quickly abandoned. While Browne kept up the attack, Claughton moved ahead to Hillock Farm. The same thing happened there: after a perfunctory return of fire, the Germans abandoned the position. Claughton opened the manhole at the top of his machine and waved a shovel in the air. A few moments later, Browne did the same. It was the signal for the supporting infantry to come on and finish the job.

Each tank had been told to return home as soon as its objective was secured. After clearing Hillock Farm, Claughton obediently turned round and was once again facing St Julien. There was no way that either Browne or Chaddock, in the support vehicle, could press on to help with the attacks further up the road, had they been so minded. The pavé was not wide enough for two tanks to pass each other side by side. Accordingly, all three headed back to St Julien, their part of the mission accomplished. But their troubles were not over. It was now 5.45am, an hour since the start of the operation. The sun had risen and the smoke was dispersing. The tanks were sitting targets for any German guns, and they had to edge back over the fallen trees which meant that progress was agonisingly slow. A number of shells fell nearby, but they made it back into the village unscathed. Browne reported that he then stopped his tank in order to dash off a message for sending via pigeon. He was later to see a copy of it: it was illegible.

Further ahead, the other tanks were engaging with their objectives. The next position up from Hillock Farm was Triangle Farm, the weakest of the three remaining targets, being less well fortified and with a smaller garrison. With his partner Kane in G31 still wallowing in the waters of the Steenbeck, it was up to Close in G28 to take on the task alone. What happened next is not entirely clear. It appears that Close reached Triangle Farm and, encountering no resistance, assumed that it had been evacuated. Accordingly, he called up the infantry. Baker-Carr's first operational report that day stated, 'Triangle Farm was not occupied by the enemy', and Bert Baker's later report supports this: 'Triangle Farm was of no importance,' it said. But when the infantry moved in to occupy the farm, it seems they did meet some resistance, and they took it only after a fierce skirmish fought at close quarters.

Unaware of this, Close carried on up the road, perhaps resolved to support the tanks ahead of him. About 500 yards north of Triangle Farm he came under machine-gun fire and his tank was ditched, most of its own guns put out of action. The crew sat tight all through the day until they were able to get out in the darkness by removing a sponson. They eventually made their way back to the camp on foot the following evening, more than 36 hours after Zero Hour.

Baker and Morgan had now reached Maison du Hibou, with its strong force of 60 German defenders. They had come under continuous heavy fire since Hillock Farm, but had not paused. Baker worked to bring his 6pdr guns to bear on the rear doors of the larger building and he fired 30–40 rounds into them. Morgan arrived to provide supporting fire from his machine-guns. The effect was devastating. Most of the occupants spilled out of the doors, to be killed or captured by the supporting troops.

At its moment of triumph, *Gorgonzola* now met the fate of so many other tanks, and became hopelessly bogged down in the mud. Baker was preparing to turn her round to return home when a burst of machine-gun fire caused his driver to swing too far over. The tank hit a tree trunk and slid on its side into a large hole by the side of the road. They were stuck. There was no way of unditching, and the ferocity of the German fire made abandoning the tank impossible.

They kept up the fight, firing the 6pdrs until the tank had subsided into the mud at such an angle that they could no longer be deployed. Baker judged that now was the moment to try to make good their escape from the tank and hook up with the infantry, taking their machine-guns with them. This they managed to achieve, still under heavy fire. They helped the soldiers establish a series of positions while the capture of Maison du Hibou was consolidated.

Baker was anxious to get a message back reporting the success of this phase of the attack, but his carrier pigeons were still inside the abandoned tank. He made three unsuccessful attempts to scramble into it under fire and retrieve them. With his fourth approach, he managed it. His report duly despatched, he reported to the commanding infantry officer, who gave him orders to retire. Leaving the machine-guns with the infantry, Baker led his crew on foot back down the road to St Julien.

They had gone barely a few paces when disaster struck. A shell landed right in the middle of the group. One of the crew was killed, and another wounded. Baker sustained superficial wounds. They kept going and eventually made it back to the camp without further incident.

Morgan had pressed on after the surrender of Maison du Hibou. He passed the ditched *Gorgonzola*, and was soon engaged in an exchange of fire with a number of German machine-gun posts further up the road. After what he estimated as about an hour and a half, and having silenced at least one gun, he turned round and returned. As he passed *Gorgonzola*, he had engine trouble of his own, but the crew fixed it and he was able to return to the camp under his own steam.

The redoubtable Coutts had meanwhile continued his solitary progress towards the Cockcroft, ready to engage the most formidable garrison on his own and armed only with machine-guns. As he approached, he came under heavy fire from three directions, and for some minutes, during which the tank's guns jammed for a time, there was a fierce exchange. With his guns malfunctioning and one of his gunners seriously wounded, Coutts now suffered the same misfortune as Baker. His tank slipped off the road and he found himself unable to move.

Just when all seemed lost, there was a remarkable development that was to determine the outcome of the entire operation. The Germans inside the Cockcroft, perhaps having seen what was happening to their comrades at Maison du Hibou nearby, were apparently unaware that Coutts in G43 did not command the same firepower as Baker in G29. They also appear to have assumed that Coutts had halted only to take aim and reduce them to smithereens, when in fact he was ditched and had no other choice. Whatever the reason, they suddenly abandoned the position and streamed out of the building. Coutts at once brought his machine-guns to bear on them. 'Killed a good many,' he reported laconically.

Coutts at once deployed his shovel through the manhole on top of the tank to signal to the infantry that the position had been evacuated, and to urge them to come up and support him – perhaps before the Germans could work out that he posed much less of a threat than they had imagined. He left the tank with his wounded gunner and started setting up positions with his machine-guns. His position was still precarious and he was in dire need of support.

His worst fears from the day before were now realised: the waving of the shovel brought no response from the infantry. He sent two men back across the open ground to exhort the troops to come on. The men returned with the dispiriting news that the infantry declined to do so. One can only imagine with what feelings Coutts himself went back and found the commanding officer to appeal to him in person. He returned with about 30 infantrymen who were able to consolidate his line of machine-guns and to hold the position with only a couple of minor casualties. Coutts and his crew remained in support until the late afternoon.

The rearmost three tanks, under Claughton, Browne and Chaddock, were now well on their way back, although the journey was anything but easy. Having dodged the shells that followed them into St Julien, they descended once more to cross the Steenbeck. Poor Willard's tank was stuck again, and so was Kane's, having failed to get across the river on the way out. Getting by them along the passable part of the riverbed would be no easy task. Chaddock and Claughton made it across, but as Browne came down the bank, his tank failed to squeeze through and came to a halt pressing against Willard's machine. He tried to swing clear but failed. He tried to reverse but failed. To make matters worse, a German counter-barrage was now concentrated on St Julien and the river, and shells were falling all around them. There followed half an hour of feverish digging with their bare hands as they pushed under the tracks everything they could find that might afford them some grip. Branches, bricks and anything else that was lying around were packed into the space as the barrage continued unabated. When at last they felt they had established an adequate base, another attempt was made to swing the nose clear. This time it worked. The crew piled back inside and completed the rest of the journey without a hitch. Morgan in G32 *Gargoyle* was the only other one of the nine starters to return home under his own power.

All the crews were shattered, regardless of whether they had made their way back on foot or in a tank. They had barely slept in two days and had been operating for hours on adrenalin, either dodging enemy fire or roasting inside their machines and expecting to be blown to pieces at any moment. They were taken back to La Lovie chateau, the headquarters of both the Fifth Army and the First Brigade tanks during the Third Battle of Ypres. Baker managed a brief message home: 'Have just come out of action and have small wounds, fingers and ears. May get in casualty list but don't worry. Quite done up and want days of sleep. My bus did splendid work.'

As the dog-tired crews tried to catch up on their lost sleep in their tents at La Lovie, they were oblivious to the arrival of the celebrated war correspondent Beach Thomas of the *Daily Mail*. He arrived when all the actors in the drama were in bed and asleep, but was treated to a detailed and heavily-embellished account of events by members of 19 Company, none of whom had come anywhere near the action. They gave full play to their imaginations, and were highly gratified to see the results in both the *Mail* and the *Times* a few days later – a gripping description of the operation, and the triumph of 'the leviathans'.

Those who had actually been at St Julien claimed they found it hard to reconcile the reports with their actual experience. But Bert Baker kept Thomas's despatch in his scrapbook, and it was actually a perfectly business-like account of the operation. Thomas was also astute enough to note that not everyone had loved the tanks, and that this little action could be the making of them: 'I notice that flippant titles have mostly vanished from the tanks. Indeed, on Sunday morning Ugly Duckling was finally changed into Swan. It is to be noted that all the tanks in this action were forced to cross rivers as well as honeycombed territory. The infantry were delighted, and they are exacting critics of the tanks. They even cheered them as they followed up in their wake and found their work done. The enthusiasm of their first appearance in September was revived.'

A stream of distinguished visitors and a torrent of congratulatory messages began to pour into La Lovie. For once, the tanks in general, and G Battalion in particular, were able to enjoy an unfamiliar sensation of popularity. 'Even those of us who had played the most modest part on 19 August awoke the following morning to find ourselves famous,' wrote Browne. It was gratifying, but Baker for one was not about to let this go to his head. His report to Miriam of his part in the battle was shorn of any embroidery. 'Had a very thin time last Sunday,' he wrote. 'Did very well. Note the name – Owl Hill. Everyone treats me as an 'ero for a few hours – modesty forbids more. One of my crew killed, my corporal wounded. The fingers going on well – bullet splinters only. G Bn has made a name for itself – see the papers.'

General Maxse, the man who had kept faith in the tanks, sent a special message of thanks to G Battalion. The army commander General Gough, who had been notably cooler, now displayed considerable magnanimity, sending a generous message via General Holland of the General Staff:

> The Corps Commander wishes to congratulate 'G' Battalion, 1st Brigade, Tanks, on its brilliant success in today's operations, of which it may be justly proud. By its good arrangements, untiring energy and gallantry, it has enabled the infantry to penetrate the enemy's defences on a front of 1,500 yards to a maximum depth of 500 yards with only 15 casualties. The Corps Commander feels confident that even greater successes are in store for the 1st Brigade Tanks in the forthcoming operations. Please convey to the officers, NCOs and men of G Battalion the Corps Commander's appreciation of their good work.
>
> Brig-Gen SG Holland, General Staff, XVIII Corps.

Gough went further, arriving in person to hear a first-hand account of the action from some of the crews, a visit recorded in the G Battalion Diary: 'The army commander General Sir Hubert Gough inspected the crews of the following officers and expressed himself very grateful for the good work they had done in the 19th inst: Coutts, Browne, Baker, Morgan, Chaddock, Close.'

Baker and the others had been lined up near their former tank park in Oosthoek Wood waiting for the general to arrive. Gough was shepherded smartly past Coutts and stopped to speak to Browne instead. Browne soon realised why: the general's first question was about whether he had been adequately supported by the infantry. Browne said he had – and when asked the same question, Baker, Morgan and Close were able honestly to agree. Coutts would have had a different story to tell, but was not given the chance to tell it.

Within a few days, Baker had moved to Wailly, some 50 miles from the frontline, to get some rest. But first there was the paperwork. He had to submit a written account of his part in the battle and fill out a Battle History Sheet. Both documents survive among his papers. Here is his description of his part in the action:

> We arrived at St Julien at 4.35 and moved off at ZERO hour, 2nd on the line. The road was very rough owing to fallen trees lying at all angles, two railways one with substantial rails torn up, and many shell holes in the pavé surface. I reached Hillocks Farm and put 6pdr shells into the ruins at 6 yards range, knocking the remaining standing walls down. We saw no Germans. With my right 6 pdr I shelled the old gun pits about 200 yards off the road. Triangle Farm was of no importance. Enemy MG fire became very fierce from R from this time onwards. I did not stop. I then picked up Hibou on my left and put my left 6 pdrs on to some doors in the larger of the two buildings. We soon saw Germans running out of the rear door. I could not get my fwd Lewis gun on to them owing to my attention being largely taken up with the difficult driving. We fired continuously on both buildings.
>
> I was about to swing and return when a burst of MG fire on the front shutters caused my driver to swing too far to the right, and catching a tree trunk we slid sideways into a large hole off the road. We could not unditch and the MG fire was too heavy to go outside. We continued firing with 6 pdrs until the left one was submerged.
>
> As the barrage was falling around us, we decided to join the infantry with our 3 sound guns and three boxes of ammunition. I took firing pins and 6 pdr spares. I left under fairly heavy MG fire proceeding through shell holes to the Warwicks' outpost line which had just reached the road. We helped to set up several strong points whilst the line across the front of Hibou was being consolidated. I made four attempts to get to my car and finally got a pigeon and some equipment out. I then reported to O/C Warwicks at Hibou who said he had no further use for my men. I left him my three guns and started off for Alberta. About 40 yards from Hibou a HE shell fell in the midst of our party and killed one of my crew, wounding another. I left my crew near Kitcheners Wood and withdrew them later according to instructions.

Here is what he filled in on the Battle History sheet:

Crew *36*
Tank *G29*
Date *19 August 2017*
Commanded by *2/Lt AG Baker G Battalion*
Unit to which attached *48th Division 14 Brigade*
Zero hour *4.45*
Hour tank started for action *2.10am*
Did you reach your objective *Yes*
Condition of the ground *Off the roads – hopeless*
Condition of enemy's trenches *Enemy only seen in blockhouses and shell holes*
Condition of weather *Very fine*
Condition of crew after action *Exhausted*
Condition of tank after action *Fit but badly ditched guns and moveables withdrawn – 6pdr strikers*
Casualties *One man killed. One officer and one man slightly wounded*
Messages sent by pigeon *Two*
Did enemy adopt anti-tank measures? *Many armour-piercing bullets*
6 pdr ammunition expended *Approx 60/70 rounds*
SAA expended *200 or 300 rounds*
No of hours tank in action *6 and a half hours*
Approximate mileage covered *3 miles*
My orders received on 18 Aug 1917 were as follows. To proceed from Belle Vue to St Julien and await Zero hours (4.45). Then to move along the S Julien–Poelcapelle road dealing with objectives as follows: Hillocks, gun emplacements, Triangle Farm, Maison du Hibou.
I suggest that in future *6pdr tank works with one Lewis for the purpose of attacking blockhouses and beg to point out that their most vulnerable part is the rear where permanent openings are made.*

The operation had been fraught, and not without pitfalls – but it had ended in a triumph for the tanks. There might have been an element of good fortune around the evacuation of the Cockcroft, but it surely owed much to the effect on German morale of the sheer sight of the tanks, and the punishment Baker was meting out to their comrades next door. The benefit of the extra firepower available to the male tanks was noted. 'All crew commanders would prefer to have Male tanks,' Hankey wrote in his report on the operation. 'The 6-pdr guns had a wonderful effect, and cleared up strong points at once. One female Tank commander spotted a gun which knocked out 2 Tanks and could do nothing to help.'

The system of sending messages by pigeon messages had also worked admirably, Hankey said, while adding drily: 'Crew commanders, in some cases, have still to realise the worthlessness of a message which does not have either the time of despatch, the map reference of the sender, or the number of the Tank on the message.'

For the doubters in GHQ, there was only one real point of interest in the hours immediately after the attack, and it had nothing to do with pigeons. They were utterly astonished at how few casualties had been sustained. These were the officers who had estimated that a successful infantry assault on the forts might cost a thousand lives, with no guarantee of success. Yet here was a telegram from General Maxse reporting the capture of all the German positions, and an advance of 500 yards across a depth of nearly a mile with just 15 dead or wounded in the infantry, and 29 casualties in all. They could not believe their eyes. Quickly a message was sent back demanding to know how on earth this had been achieved. No doubt with considerable satisfaction, Maxse sent a reply comprising a single word: 'Tanks'.

8
'ONE OF THE BEST STUNTS OF THE SHOW'

The Kaiser and Hindenburg happened to meet
And William remarked: 'I admit
I don't think we're doing
As well as we did
And it's troubling me more than a bit
What is the reason for this?' murmured he
So Hindenburg sobbed as he said, 'well you see....

I fear we have been somewhat circumvented
Our frightfulness has evidently failed
Our victorious aspirations have diminished
Our advance is inadvertently curtailed
The enemy is encroaching on our salient
We are cornered, outmanoeuvred and outflanked
Our strategical position is imperilled
In other words, WE'RE TANKED'.
(Anon)

It is easy to exaggerate the importance of the events at the Cockcroft on 19 August 1917. The operation was certainly a striking success. 'A very memorable feat of arms,' was the verdict in the weekly *Tank Notes*. But in strategic terms, it was a minor affair – one of a hundred cameos that punctuated the four years of war, but with no overall significance in terms of the balance of power. It has a special place, however, in the story of the tanks.

True, those who were determined to be unimpressed by the tanks remained unimpressed. For them, the Cockcroft was just a stunt, another showy but ultimately superficial performance by the new arm. Some went too far the other way, seizing on the operation as a winning formula that could be replicated with the same results. That this was mistaken thinking was evident all too soon. A month later, a similar task force was sent out on a similar mission at Langemarck–Poelcapelle, north-east of St Julien. This time the Germans were waiting, and without the element of surprise the attack was not a success.

At the Cockcroft, the tanks had not ticked every box. The attack had been on a small scale – only a handful of machines. As a destroyer of barbed wire, a crosser of trenches and a crusher of machine-gunners, the prowess of the tank had not been put to the test. When the tanks had left the comparative stability of the road, they had invariably become ditched in the mud in a way that had become all too familiar in the previous months.

Even so, they had made a number of important points. They had shown how vital was the element of surprise. For once, an operation had not been preceded by a sustained artillery barrage, of the sort that softened up defences but also gave the defenders ample notice of where to expect the attack. Arriving without warning, the tanks had caught the Germans on the hop. They had never recovered.

Linked to this was the effect of the physical appearance of the machines. Although it was a year since the first tank had lumbered into view on the Somme, most Germans had yet to see one at close quarters. When they did, they found it a terrifying prospect, and their first instinct was to surrender or flee. This was what had happened at the Cockcroft itself, which was arguably not in immediate danger when the garrison took to its heels. Coutts was on their doorstep, but the position was strongly fortified, he was on his own, he was stuck, and he had no 6pdrs. Yet his very presence, and an awareness of what was happening to their comrades a short distance away at Maison du Hibou, was enough to send the soldiers stampeding out of the fort and completing the rout.

Another key outcome was the way tanks and infantry had shown themselves to be highly effective when working together in close cooperation – notwithstanding the experience of Coutts. The tanks made the breakthrough and drew the fire, the infantry made good their gains. Swinton had always said that the prime function of the tanks was to offer protection to the foot soldiers. If nothing else, the fact that the infantry had sustained only 15 casualties, whereas a conventional attack might have cost a thousand, was bound to give the generals pause for thought. 'It was a brilliant little exploit, and the casualty figures pleaded too loudly to be ignored,' said Williams-Ellis. 'It is probably no exaggeration to say that it was in some measure to the tanks that won the little Battle of St Julien that the Tank Corps owed the opportunity of winning the Battle of Cambrai.'

Browne agreed. 'Indirectly, the Cockcroft led to Cambrai.' He, too, believed the aspect of the action that would have been most striking for the higher command was the small number of casualties. Up until that point, the infantry had been sustaining heavy losses for no appreciable gain. For three weeks they had been battering the line of fortifications to no avail – and further defensive lines lay beyond. 'And then had come what seemed a sudden and quite startling gleam of light,' said Browne. 'In an hour and half, all these initial bogies had tumbled down like ninepins, at the ridiculous cost of fifteen wounded infantrymen and a few tank Corps personnel.' The action aroused intense interest across the army, proving as it did the potential of the tanks to reduce losses. The Cockcroft did not change the course of the war, or even immediately change the way the tanks were used. As Browne observed, 'dozens and scores of tanks were thrown away in the Salient after the Cockcroft with no adequate return for the sacrifice.' But it certainly changed the fortunes of the tanks. 'There was no more overt talk of abolition or even of reduction.' They would now be plumbed into the planning of future attacks as a key component, rather than an auxiliary of dubious value.

For Bert Baker, there were two legacies of the action, one short-lived, the other longer lasting. The first was an injury to his hands and arms, cut by the splashing of metal fragments that flew around the interior of a tank when it came under fire.

The wounds cannot have been too serious, because within ten days he reported that they were 'nearly better'. They were slow to heal completely though, and a doctor later reopened one wound and found a splinter of metal still lodged inside it.

While he was recovering, Baker was given some light duties as an instructor, which he detested. He wanted to get back to the action. 'Fairly got the hump with instructing and want to get back to Bn,' he wrote, only a week after the Cockcroft. 'Hate the people at the School – very unsociable and worried about their jobs, afraid we shall get them and they will be sent up the line! Goodness knows, we don't want their jobs. Am applying to CO in the morning to be allowed to return to Bn.' All in all, he is uncharacteristically grumpy: 'Food rotten, post delayed. No letters since I've been here.' He is still talking about buying a Brit Warm overcoat and asks to be sent a Primus stove. It would be mid-November before he acquired both, the stove sent by his brother in-law Cally, Nellie's husband. A welcome high point was a dinner to celebrate the 'show' at St Julien. 'Passed your photo round for signatures,' he told Miriam. 'Must save it as a souvenir.' He later sent her the menu from the evening.

He would have been further cheered by the second, and more enduring, consequence of that early morning at the Cockcroft. He learned of it when his request to return to the battalion was finally granted in mid-September. 'Back to Battn and told on arrival I'd got an MC for the show on Aug 19th. (Gazette came through on Sept 15). Very bucked.' He also thought he might be promoted to first lieutenant, but did not expect to hear about this for some time.

Miriam had already been given an indication that he was to be decorated via a letter from one of Baker's comrades, sent to her ten days after the Cockcroft. 'One of our officers, Lt Fearnley, has gone home, he's oldish, 40, and has gone back as instructor,' Baker had told her. 'Has promised to get in touch with you.'

Fearnley kept his promise, and once back in England sent a charming letter to Miriam, which told her more about the action than she had been told by her fiancé:

> 28/8/17 The White Hart Hotel, Lincoln.
> Dear Miss Potter,
> You are no doubt wondering who this letter is from so I will explain.
> My name is Fearnley and I am in 'G' Battn of the Tank Corps. I am in England for a short time on duty and a promised a 'friend' of ours 'Charlie' Baker by name that I would drop you a line to tell you all about him. (As a matter of fact I believe 'Charles' is only his regimental pet name but he tells me you will understand who I mean!)
> Well, here goes:-
> 'G' Bn are at present in La Lovie Camp about 2 miles from Poperinghe and have been in all the scrapping on and off since July 31st.
> 'Charles' was not actually in action himself until last Sunday Aug 19th but on that date he took a glorious part in the most successful tank action that

has taken place.
A few days before this the Infantry had been in action in front of St Julien but had been held up by Hun machine guns in concrete emplacements. They then suffered very heavy casualties.
On the 19th 'G' Battn went into action on the same front and destroyed or captured all the offending machine guns. The Infantry (5 battalions strong) then advanced and occupied the position with a total loss of 1 killed and 15 wounded!
'Charles' had one of the most difficult tasks to perform and did his job so well that he has certainly earned and will I believe receive a Military Cross for his exploits.
(He did not tell me to say anything about this and would probably be very cross if he knew I had mentioned it.)
You will be pleased to hear that when I left (Aug 22nd) he was very fit and well and in high spirits. I had dinner with him on the Monday evening and he was never better in his life. His name may possibly appear in the casualties as he got one or two small splinters of the armoured plating in his fingers, but it is nothing to worry about and his 'wounds' are no more than very slight scratches.
Please forgive me for writing this rambling epistle, but I thought direct news of his whereabouts and recent doings would be of interest.
Trusting that you will continue to have good news of him.
I am yours sincerely,
N Fearnley, 2/Lt.

With the medal came an official citation, one of the first to appear in the *Tank Corps Book of Honour*:

T 2nd Lieut BAKER, ALBERT GEORGE. 'G' Battn. Awarded M.C.

August 19, 1917. Operations in the Ypres Salient. For conspicuous gallantry and devotion to duty. He reached his objective – a strong concrete emplacement – and, by getting behind it and firing his 6-pndr guns, he was able to drive the enemy out. Although his tank was ditched, he was able to inflict severe casualties on the enemy, who were running away. The remainder of the enemy surrendered to the infantry, who were able to capture and consolidate the position. He and his crew assisted the infantry in consolidating the position by manning shell-holes with the guns from his tank for the rest of the day.

Harry Coutts and Tommy Morgan were also awarded the Military Cross for their actions on the morning of 19 August.

Baker had left *Gorgonzola* gently sinking into the mud outside Maison du Hibou. It would achieve local celebrity status as a post-war landmark on the road out of St Julien. For now, though, he needed a new machine, and went to the workshops at Érin to draw one. It would bear the same name. '*Gorgonzola* a terrible name, but must stick to it for luck,' he told Miriam. She sent him a sprig of heather for additional good fortune, and he kept it by him at the front of the tank. His arms were now better, though stiff.

While Baker was nursing his injuries and making a fuller acquaintance of *Gorgonzola 2*, planning was well advanced for another appearance by the tanks. This time – at last – it was designed to take advantage of their potential for making a surprise attack in large numbers and on firm ground, surging through the German defences and making a breach for the infantry to push through. It was the sort of operation Swinton and others had been recommending for more than a year. Perhaps the success at the Cockcroft, limited though it had been, really had done something to turn the tide and to make the senior commanders more amenable to discussing a properly joined-up combined arms attack.

The focus of the new offensive was the town of Cambrai, about 50 miles south of Ypres. It was the main German base in the region, and an industrial centre with good road and rail links to all parts of the frontline. Until late 1916 it had been more than 40 miles behind the fighting, but that had changed over the previous 12 months. The scale of German losses at Ypres and elsewhere had been just as horrific as those of the Allies. As winter set in, the Germans sought to reduce their commitments by withdrawing to a new and shorter defensive line. It was called the Siegfried Stellung, although the Allies always referred to it as the Hindenburg Line. It reduced the length of the German defences by 30 miles, and it brought the frontline very close to the western outskirts of Cambrai. The Germans began withdrawing to their new positions in early 1917, destroying villages, roads and anything else that might be useful to the Allies as they went.

Cambrai had so far escaped the ravages of war. In personnel terms, the Germans were believed to be weaker here than elsewhere, the sector often manned by units recovering from action further north. The presence of so many battle-weary troops gave the town the nickname 'the Flanders Sanatorium'. The Germans took comfort, however, in the size and scope of the defences they had laid down along the new line. There were three interconnected rows of trenches, cut deeper and wider than usual to thwart a tank attack. Each trench was protected by its own vast expanse of heavy-duty barbed wire, up to a 100 yards wide in places. The line was punctuated by concrete bunkers and large dugouts. It was generally considered to be impregnable.

Such was its strategic importance though, that British planners were soon eyeing Cambrai as a potential target for an attempted thrust through the Hindenburg Line. Plans were sketched out for a combined Anglo-French attack, but not pursued. At that time the priority was still Ypres.

It is difficult to disentangle the chronology and decision making that brought the battle plan to fruition many months later. It was a combination of disparate ideas that eventually coalesced into a firm proposal. The prime mover in the process was General Sir Julian 'Bungo' Byng. A veteran of the Boer War, Byng had been promoted rapidly through the senior ranks since 1914, and his recent successes at the head of the Canadian Corps had been rewarded with command of the Third Army outside Cambrai. Byng was an imaginative and resourceful commander. He was actively interested in, rather than resistant to, the fundamental changes in warfare that the mechanised age was speedily ushering in. He was ready to embrace and exploit them. Few of his fellow veterans of earlier wars were ready to make this journey. Their formative years had been spent putting down local difficulties and keeping the natives in order in remote corners of the British Empire. By the time they were running the British Army, they found themselves managing huge forces in the field, and fighting battles that lasted weeks and months rather than hours – battles featuring a whole range of tools capable of mechanical slaughter on an industrial scale. The rifle, the bayonet and the cavalry charge had been superseded by the machine-gun, the long-range artillery shell, poison gas and – now – the tank. This was not war as they had known it all their lives. It was too much to expect most of them to make a smooth transition from the one to the other. Byng was one of the few who did.

The character of the campaign on the Western Front had been settled at an early stage. Winding hundreds of miles south from the Belgian coast, the lines of trenches made it all but impossible for either side to strike a decisive blow. Battles developed a pattern: an offensive by one side would make early gains before petering out in the face of counter-attacks, until the fighting eventually juddered to a halt with both sides occupying roughly the positions in which they had started. The new warfare overwhelmingly favoured the defender. An entrenched enemy with ranks of barbed wire in front of him and a machine-gun in his hand could not be dislodged, or at least not without unconscionable losses. This lesson had been absorbed but slowly, and only after dense masses of infantrymen advancing slowly across the open and muddy ground of No Man's Land had been cut down in their tens of thousands in one action after another.

Byng dusted off the discarded plans for an attack on Cambrai. He listened to Elles and Fuller when they told him what the tanks were capable of, if only they were deployed properly. And he absorbed the ideas of another innovative thinker, an artilleryman, Brigadier-General Hugh Tudor. Byng integrated the pieces into a whole that constituted a step change in the way an attack was planned, coordinated and carried out. Cambrai would be different. It would use all the mechanised weaponry available – static, mobile and airborne. It would be meticulously choreographed and prepared in great secret. It would involve all arms working together in full cooperation. Critically, the enemy would not be forewarned: the success of the attack would owe much to the element of surprise.

For Elles and Fuller, Cambrai offered the tanks a tempting target that would at last give them the opportunity to show what they could do if conditions were in their favour. They proposed assembling a force of machines many times larger than anything that had been seen so far, numbering several hundred tanks. The Hindenburg Line outside Cambrai was in a sector almost untouched by the war. The untended fields were overgrown with coarse grasses and weeds, but the land had not been pulverised and pitted by millions of artillery shells. Nor was it low-lying and vulnerable to the flooding that had been the curse of the Somme and Ypres. It was rolling chalkland with few hedges – perfect terrain for the tanks. The open land was punctuated in places by copses and larger woods, and by a number of villages. There were some canals and a number of small streams to be reckoned with. But otherwise the sector recommended itself strongly as a landscape in which the tanks could prosper.

Nor were the tank men deterred by the impressive defences of the Hindenburg Line. Crushing barbed wire, flattening machine-gun nests in their redoubts and creating a path for the infantry was exactly the role that Swinton had envisaged for them from the start. There were obstacles to be overcome, certainly – the waterways, and German trenches reported to be wider and deeper here than elsewhere on the front. But they were confident these could be overcome. Certainly, the principal feature of the defences – belt after broad belt of barbed wire, nowhere less than 50 yards wide – should not pose too much a problem for the 30-ton Mark IV tanks.

Much still depended though on taking the defenders by surprise, and that would be impossible if the offensive began in the now-traditional way, with a massive artillery barrage. In its small way, the Cockcroft had demonstrated how much more effective an attack could be if the tanks loomed up in front of the enemy in the dawn light when they were not expected. Fuller drew up a plan for a surprise 48-hour raid, led by tanks, the objective of which would be the capture of strategic positions to the west of Cambrai without directly attacking the town itself. But he struggled to convince the generals that the plan would work without some form of artillery bombardment to precede it. Such a barrage would mean the element of unexpectedness, if not lost altogether, would be severely compromised.

It was Tudor who solved the conundrum. When an artillery barrage began, it took the guns time to find their range and bear accurately on their targets. This was a process known as 'registering'. Weather conditions, the performance of individual batches of ammunition, the calibration of individual guns – all were variables. The gunners seldom hit the target at the first time of asking. They had to fire several registering rounds while forward observers or air crews reported on the results and gradually helped them settle on the target. All this gave a degree of advance notice to the defenders that an attack was imminent in a particular sector. They knew what was coming. The Cambrai planners were adamant that the enemy must be given no notice at all.

Tudor exploited some of the new technology that had recently become available to develop a system of unregistered firing called 'silent registration' or 'map shooting'. Targets, directions and ranges were all plotted by trigonometry and tested by air photography and reconnaissance. The results were issued to each battery, to allow them to train their fire at a point identified on a map rather than by a practical process of trial and error. A further series of mathematical calculations was designed to minimise the variables, such as testing the muzzle velocity and calibration of each gun. The effects of different atmospheric conditions were also factored in. None of this had been done before, and it meant that Byng could support his tanks and infantry with an accurately directed barrage that, critically, could be synchronised with the start of the attack rather than preceding it, and so forewarning the enemy.

In this way, the plan evolved into a genuinely combined operation involving artillery, tanks and infantry, and in due course, aircraft as well. As such, it would create a template for the next 100 years of mechanised warfare. That is why the Battle of Cambrai has become an irresistible subject of study for generations of historians and military analysts. It was a dramatic battle in its own right: but it was also the moment that all the confusion and muddled thinking of the previous three years resolved themselves into a coordinated strategy for employing the new tools of warfare in a fully integrated way.

In spite of the prominent role apportioned to the tanks, it was not a tank battle. The tanks made a potent early impact on the course of the fighting, but for various reasons that was not sustained. Cambrai was a major infantry engagement. But it was the first battle in which the tanks played a strategic and influential role, initially at least, and it ended any doubts about their potential as a key battlefield weapon.

The plans were fully developed by September 1917. Haig approved them in principle, but waited to see whether any breakthrough was likely to be forthcoming in Flanders. The news from there, however, remained stubbornly bad. It became evident to him that if he was to continue tying up the German defences while the French Army recovered, a new point of attack was required. Time was running out: the autumn was already well advanced and if he left it much longer, the attack would have to wait until after the winter. Operation GY, the raid around Cambrai, was authorised on 13 October.

All this planning was happening way above the heads of the tank crews themselves. As with all soldiers, their experience of a campaign was their own immediate location and circumstances, the micro-action that was going on in their pocket of the battlefield. They were not thinking big strategic thoughts. They were thinking about getting the job done and living to tell the tale, and not necessarily in that order.

So, when G Battalion began moving south out of Belgium, they were still completely oblivious of what that job might be. The imperative for secrecy meant that only the most senior officers would know the details of the attack until the last moment. By the end of October, the battalion was camped under canvas south of the Somme, with the crews hearing rumours that they would be there for the winter. 'Then we go and finish the war with a mighty push' Baker recorded. But only a few days later, they were moving south again. As the weather became colder, Baker was glad finally to acquire his British Warm and also to receive the requested Primus stove.

The movement of G was part of a monumental organisational effort in preparation for Operation GY. Tudor was refining his calculations in readiness for map shooting. Reconnaissance missions were scouring every inch of ground in front of the Hindenburg Line. Hundreds of tanks, thousands of troops and a gigantic mass of materiel were slowly making their way to the rallying points. And all of this had to be done without arousing the suspicions of the defenders.

A priority was getting the tanks and the infantry to practice working together. It would be too risky for them to do this for the first time in the heat of a real battle. Many of the troops had yet to see a tank, and had received mixed messages about how effective they were likely to be. For the tank commanders, the problems of vision and of communicating with each other, let alone with their supporting troops, had yet to be surmounted. Section commanders would be appointed – tank officers who would walk in the open with a group of three or four tanks, directing their efforts and making sure they were joined up with the troops.

Zero Hour was set for 20 November. By the end of October, G Battalion were at the training grounds at Wailly near Arras, working with the infantry. Work was also being done to prepare for their arrival in due course in Havrincourt Wood, several miles south west of Cambrai. This was where much of the force would assemble in the days leading up to the attack. Baker's letters and diary entries tailed off at this point. The tank men were fully aware that something was in the wind; they just didn't know what it was, and they would not know for some days to come. Baker noted his promotion to full lieutenant on 10 November, then added: 'no chance of writing for several days, possibly a Field PC.' These were pre-printed postcards that allowed the men to reassure those at home of their welfare by ticking one of a series of statements. 'I have been admitted into hospital sick/wounded and am going on well/hoping to be discharged soon/being sent down to the base' was one example of the options. No words were permitted. If the sender entered anything other than a tick, the card would be destroyed for fear of divulging operational details if it fell into the wrong hands.

As the Zero Hour for Operation GY neared, work was continuing to resolve the many practical obstacles that lay ahead. For once, the cloying mud was not one of them. More worrying was the unusual dimensions of the enemy trenches. The Germans had realised that one way of stopping the tanks bridging their trenches was to make them much bigger. Aerial photographs had revealed that some of them were 15 feet and more in width – too much for a tank to straddle. If the nose of the machine crashed down into the trench, it would be very difficult to raise it again and get out on the other side. A key plank of the attack was that the tanks would punch through the trenches to allow the infantry, and perhaps the cavalry, to pour through the gaps. If the trenches were too wide to negotiate, the advance would falter, literally at the first hurdle.

An ingenious yet almost medieval solution to the problem was devised. The workshops at Érin were instructed to make hundreds of fascines – cylindrical, closely-packed bundles of brushwood about 10 feet long and 4–5 feet in diameter, each weighing not far short of two tons. The name derived from the Latin word for bundle. The branches were secured with iron chains, and tightly compressed by attaching the chains to two tanks and having them pull against one another. They had been used before in a limited way, for example laid in advance to provide a solid base for the tanks on the River Steenbeck at St Julien. Now they would be carried by the tanks themselves. The fascine would be mounted on the nose of the tank, ready to be dropped when it reached an obstacle. A useful secondary advantage was that the fascines made the tanks look even more fearsome than before.

The trenches were too wide and deep for the fascines to make a bridge across them, so the idea was to make the obstacle shallower and narrower, and therefore traversable. Advancing to the edge of the trench, the tank would release its fascine by means of a lever inside. The brushwood bundle would topple into the trench, and so make it possible for the tank to drop its nose down, gain traction from the fascine, and then lift the nose up and climb out on the other side.

It was crude but effective. The drawback was that each tank could use its fascine only once. A protocol was devised to enable a number of tanks working together to cross successive lines of German trenches. They would advance on the trench in groups of three, flattening the wire and using grappling hooks to drag it clear. Each trio of tanks would be supported by a company of infantry. The lead tank would approach, drop its fascine, and cross the trench. It would then turn and move along the line of the trench, enfilading the machine-guns from the rear. While the lead tank was drawing enemy fire, the second tank would cross the trench using the same fascine, the position of which would have been marked by red and yellow flags, planted at the edge of the trench. This tank then advanced to the second line of trenches, where it would drop its own bundle and the manoeuvre would be repeated. The third tank would cross the two fascines already laid and head for the next line of defence. In time, all three tanks would be reunited at the far side of the Hindenburg Line. The infantry would be following at close quarters to mop up the remaining resistance and occupy the trenches section by section. In the three weeks before the battle, the workshops at Érin were working flat out to make 400 fascines in time for the start of GY. The bulk of the work was done by a thousand workers from the 51st Chinese Labour Company.

Now began in earnest the massive logistical operation to move men and machines, guns and supplies, to their final positions outside Cambrai without alerting the Germans to the prospect of an all-out attack. The tanks were still at Wailly, trying to pack in as much training with the infantry as they could before the move began, practicing and talking together in a way that was entirely novel. The tanks would have to be transported by rail more than 20 miles to the south-east of Wailly, and then make their own way to their lying-up positions ahead of Zero Hour on 20 November. Timing was important: the weather was cold and damp, and it was important not to get the men to the starting line too early, and leave them hanging about getting tired, cold and wet.

The Tank Corps would be fielding more than 400 tanks – by far the largest number so far assembled. They were first transported on 36 trains to Bray-sur-Somme, east of Amiens, and then transferred to trains that ferried them up to Bertincourt and Ruyaulcourt. From there, they made their way under their own steam to the lying-up points about five miles away in Havrincourt Wood.

All this had to be done under cover of darkness and as quietly as possible. It was a lengthy and complex operation that took a number of days to complete. *Gorgonzola 2* seems to have been among the earliest tanks of the First Brigade to reach its position in the wood, because Baker and his crew spent three cold November nights huddled under the nose of their tank, with no tents, no lights and no fires. 'You can guess how glad we were to start,' he wrote later, giving some indication of just how uncomfortable the experience had been.

Baker and his fellow members of G Battalion spent this dismal period in the 2,000-acre Havrincourt Wood, on the edge of a village of the same name. The Hindenburg Line ran through the village. For fear of being heard by the enemy if they ventured any nearer, the tanks formed up at least 1,000 yards short of the line. They were not short of company: by 18 November, 378 tanks and 98 reserve machines were in place along the line, covered with camouflage netting. There were artillerymen with a thousand guns, who would lay down smoke and high explosives as the attack started, the barrage being shifted to keep just ahead of the advancing tanks. The infantry arrived too, some of them having made three or four consecutive night marches before they reached the wood. A supply dump was set up for the First Brigade, containing 165,000 gallons of petrol, 55,000 pounds of grease, five million rounds of small arms ammunition and half-a-million rounds of 6pdr shells. A screen of brushwood and foliage two miles long was built in the wood to conceal this extraordinary concentration of armour. The scene was alive with thousands of men creeping around among the dripping foliage. It was bitterly cold. They concentrated on staying warm and fed, eking out their rum rations and, in the case of the tank crews, trying to ensure that their machines would be ready to roll in the early hours of the morning. It is hard to imagine that many of them managed much in the way of sleep, and they must have felt shattered before the fighting even began. Baker would later report that he had gone four days without rest.

Such was the mania for secrecy that on the eve of the attack most of the men hunkering down in Havrincourt Wood and at other points along the line of attack were only just learning the details of the mission that lay ahead of them. All officers and men of the First Brigade had been sent a message marked 'Secret' by Baker-Carr a few days earlier. Designed to pep them up for the battle ahead, even at this late stage it was frustratingly short of details as to the nature of that battle.

> I desire to impress on all ranks, the enormous importance of the operations which we are about to undertake.
> It is impossible to foresee the results that may ensue, in the event of a complete success, not only as regards the present Battle but as regards the organisation of the whole army.
> The success or failure of these operations is largely in the hands of the Tank Commanders.
>
> The Battle is built up around the tanks, and on the skill and determination of the crews may depend the lives of thousands of our comrades.

> No effort should be spared, no sacrifice should be considered too great in order to achieve our object. If the Battle is successful, it will probably last many days and the greatest determination and endurance will be needed from you all. Personal courage I know you all possess, but more than this is required to carry out a most difficult and novel type of operation.
>
> The Divisions with which we are working are all that could be desired, and Tank Commanders can go ahead with the utmost confidence that they will be loyally supported.
>
> The period of training has been short but full advantage has been taken of it and a most favourable impression created among all the ranks of the infantry.
>
> The 1st Brigade during the past three months has been able to accomplish a great deal in spite of the most adverse circumstances. The conditions under which we are now to operate are most favourable and the result of these operations will be influenced to a very large extent by the skill and determined action of the Tank Commanders and their crews.
>
> I wish the best of luck to you all.

The implied sub-text of Baker-Carr's message was that this action was likely to be make or break for the tanks. For the first time, they had been given pretty much everything they wanted: hundreds of machines, dry and firm going, close infantry support. They could not afford to fail now.

Williams-Ellis reported that the crews understood the message. 'It was generally realised that the Tank Corps had, in this action, a very great deal at stake; it risked not merely machines and the lives of its officers and men, but its very existence. If the tanks failed to make good this time there is no doubt that this type of mechanical warfare would have been abandoned, for some time at least.'

Hickey's comrades in H Battalion also got the point, even if the nature of the forthcoming battle still remained a mystery. 'The place was not stated; but we knew that the tanks were to be given an opportunity to prove their worth on firm, suitable ground. If they failed this time, they were done for.'

The tank commanders had to wait until the eve of battle for a more thorough briefing, and a first chance to inspect maps and aerial photographs of what would confront them once they emerged from the wood. Some of them did not even know where they were, let alone where they were going. They must have spent the last few hours before the attack frantically poring over the maps and trying to commit the details to memory. There would be no chance to refer to them in the dingy half-light inside a bucking and roaring tank.

Their orders were remarkably detailed – so much so that it is hard to believe they could have been absorbed fully in those final hours before the start of the battle. They used the colloquial place names that had been bestowed on various landmarks by the British. An extract from the orders issued to G Battalion by Major Fernie makes the point:

No 2 Section advances on the SUGAR FACTORY, the left tank paying special attention to ETNA and VESUVIUS, the left pair tackling the two trenches to the left of the railway in K.276, the right pair skirting the outskirts of the village, blocking the road at F.21.d.60

No 4 Section left pair pass to the left of the village; right pair will move against BOGGART HOLE where they will swing to the left, regaining their line at the top of the bank, the right tank tackling SNOWDEN and going straight up the village, the left tank entering from the road at K.27.c.88

Sections 2 and 4 must be careful not to become entangled in the village, only the right pair entering it.

The Barrage Table must be carefully studied, and owing to the fact that the targets have not been registered, Tanks should keep at least 300 yards behind the barrage.

On reaching the 1st objective (Blue Line) at Zero +85, there will be a pause of 50 minutes, during which the Section Commanders will reorganise their sections. The Reserve Section will come up, and the survivors, at Zero +135, will proceed forward to the attack of the 2nd objective (Brown Line) which should be at Zero +185

Later instructions will be issued as to the further advance of survivors, and as to rallying.

SIGNALS
Infantry required by tank – Flag waved from manhole
Tank broken down, don't wait – shovel waved
through manhole and left standing
Tank wanted by infantry – helmet on rifle held above head.

Late in the evening came another message, rather shorter and more direct, from the commander of the whole Tank Corps, General Hugh Elles. Entitled 'Special Order No 6' and marked 'Distribution to Tank Commanders', the note was handwritten in pencil on thin duplicating paper:

1 Tomorrow the Tank Corps will have the chance for
which it has been waiting for many months, to operate
on good going in the van of the battle.

2 All that hard work and ingenuity can achieve
has been done in the way of preparation.

3 It remains for unit commanders and for tank crews to complete
the work, by judgement and pluck in the battle itself.

4 In the light of past experience, I leave the good name
of the Corps with great confidence in their hands.

5 I propose leading the attack of the centre division.

Hugh Elles

It seems Elles, too, was conscious of the wider context, and the implications for the tanks if they failed now when circumstances were for once propitious.

Special Order No 6 became celebrated for the manner in which it was translated by a newspaper sub-editor when the text of it reached London. His summary of the message for headline purposes was: 'England expects every tank to do its damnedest'. When Elles later came to hear of the way his message had been abridged, he was appalled. 'A vulgar and impertinent travesty,' he called it. He would have been better advised to embrace it, since it was to stick with him for the rest of his life.

As the hours ticked away to 6.20am the following morning, everyone was now aware of the plan of battle. As with most such plans, the opening moves were meticulously set out, but things became rather vaguer after that. Specific objectives were set for Day 1, in the shape of Blue, Brown and Red lines drawn on the maps issued to the commanders, Blue denoting the initial objective, Brown the intermediate and Red the positions the attack hoped to reach by the end of the first day. Beyond that, gains would be exploited as far as the situation on the ground permitted.

Fuller's idea of a brief raid rather than a full-scale offensive had been retained. This is how he summarised its aims: 'To destroy the enemy's personnel and guns, and demoralise and disorganise his fighting troops and reserves, and not to capture ground or hold trenches.' The attack would proceed for 48 hours, and then a decision would be taken about whether to consolidate positions or try to exploit the situation further. The objective was not to take Cambrai, but to isolate it and cut off its communications channels. This would cause severe problems for the German transport networks. It was to be achieved by breaching the Hindenburg Line in a number of places and capturing a sweep of villages to the west of the town. On the western flank, this advance would culminate in the capture of Bourlon village and the adjoining Bourlon Wood, a strategic vantage point from which the Germans controlled their artillery positions. Taking the wood was an objective set by Haig for the first day, although Byng was not alone in considering it too ambitious a goal. On the eastern flank, the plan was to secure canal crossings at Marcoing and Masnières so that the cavalry could move further east as far as Walincourt. If everything went spectacularly well, there was the opportunity to attack Cambrai itself and drive further north towards Valenciennes.

Byng had a huge force of tanks, but only six infantry and two cavalry divisions to attack a front six miles long. Even before the start, this did not seem like enough to achieve the most stretching of his objectives. It certainly did not allow him to hold substantial forces in reserve for when those spearheading the attack became exhausted. Everything would be thrown at the opening advance. This would prove to be a debilitating weakness.

For some, this want of resources was further evidence that Haig and GHQ were still reluctant to put their full support behind the tanks. Browne, for one, was disgusted: 'The plan was stamped plainly with that spirit of compromise, due to ignorance and consequent mistrust of the capabilities of tanks,' he wrote. Having lost 250,000 men at Ypres, GHQ did not have the courage of its convictions. Even if it went well, Browne argued, the next phase would be beyond the capability of six divisions. The capture of Cambrai and a move forward to Valenciennes would take three times as many men. Browne was also disdainful of any plan that put faith in the cavalry, whom he regarded as obsolete in the age of mechanised warfare. 'As an offensive weapon, a man on a horse is an anachronism in any modern battle fought in an in an enclosed and cultivated country where everybody else is under cover. He cannot see his enemy, but he can himself be seen a mile away and what is more pertinent, can be shot at that distance.' He was right on both counts.

Baker-Carr, Browne's equal when it came to mistrust of the high command, agreed that the size of Byng's force was evidence of a 'characteristically lukewarm' attitude. He also pointed out that the divisions allocated to Byng were still recovering and refitting after being badly mauled at Ypres. For him too, it was clear that the commanders still had little faith in the tanks. His sense of foreboding deepened when General Harper, no lover of the tanks, but with command of a key part of the infantry, told him that he considered the battle plan 'a fantastic and most unmilitary scheme'. Harper's lack of faith would prove costly once battle was joined.

But Haig's failure to supply Byng more generously was being forced upon him by other events, rather than indicating a want of confidence in the tanks. He had after all been one of their stoutest defenders. As preparations for Cambrai gathered pace, the Germans were winning a significant victory at Caporetto in northern Italy. It left the Italian Army in disarray and in headlong retreat. Haig was immediately put under pressure by the War Office to send reinforcements south to help them. He resisted, arguing that the Cambrai raid could ease the pressure on the Italians by keeping German resources occupied elsewhere. While he was making, and eventually winning, these arguments, he may have felt that he could not afford to commit any more effort to the Cambrai raid.

Gorgonzola 2, Baker's tank, was in one of two composite companies, each of 30 tanks, that had been created from D, E and G battalions. They would work with the 62nd Division of the infantry in the most westerly part of the line. One company, under Major Broome, would operate with the 185th Infantry Brigade on the right of this sector. The other, under Major Fernie, and with Baker's *Gorgonzola 2* among its number, would fight alongside the 187th, on the left. The first objective on emerging from the wood was the village of Havrincourt itself. After breaking through the Hindenburg Line there, Fernie's company would head for the villages of Graincourt and Anneux, and thence to Bourlon Wood about five miles distant. Given that the story of the past three years had been one of thousands of lives lost for a mere few yards of gain, it must have seemed a scarcely credible ambition for men who had already spent three cold nights in the open with little sleep and only a tot of rum to warm them.

By midnight, the camouflage nets had been removed, and the tanks began to move forward to their final pre-battle dispositions. They crawled along in second gear at a snail's pace in order to keep the noise down. It was a cold and dark night, with a dense ground mist. The tanks set off in long columns, but gradually peeled off into smaller groups and eventually into twos and threes. By 5.00am, 80 minutes before Zero Hour, they were all in place at intervals of 100 yards or so, in a continuous curving line six miles long. Now it was just a question of waiting, running the engines every so often and rolling backwards and forwards so that the tracks wouldn't freeze.

It was a nervous wait. A short distance from Bert Baker in *Gorgonzola 2*, in another of the tanks of G Battalion, was Gunner W.E. Harrison. He was later to record what it was like waiting in the darkness for the signal to attack: 'The early streaks of dawn began to show themselves, disclosing for the first time the long line of tanks as far as the eye could see, right and left, the huge fascines making them look all the more fearsome. The dawn was stealing up. Trees and long grass gradually became visible. Partridges began to call to one another. It was indescribably still. From now onwards the minutes crawled. The suspense was terrible. The tension as watches ticked the night away was almost unbearable.'

As Baker stood next to his tank waiting for the first streaks of day, his thoughts must surely have returned to another dawn, four months previously, when he had again been standing in readiness for action in the ruins of St Julien. Then, he had been part of a small deployment of fewer than a dozen tanks, waiting to carry out a limited raid on fortified gun posts. Now he was part of a vast army, waiting to embark on a major battle. Perhaps he had time to reflect that, but for the success of the Cockcroft raid in July, there might not now be such a huge gathering of tanks assembled in Havrincourt Wood and beyond, waiting to spearhead a large-scale combined attack. In any event, he must surely have been sharing the same feelings as everyone else who was poised for the signal to advance: that strange sensation in the pit of the stomach, the apprehension and the adrenalin surge when they contemplated what lay ahead.

Daniel Hickey, also experiencing those sensations a little further down the line with H Battalion, felt that the success of the whole enterprise would turn on whether or not the enemy had got wind of it. 'If not, the attack would be a walk-over. If he had, however, he would be prepared with light guns in forward areas, machine-guns with armour-piercing bullets, tank traps and extra troops, so that the operation might end in disaster and put paid to the Tank Corps.' He noted that the fascines, on which the whole plan depended, had never been tested in battle. As he too waited in the damp and cold for the skies to lighten, he did not much care for the odds. 'The whole Corps was being risked in this one hazardous operation to prove the worth of the tank.'

Hickey's company commander, Major Gerald Huntbach of H Battalion, located in the middle of the line, was suddenly aware of someone approaching.

Zero Hour was only a few minutes away. 'A lithe figure strode past the infantry and the rear tanks, pipe aglow, and an ash stick with mysterious cloth wrapping tucked under his arm,' Huntbach recalled. 'Unheralded, unexpected, then and there and unattended, Brigadier-General Elles arrived. "Five minutes to go," he said. "This is the centre of our line and I'm going over in this tank." He tapped *Hilda*'s offside sponson. I swung the door open and informed Leach [the tank's commander] of his distinguished passenger. The General glanced at his wrist. Shaking out his stick he disclosed the brown, red and green flag, soon to be historical, and then he squeezed through the doorway.'

The flag was of Elles' own devising: brown, to signify earth or mud, red to represent fighting spirit, and green for fields, or good going. It symbolised the aim of the Tank Corps to fight its way through mud and blood to the green fields and open country beyond the German lines.

At 06.20am, with the sky lightening through the lingering mist, the silence was broken. Harrison recalled 'tank gunners with their fingers on the triggers and the drivers' hands on the throttle lever waiting for the signal. A big gun somewhere suddenly went off. This was the knock at the Kaiser's door, and we roll into action. Suddenly the air itself seemed to reel under a colossal blow, a dull and curiously mellow roar broke forth and continued with a peculiar rhythm. The atmosphere became alive with the scream of shells. Four hundred tanks with platoons of infantry following them up were going forward. So opened the secret surprise Battle of Cambrai.'

A thousand guns were raining shells on the outpost line, the first line of trenches. The shells landed with precision. All the work that had gone into refining the unregistered shooting was paying off. But the Germans remained where they were. They expected the bombardment to last for some time, perhaps days, before any assault would start. That was how all previous battles had started. But this time, it was different. The tanks were already on the move, and within minutes were at the fringes of the massive barbed wire defences.

The rout of the German defences that followed was of a scale that must have been beyond the dreams even of Elles and Fuller. The Germans had long suspected that an attack might be coming outside Cambrai, but they had no notion of the nature and scale or timing of it. Their defenders were caught completely off guard. One can imagine their feelings as, with shells cascading down on them, there emerged from the mist the awesome and terrifying apparition of tanks as far as the eye could see, making short work of the defences they had thought impregnable. The tanks rolled through the wire, crossed the trenches and pressed further forward with the infantry in close support, entirely according to plan.

It was, as Hickey might have said, a walk-over. 'When we reached the Hindenburg main trench, the tank was surrounded by groups of the enemy eager to surrender themselves and their arms. One Jerry tried to hand his rifle through the front porthole; but we were not collecting souvenirs and directed him and his companions to go further on to the infantry. We crossed the Hindenburg main and reserve trenches according to plan. The fascines were a great success;

and the infantry were able to advance through the gaps which the tanks had made.'

The account of Gunner Harrison of G Battalion captured the fear, discomfort, chaos and sheer adrenalin-fuelled excitement of the early advance: 'We kept rolling and creeping forward until we came to a great ditch: the Hindenburg Line. The huge beds of barbed wire were flattened down by the tanks, platoons of infantry following close up.

'As the lip of the tank went over the great trench, our fascine was loosed and rolled over the parapet to the trench floor. It was an enormous trench and there was one horrid moment when our tank dropped on to the fascine it seemed to be touch and go if we could get over. The crew were firing their machine guns like hell up the trench right and left. My God it was hot inside. Down the whole line tanks were dipping and rearing up and clawing their way forward into the fearsome battle. The Germans were running, panic-stricken, casting away arms and equipment. It was very, very exciting. I suddenly thought of the two pigeons and sent a message: "Hindenburg Line crossed". My word, the poor pigeons were glad to get out.

'The Hindenburg reserve trenches with their own massive entanglements went the same way as the front trench. Looking through the periscope I saw lots of tanks on fire – they had direct hits. It is now daylight. I saw masses of small trenches and redoubts and tunnels. It was very thrilling chasing after machine gun positions and shooting them up. By midday we had got through all these trenches and redoubts ok, but we suddenly spotted a tunnel. It was very wide and I think it led to the front trenches. We saw a hell of a lot of Germans running up it, so we helped them on their way by firing our Lewis guns. I will leave you to guess what the tunnel was like. Nothing but a shambles. The periscope which I was looking through was shot to pieces by machine gun fire.'

Douglas Browne of G Battalion also gave a memorable account of these early successes: 'The immediate onset of the tanks was overwhelming. The German outposts, dazed or annihilated by the sudden deluge of shells, were overrun in an instant. The triple belts of wire were crossed as if they were beds of nettles, and 350 pathways sheared through them for the infantry. The defenders of the front trench, scrambling out of dugouts and shelters saw the leading tanks almost upon them, their appearance made the more grotesque and terrifying by the huge black bundles they carried on their cabs. So far our following infantry had found little to do beyond firing on the fugitives and rounding up gangs of half-stupefied prisoners. It was now broad day, the mist was thinning, and everywhere from Havrincourt to Banteux on the canal was rout and consternation.'

It had not all been plain sailing for Baker and his comrades in the two composite companies. Of their 60 tanks, ten had failed even to make the starting line. They had to travel through the whole length of the wood to do so. Four were stymied by mechanical trouble, three fell foul of tree stumps, one was late, one got stuck and another was hit before it got going. The remaining tanks had been late starting, but they caught up the infantry and all were at the first objective, the Blue Line, by around 8.30am – just over two hours after Zero Hour. They were through the first line of trenches. *Gorgonzola 2* was now one of six tanks lined up for the second stage, which began a few minutes later, even though fighting was continuing in Havrincourt village. By 10.20am, around 40 tanks had reached the Brown Line, the second objective, and were taking hundreds of prisoners as they advanced. Baker paused at the support line to send a message back to headquarters via carrier pigeon. It read:

> To HQ 1st Tank Bde
> 20 Nov
> Our infantry (more required) consolidating on Hindenburg Support
> Enemy infantry retreating towards Graincourt.
> Enemy artillery very weak
> Tanks visible – about a dozen.
> My tank – setting off for Graincourt.
> Ground good.
> Wire plenty.
> From A G Baker, G 29
> Cross rds Hindenburg Support.
> Time 10.30 am.
> (signed)

Arms, armour and infantry were now operating as planned in a fully-coordinated manner. They were joined by the Royal Flying Corps, dipping so low on their strafing runs that one pilot recalled having to hop over the tanks. They kept up their harrying all through the day.

Behind them, the garrison in Havrincourt village, a mile from the start point, was putting up stern resistance, and several tanks were lost as the Germans fought back from the cover of a fortified chateau. The fighting was intense, but the infantry were able to capture the chateau and the village by around 10.30am. By now the Hindenburg Line had been breached in a number of places and the tanks had pushed through the next line of trenches, the Brown Line. Baker and his company had an unhindered run to the next objective, the village of Graincourt-lès-Havrincourt, usually referred to simply as Graincourt. From the Brown Line to Graincourt was about three miles over the rolling chalklands, up a rise and then a long descent into the village. Although those inside the tanks would have felt as though they were barrelling along, in reality that three-mile run was still an hour's drive away.

As the tanks approached Graincourt, the advance in this sector met its first substantial check in the form of two German field guns strategically placed on the outskirts of the village. They were 77mm Feldkanone, each with a crew of four firing their 3in (77mm) shells into the line of approaching tanks. With the tanks able to manage no more than a brisk walking pace, the German gunners were able to target them at leisure. In a matter of minutes, they destroyed or disabled at least six tanks. They needed to be neutralised – and quickly.

Baker and the crew of *Gorgonzola 2* knocked out at least one of the German field guns, and possibly both. Accounts vary as to exactly what happened, but it seems that *Gorgonzola 2* and another tank from G were ordered to peel off and deal with the guns that were causing so much damage. This second machine is thought to have been *Gordon*, the tank commanded by Harry Coutts, another of the heroes of the Cockcroft action. The history of G says: 'Six tanks were put out of action by direct hits from two of the enemy's light field guns mounted in front of Graincourt, and these guns were in turn knocked out by 6-pounder fire from two tanks of the 20th and 21st Companies.' Browne's version reads: 'Two German field pieces concealed near the village were happily spotted by Charles Baker from the dust thrown up by the blast of their first discharge, and a few 6-pounder rounds drove away the gunners.'

Baker certainly put one of the guns out of action as well as scattering its crew. He achieved this by working his tank round into such a position as to be able to fire on the guns with his 6pdrs. It is worth reflecting what an extraordinary feat of marksmanship this was, by Baker and by Gunner Philip, who was manning the 6pdr that was brought to bear on the German field guns. The maximum running time for a crew before they needed a break and some fresh air was about three hours. *Gorgonzola 2* had already been running for twice as long as that, its crew bucketing along in their red-hot iron box, their ears deafened by the engine noise, their bones jarring with every obstacle. The cabin would have been filled with the smell of burning oil, petrol and exhaust fumes, sulphur and cordite from the ammunition. Steam from the cooling system would fill the confined space. Inside, it would have been almost pitch black. The two front shutters that afforded the driver and commander a view of where they were going would be closed during the battle, as they offered targets to enemy gunners. They would be peering through a couple of narrow slits instead. Once the fascine had been dropped, they could use the periscopes, but these too were vulnerable and of limited practical use. The gunners had only those three little holes to squint through, each only one millimetre wide. Their view outside was obscured by the autumn mist, and by the smoke of battle. What was called 'target acquisition capability' – essentially, being able to focus on what you wanted to fire at – was extremely limited. The German gun was about 600 yards away and was firing at *Gorgonzola 2* as Gunner Philip was straining to locate it through a tiny gap and trying to bring his 6pdr to bear on it. The fact that he was able to home in precisely on such a small and distant target while under fire and half-blind was a stupendous effort. But he did it. Both guns were disabled, and the road to Graincourt lay open. The Germans continued to put up stiff resistance, but the tanks and supporting infantry were able to advance and capture the village.

They had now advanced nearly four miles from the start line. At three in the afternoon, Baker took out his message pad and deployed his second pigeon to update headquarters:

To HQ 1st Bde Tanks.
Message No 2; 20 Nov.
Our Infantry have taken Graincourt
Enemy infantry retreated on all sides of village.
Enemy artillery nearly nil
Tanks visible – Giggle II, 3 unknown.
My tank On Hind. Support. Nearly out of petrol, otherwise fit.
Ground good
Wire well crunched.
From A G Baker
Graincourt

The same sensational gains were being made along the whole front, with one exception. A mile or so north-east of Havrincourt, the combined assault was making little headway at the village of Flesquières. One possible reason was that the attack here was not as combined as it might have been. This was General Harper's sector – the man who had disdained the plan as fantastic and unmilitary. He was not prepared to sacrifice his 'little fellers' as he was wont to describe his men, by attaching them too closely to the tanks – an arm in his mind associated only with failure. Accordingly, he ordered them to stay 400 yards in arrears, leaving the tanks fatally exposed when they came to Flesquières Ridge. The Germans were on the other side of the ridge, and tank after tank was destroyed as it crested the top and offered a tantalising silhouette for the enemy gunners to aim at. A legend later persisted that a single German officer manning a field battery destroyed 16 of the tanks single-handed before he was killed. Baker-Carr was among those who believed that had the infantry been in close support, they would have been able to knock out this battery straight away. Many others agreed, and blamed Harper both for unnecessary losses and the failure to take the village. This analysis may underestimate the strength and determination of the well-trained and well-positioned anti-tank gunners confronting the attackers. Either way, the losses of tanks and men were very large. The Germans withdrew from the village during the night, the other Allied advances having left them isolated. The infantry took control of it the following day. But the failure to capture it on the first day was a significant setback.

By the end of the morning, most of the Blue and Brown Line objectives had been taken. The tanks had sustained heavy losses, but they had more than done their jobs, and infantry losses were very light by the shocking standards of most battles along the Western Front. The Hindenburg Line was in tatters, and the troops had advanced a scarcely-credible seven miles. They had taken 8,000 prisoners and captured 100 guns. Progress was not uniform, but the tanks had managed to take Fontaine-Notre-Dame, virtually a suburb of Cambrai itself. Graincourt, taken thanks to the destruction of the defending field guns by Baker and his companion tank, represented another of the farthest points of the advance.

Within a few minutes of its capture, Brigadier-General 'Boy' Bradford –

at 25 the youngest general in the army – was in Graincourt, and eager to press on further. The infantry were already pushing towards the next village, Anneux, and Bradford wanted to know what was happening further ahead in Bourlon Wood, their final objective. Bradford put Baker in charge of a patrol of three tanks, with orders to go to the wood to report on the situation there. Baker returned after about an hour to tell the general that the Germans were retreating rapidly towards Cambrai, and there was a wonderful opportunity to occupy both Bourlon village and Bourlon Wood.

It was a pivotal moment. By the time Baker made his report, Bradford had already received orders not to press the advantage beyond Graincourt. This could have been prompted by a desire not to create too great a separation from Harper's forces, still stalled at Flesquières. In any case, it was already dark and the men were simply too tired to make another advance. Bradford complied. The opportunity was lost, and the subsequent costs would be great.

Baker-Carr was one of those frustrated that the advantage had not been pressed home, and thought that fatigue in the ranks of the infantry was the main reason. 'Tanks, their crews perched outside on the roof, pushed on a long distance in front of our high-water mark without meeting any opposition, but the infantry, eager and victorious though they were, were physically incapable of going any further.' In Baker-Carr's view, this should have been the cavalry's moment. If they had followed the armour and the troops, he was convinced that Bourlon village, Bourlon Wood and perhaps even Cambrai itself could have been taken. But the cavalry were conspicuous only by their absence – 'astounding inactivity', he called it – and the chance was lost. There would not be another. At the end of the day, the tanks were withdrawn as far as Hindenburg support line, a position they had blasted through without ceremony several hours before.

These regrets notwithstanding, there was no doubting that the day had been a triumph of British arms. Even Baker-Carr called it 'one of the most remarkable victories in the annals of the British army'. 'The attack was a stupendous success,' according to Fuller, one of its architects, and it was hard to disagree. The weekly *Tank Notes* called it 'one of the most astonishing battles in all history'. The gains made dwarfed anything achieved over the previous three years, comfortably the greatest and most rapid advance made by British troops since the war had begun. Casualties were mercifully light by comparison. The Allies seemed to be on the verge of a great victory. When the news reached London, church bells rang out in celebration. For Fuller, as for later historians, the bells were irresistibly symbolic: 'When the bells of London pealed forth in celebration of the victory in Cambrai, consciously or unconsciously to their listeners, they tolled out an old tactic and rang in a new epoch in war, the epoch of the mechanical engineer.'

The day of the tanks had come at last. 'The battle had been the vindication of the Tank Corps,' wrote Hickey. 'The tanks had proved their real worth, and succeeded beyond the most sanguine expectations. The enemy was on the run for the first time in the history of the War.'

In the hour of success, Elles had the magnanimity and class to remember Ernest

Swinton, the man who more than anyone else had made possible the successes the tanks had enjoyed that day. He telegraphed Swinton at the Committee of Imperial Defence, his message being delivered at a quarter to eight that evening. It read simply: 'All ranks thank you. Your show. Elles.' Swinton said that it became one of his cherished possessions, but even in that moment of elation he harboured doubts about what might happen next. He said he told Hankey: 'I bet that GHQ are just as much surprised by our success as the Boche is, and are quite unready to exploit it.'

Haig was also generous in his praise. As part of a wider message congratulating the forces on their early gains, he made a point of singling the tanks out for commendation: 'In this battle, for the first time, the tanks have been afforded an opportunity of working in large numbers. Without them the complete surprise gained would not have been possible and could not even have been attempted. Their performances have entirely justified the trust placed in them.' No doubt the likes of Elles, Fuller and Baker-Carr had to bite their tongues when they read this, and privately rue the fact that Haig had not listened when they had made exactly these points more than a year earlier. Nor had they ever really felt that much trust had been reposed in them before 20 November 1917.

The generals on the ground were looking at the bigger picture. They were all too aware that their gains, spectacular though they undoubtedly were, fell short of what had been hoped for from the first day. Flesquières had been a costly delay, Masnières further east had held out, and no attempt had yet been made on Bourlon Wood. The element of surprise was now gone. German reinforcements would be coming soon. The British troops were worn out from fighting and lack of sleep, and there were no reinforcements available. The momentum was already beginning to ebb away.

Everyone on the battlefield was exhausted. Some of the tanks had been running for 16 hours, bucking and buffeting as they advanced. Their crews were also spent. It was the severest test the Mark IV engines had faced, and although they proved more reliable than the Mark Is, and were blessed with much better ground, running for so long at such high temperatures was too much for many of them, and they succumbed to engine failure. Those that didn't were out of petrol, water and ammunition and had advanced way beyond their supply dumps. Their ability to contribute further to the mission was now severely reduced. They had made the breakthrough, but disabled tanks littered the battlefield, those remaining were reliant on long supply lines to carry on and they had no reserves to relieve them.

Only about half the tanks that had rumbled forward at dawn were still serviceable. Around 180 of them were out of action altogether: 65 disabled by enemy fire, 71 the victims of mechanical trouble, 43 stuck in trenches. The First Brigade alone had lost 40 tanks, most of them at Flesquières. G Battalion had taken its fair share of the damage, losing 17 tanks, 12 from direct hits – many of them outside Graincourt. Another 17 were immobilised by mechanical failure.

The tanks would not have anything like the same effect again as the battle developed. In spite of their immense impact on the first day, from this point on the Battle of Cambrai would be principally an infantry engagement. As the *Tank Notes* stated, the battle had not been won but as far as the Tank Corps were concerned it was 'tactically finished' – already at an end. 'No reserves existing, it was not possible to do more than rally the by-now very weary and exhausted crews, select the fittest, patch up composite companies and continue the attack on the morrow.' In the few hours remaining before the resumption of hostilities, there was little respite for sleep. The machines had to be refuelled and rearmed and their engines worked on to ensure that they would be ready to go again in the morning. The men would spend another night in the open, conditions made more miserable by the cold rain. The battlefield was quiet after the frantic action of the day. But across the November night came the sound of German troop trains pulling into Cambrai station, bearing reinforcements to be thrown fresh into the fray.

On the morning of 21 November, the tired crews and patched-up tanks of G Battalion set off again, moving through Graincourt to the next village, Anneux, just over half a mile up the road. It was rapidly secured, and the tanks once again pressed on to the edge of Bourlon Wood before retiring. Further gains were being made elsewhere along the front, but the main feature of the day was the ferocity of the German counter-attack, which forced the British to relinquish some of the ground they had made the previous day. By dusk, Operation GY's allotted 48 hours were up. Haig and Byng had to decide whether to call it off, as per the original plan, or press on to exploit what had been achieved. In particular, their thoughts were concentrated on Bourlon. If they could take the ridge there, they could make a decisive shift in the balance of power, and be well satisfied with the success of the operation. It would have been hard to give up the spectacular gains of the previous two days, and after the triumphant pealing of the bells the nation was now expecting the victory to be completed. Haig decided to carry on. After a day of preparation, there would be another attack on Bourlon on 23 November.

The frontline for this second phase was almost as long as for the initial onslaught, although the resources at Byng's disposal were now greatly depleted. The objective was to recapture Fontaine, which had been held only briefly, and take the area around Bourlon – village, wood and ridge. November 23 was another cold, wet and windy day. The Tank Corps managed to muster 88 machines, ten of them from G Battalion, to fight in the Bourlon sector. Congestion on the roads hampered logistics, and G's tanks were late setting off because they had had to wait for supplies of fuel and ammunition. They caught the infantry up and helped them make significant inroads into the wood. But their usefulness was now all but exhausted, and their dog-tired crews had fought to a standstill. Their capacity to protect the infantry was now considerably blunted. They had spearheaded the attack on the first day to glorious effect, but in a built-up area like the streets of Fontaine, or among the dense forestation of Bourlon Wood, they could no longer forge ahead or provide cover for the following troops. As the *Tank Notes* had declared, from a tactical point of view, their contribution to the fighting was over.

Gunner Harrison's tank was one of those that advanced to the edge of Bourlon

Wood in this second phase of the assault. There its progress came to a sudden and horrific end. 'The outskirts of the wood had been booby-trapped, and land mines laid,' he recalled. 'My tank went over one of these. There was a large flash, some which came into my face, a large explosion, and seconds afterwards the tank was on fire. I was operating a Lewis gun in the left-hand sponson under which were two small double doors. I opened these and fell on my backside and pulled my feet through and out. The heat was dreadful. I grabbed the leg of a gunner and pulled him out. The poor chap was burned and wounded. There were no other survivors.' It was a hideous reminder of the vulnerability of the crew if a tank was engulfed by fire.

While a terrible battle now developed in Bourlon Wood, G Battalion's tanks were withdrawn, all the way back to their starting point in Havrincourt Wood. It was not quite the end of their involvement in the battle. As the Germans began to make good the gains of their counter-thrust, the battalion moved half-a-dozen miles to the south-east, to Dessart Wood near Fins, where they helped strengthen the right flank of the frontline. The narrative history of G Battalion records: 'Very severe weather followed with frost and snow, and for a fortnight the tanks occupied the wood, and did useful service in salving and towing back by night guns which had been abandoned in and about Villers Plouich under pressure of the counter-attack. On 14 December, the Battalion was relieved; the tanks were entrained at Fins and taken to Plateau, whence they were driven to Bécordel, the Battalion going into winter quarters at Méaulte, near Albert.' G had lost one officer and ten other ranks during nearly four weeks of action. Thirteen officers and 68 other ranks were wounded.

The tanks had left Bourlon, but the fighting there was far from over. For the next few days there was desperate action in the wood, by the end of which the ground was strewn with dead bodies, Allied and German. In worsening weather, the initiative was shifting to the Germans, and on 30 November they launched a huge attack, intending to win back all the ground they had lost to the British. Attack and counter-attack followed, with appalling losses on both sides, until Haig and Byng decided to call a halt before the weather did the job for them. A strategic withdrawal in the first week of December saw them pull back to the line of Flesquières Ridge. The Germans built new trenches opposite. Both sides settled into their new positions. The battle was done.

We left Bert Baker and *Gorgonzola 2* leading a reconnaissance party to Bourlon Wood at the behest of General Bradford, while the church bells rang out in London. Exactly what happened to him in the next few days is not clear. There is an understandable gap in the Tablet entries, and they were not resumed until three days later. As his tank appeared to be intact, he would probably have been involved in the capture of Anneux the following day and subsequent advance to the edge of Bourlon Wood, before withdrawing with the other G tanks to Havrincourt Wood. At some point, the journey back took him through Graincourt, where he stopped to examine the German field guns he had disabled, and admire his handiwork. He hitched one of the guns to the back of his tank and towed it back as a trophy. The gun would have a history of its own, as we shall learn later.

When Baker did find the time and energy to pick up a pen, the entries told of elation, but also physical and nervous exhaustion. 'Have just finished a big battle,' he wrote to Miriam on 23 November. 'Am untouched as far as wounds go but very shaky, only natural being without sleep for 4 days. Had one night's rest!! Am now back in camp and very thankful to be alive. My bus has done one of the best stunts of the show. Two of us captured Graincourt and a battery of guns. Feel I can't write. Have sent field PC in case this doesn't go through. Lox has gone back very seriously wounded. We've had a glorious victory for the tanks.'

A couple of days later, he apologised for not having been able to write to her before the action started. Now the news came pouring out of him. 'Sorry, the post is all astray, but the show was so secret that even we tank commanders didn't know exactly what was on until 2 days before – all post was stopped. Also we've been living in German dugouts and our tanks for a week. We are now bivouacked in a wood. I'm in command of a Section and don't ride in a tank any more. Lox will be much missed – he's pretty bad.' Loxley would survive, but at the cost of an amputated leg. 'We've had some good officers killed and many wounded. Only one in my tank escaped – myself. Very busy pulling things together, tanks in an awful state.' Although not wounded, he adds: 'have had rheumatism in my arms and shoulders and much nose-bleeding.'

Living out of doors in a chill and wet November with no chance to change your clothes could certainly account for the rheumatism. Conditions were now only a little better. 'We captured a stove from the Germans and it's now under the tank. No tents even – but we now have lights and fires.' By 5 December, he was clearly a part of the salvage operations in Dessart Wood. 'Very rough, still sleeping out. 3 days without a wash or shave. In the line all night pulling guns.'

As a newly-promoted section commander, he would now have had responsibility for a group of three or four tanks, ensuring that they worked together and offered the best support possible to the infantry. There was also talk of a promotion to go with these new responsibilities. 'I'm in for a Captain – £10 a month better off.' He had also been summoned once again to give an account of his part in the action to his commanding officer. 'I was lugged up before Gen Elles to tell him about the Graincourt guns.'

There were congratulations for all the crews of the First Brigade from their commander, Baker-Carr, in a message dated 26 November:

> I cannot adequately express my admiration for the splendid courage and determination displayed by all tanks of the 1st Brigade during the recent operations.
>
> The complete success which we have attained is principally due to the magnificent spirit both of the Tank Corps and the infantry.
>
> Without the support of the infantry we can do nothing, and we must bear in mind their difficulties and offer to them the highest praise for the splendid manner in which they have supported us in an entirely new and to them

experimental battle.

Our losses have been heavy, but we have the satisfaction of knowing that those who have nobly laid down their lives have saved the lives of thousands of comrades.

When we go into Battle again, as I hope we shall shortly, we shall start with a feeling of mutual confidence based upon past experience, and with the knowledge that whatever happens the 1st Brigade will maintain the reputation which it has already won.

It is a great source of pride to me to command the 1st Brigade all the Battalions of which have proved themselves worthy of the utmost confidence, not only as regards pluck and determination but as regards their skill and endurance.

A week later though, and it was a different story. The news of the strong German fightback was dispiriting. 'Sad happenings on 1st Dec, stopped our leave and no chance of going back to reserve village yet. We are all very depressed at Dec 1st and conditions are bad with the cold weather.'

By 7 December, some of the tanks had started the journey back to their winter quarters in Méaulte, near Albert. Baker was still in Dessart Wood. 'Still up the line and am 2nd in command of Coy and very busy. Shaving tackle and kit came yesterday, and we broke the ice to have a good wash and clean up. Very refreshing in spite of cold.' A week later, he too was on his way. 'Going back today and waiting for train. Last 2 weeks very anxious time for all. Haven't had clothes off since Nov 14 and shall be glad to see my pyjamas again.'

He did not have much longer to wait. Three days later he was in Albert. 'Baths and stoves in huts. Lots of snow everywhere.' He was able to enjoy his first bath and decent night's sleep for a month. Winter had set in, and the fighting season was finished. But in London, the inquest – and the recriminations – were only just beginning.

9
'GOOD OLD G!'

*When the HB MGC**
Goes back home across the sea
There's a lot of us will offer up our thanks
For it's us wot won the war
Why if they'd sent us more
We'd 'ave 'ad peace long before
Bless the Tanks!
**Heavy Branch, Machine Gun Corps*
(Anon)

One minute the British had been advancing on Cambrai at unprecedented speed, slicing through the German defences at will and scoring a victory so overwhelming that it had the bells of London pealing in jubilation. The next they were in reverse, the Germans were fighting back with unexpected potency, and the premature ringing of the bells felt like a national embarrassment. The swathe of villages that had fallen during the relentless advance on the first day of the battle were relinquished one by one, as the British were forced back to positions along the line of Flesquières Ridge. And, depressingly, the attack of combined arms that had promised to restore mobility and dynamism to the battlefield had once again given way to the familiar pattern of entrenched and static forces facing each other across No Man's Land.

It might not have been a defeat, but it certainly felt like one after the triumphs of the first day. Heads must surely roll, and an official inquiry was set up to determine what had gone wrong and who was to blame. Byng did not endear himself to his men by suggesting that there was nothing wrong with his plan or his commanders, but that the troops had lacked the necessary fighting qualities, 'staunchness' in particular. It was an unjust accusation, given the speed and extent of the original advance and the tenacity and courage repeatedly demonstrated by the infantry in resisting the German counter-attack, even as they were pushed back again.

To his credit, Haig came to the defence of his men and took responsibility himself. He concluded that he had asked too much of them when he had decided to press on after the 48-hour mark, in the hope of taking the considerable prize of Bourlon Wood. The lower ranks were not at fault, he said. 'I feel, after careful consideration, that all the blame for the mishap must rest on my shoulders. It was I who decided on the 22nd that Bourlon Wood should be attacked. The occupation of this position at once increased our front and threw extra work on our troops. As events on the 30th show, many of the men were very tired and unable to resist the enemy's blow, as I believe they could have done had they been fresher.'

One obvious explanation, implicit in Haig's words, was that there had been insufficient reserves to consolidate and exploit the early gains. Fuller wrote later that to attack without reserves was like playing cards without capital: a gamble, pure and simple. The attack had been front-loaded in order to ensure that it broke through the Hindenburg Line. In the event, this had been achieved relatively easily, and the advance had pushed well beyond the Line across the whole front, with the exception of Flesquières. But by the end of the day everyone was exhausted, and there was no one to press home the advantage. Haig decided to try anyway, but as he admitted, it was asking too much. Later appraisal would point the finger at the failure of the senior commanders to take sufficiently seriously the prospect of the German riposte. There had been plenty of intelligence to suggest that it was coming, but they underestimated the scale and ferocity of it. The result was that the battle, in Browne's striking phrase, had been 'no more than a brilliant but disappointing fragment'.

But Bert Baker was correct, too, in his assessment that it had been 'a great victory for the tanks'. Seen through that prism, much had been achieved. The tanks had been at the heart of everything that had been successful about the initial advance. They had crushed the barbed wire, spanned the trenches, terrorised the machine-gunners inside them and spearheaded an advance of several miles to the very edge of the final objective, Bourlon Wood. Where they had operated as planned, in close concert with the infantry, they had prospered, and no doubt saved many thousands of lives. When the tanks became isolated from the infantry, as at Flesquières, and later at Fontaine, things had not gone anything like as well, and their losses had been great. All the potential advantages of the tanks acting in numbers on good ground, as envisaged by Swinton, had been fully demonstrated. But their limitations and shortcomings – also foreseen by Swinton – had been evident as well. The tanks had performed sensationally at the head of an advance, but they could not operate in the density of Bourlon Wood, and they had proved appallingly vulnerable in close combat in narrow streets. The Germans had quickly learned to take advantage of their slow and ponderous progress, disabling them by creeping up alongside and throwing bags of grenades under their tracks. The perennial problem of poor visibility had made it difficult for the tanks to identify their targets.

For all this, they had been properly put to the test at last, and had proved their mettle. The tanks had established themselves as a formidable weapon, and demonstrated that combined operations would be the way war would be waged in the future. They had shown their potential to bring mobility back to the battlefield: there would be no future conflicts involving men hunkered down in trenches over years of stalemate. However, there had been a price to pay. The dozens of abandoned hulks spread across the battlefield provided much food for thought for the tank tacticians such as Fuller. Many refinements of tactics and design would be needed before the tanks could be used to even greater effect. And in the next phase of the war, they would find themselves required to operate in an unfamiliar defensive role, rather than spearheading an attack.

All this lay ahead. For now, the tank crews were able to draw breath and recover at their winter base in Méaulte. Their quarters were far from luxurious, and the weather was bitterly cold, but the conditions represented a major improvement on sleeping in the open ahead of a big battle. Baker went so far as to describe as 'very comfy' the huts in which the officers were billeted, on a hillside overlooking the village. 'We've all made furniture for the mess,' he reported. 'I made a settee for 4 out of old boxes and sacking and a mattress.' Browne thought Méaulte 'an unholy spot' and described the conditions as Arctic. 'Heavy snow fell, and the road up to the camp was a slope of ice for weeks. Fuel was short and leave many months overdue.' Daniel Hickey, wintering in the neighbouring village with H Battalion, also remembered the period without affection. 'The sharp cold made fires essential. No coal was issued to us, and we had to rely on timber salvaged from derelict dugouts to keep the stoves going. Everybody was out on the scrounge.'

Hickey said the crews regularly made the short walk to the ruined town of Albert, where the inhabitants had begun to return, and shops were opening again. Camembert cheese was a popular purchase. Once or twice they managed to hitch a ride into Amiens, 25 miles away, to do some Christmas shopping. It is likely that Baker made more than one of these trips, since his post-war correspondence referred to visits to Charlie's Bar, a well-known Amiens watering hole.

Baker was also able to renew acquaintance with *Gorgonzola 2*: 'Saw my old tank at tank park today,' he told Miriam. 'Took out the sprig of heather hanging over the driver's seat – the one you sent. It was certainly lucky – although the old bus is knocked about a bit, having glass periscope broken – 5 gun sights smashed to pieces. Much damage inside.'

Christmas Day brought not only a 'good dinner, turkey etc.' but also good news about one of his crew, the gunner whose shooting had been so remarkable on the first day of Cambrai. 'My gunner got the MM [Military Medal]. Philip by name and only one other MM in the Coy. He fired the gun that put the Gerries out in Graincourt. A good Scotsman.' *The Tank Corps Book of Honour* records the citation accompanying Gunner D.T. Philip's medal: 'For conspicuous gallantry and devotion to duty. On November 20, 1917, west of Graincourt, though wounded, he served his 6-pndr gun in a most cool and gallant manner. He knocked out an enemy field gun at about 600 yards range which had already knocked out several tanks close by, and which was at the time firing at his own tank.'

There was further cheering news early in the New Year. 'Rumours of another medal and leave,' Baker reported, after making a brief visit to Amiens. And the next day: 'I've been given bar to MC.' And that was the sum total of what he had to say about this signal honour. The official citation was somewhat fuller:

> T 2nd Lieut BAKER, ALBERT GEORGE, M.C. 'G' Battn. Awarded Bar to M.C.
>
> For conspicuous gallantry and devotion to duty. He handled his tank with most conspicuous dash on November 20-21. He did especially fine work on Nov 20. When other tanks of his Company received direct hits from an anti-tank gun just west of Graincourt, he manoeuvred his tank so that he

> eventually knocked the gun out. This act enabled the infantry to complete the capture of the village, following after Lt Baker's and other tanks.

A dinner was given to celebrate the awards to the officers who had been decorated. '1 DSO, 2 Bars and 5 MCs for Bn – wonderful record for 50 officers,' said Baker. He was scheduled to go on leave by the end of January, and hoping to have his captain's pip confirmed by then. He got his pip, the leave duly materialised and Captain Baker was back in England before the end of the month.

It seems likely that during the fortnight or so he was at home, Bert and Miriam became engaged. There is no direct reference to it in the Tablet – in fact, he made no entries for more than a fortnight. He was with Miriam during this time, so they obviously wouldn't be writing to each other, as they had been doing very regularly since the start of the war. But later entries show that they were actively planning a wedding and that they did not intend to wait until the end of the war. They would try to arrange it during a later period of leave.

News of Bert's latest heroics had reached Derby before him, and Miriam was not the only one pleased to see him back in his adopted home town. Derby's local newspaper had already reported his new honour, coming as it did so soon after the first award, with considerable pride: 'This is a unique distinction for Derby. Captain Baker is expected home on leave shortly, when he will be assured of the hearty congratulations of his friends, fellow employees and townspeople.'

Foremost among those offering these hearty congratulations were his peacetime employers, F.W. Gilbert Ltd, and their staff. They, too, were proud of the exploits of their former chief analyst, and gave a dinner in his honour while he was back in Chellaston. This was also the subject of a report in the newspaper:

> A social evening was held on Thursday at Ramsden's Café, Derby, at which Messrs F.W. Gilbert Ltd entertained some of their employees at a dinner to meet Capt Baker MC of Chellaston, who was over from the front on short leave.
>
> Mr F.W. Gilbert presided and Mr A. Foster was in the vice-chair. At the conclusion of an excellent war-time repast, the Chairman proposed the loyal toasts and Miss Gilbert sang a verse of the National Anthem.
>
> The Chairman then proposed the toast of 'Our Guest' and intimated with what pleasure he met Capt Baker after having been so successful in his duties in charge of tanks during very heavy fighting that had been taking place in France, and hoped it would not be long before they were able to meet after a glorious victory for our country.
>
> In conclusion he asked Capt Baker to accept a cheque as a small acknowledgement of the high regard in which the firm held him.
>
> Miss Gilbert, in a happy little speech, said they were honoured by having Capt Baker MC with them. Her fellow employees had requested her to present Capt Baker MC with a token of their high regard for the splendid services and brilliant feats which he had performed for King and

> country. She sincerely hoped this horrible war would come to a speedy conclusion and allow Capt Baker to do those duties which she had been endeavouring to carry out in his absence.
>
> She had much pleasure, on behalf of the staff, in asking Capt Baker to accept a silver-fitted suitcase and she added: 'May he have a speedy return to Blighty after a glorious victory for England's fight for right against might.'
>
> Messrs Brigham, Foster, Bates and Stringer, together with Miss Kilgower, supported in a few well-chosen remarks.
>
> Capt Baker replied in a very soldier-like manner, intimating that he preferred deeds to words, and he cheered up the whole of those present by his optimistic speech and his emphatic declaration that we were safe to win, and if it were left to those at the front they would soon have the Boche on the run and back in his own country. What he particularly wished to impress upon all was the desire that all those in this country should stick it, buckle up their belts a little tighter, contribute their money, and generally do their bit. They could depend upon it that the Tommies at the front would do the rest. He thanked the firm, and more especially the staff, for their gifts, which would always be valued by him. That evening would go down as a red-letter day in his memory.
>
> An old employee in ex-Corporal George Woodfield of the Coldstream Guards, who was wounded in France and thereby rendered unfit for further military service, was then the recipient of a small present in acknowledgement of his services to which he suitably replied. Miss Gilbert presented Capt Baker's fiancée (Miss M. Potter) with a small token to commemorate the occasion.

It is evident from this final paragraph that Bert and Miriam were indeed engaged by this time. We still have the suitcase, although all the fittings from the inside are gone. The inscription on a silver plate by the handle reads: 'Presented to Captain A.G. Baker MC, to commemorate his distinguished services to his country, by his colleagues, the staff of F.W. Gilbert Limited, January 1918.'

In this report of his speech, we hear the authentic voice of Bert Baker for the first time. The extracts he later transcribed into the Tablet were brief and generally business-like. Now we hear him speaking, and displaying the same positive thinking that ran through most of the entries in the Tablet. Considering he 'preferred deeds to words', it was a speech that seemed exactly suited to the occasion, and was no doubt just what his audience hoped to hear.

By the time he returned to his battalion in February, G Battalion's eight-week sojourn at Méaulte was almost at an end. The tanks would soon be moving again, amid rumours of a massive spring offensive by the Germans. It had been a formative period for the tank men. Rest and recuperation had been the orders of the day. But it had been invaluable as an exercise in what these days we would call bonding. The officers and crews had been together for months, at Bisley, Elveden, Bovington, and then in France. Their ties of comradeship had been deepened by their joint experience of hardship and of battle, by elation at their recent successes, and by their very survival. This spirit was increased by the celebrations for Christmas and the New Year, and games of football when the snow permitted.

As the narrative history recorded: 'The stay at Méaulte was not remarkable for the occurrence of any event of importance, but it ... was productive of a salutary drawing together of the units of the battalion into a closer feeling of comradeship. It was beginning to be felt that the Tank Corps, for all its newness, was acquiring traditions; and a sense of having in some degree shared in the making of them began to diffuse through the Battalion a better realisation of its corporate identity, a common pride in what had been achieved, and a common faith in the possibility of greater achievements to come.'

Baker-Carr also commented on this growing morale: 'Each tank crew was a definite permanent entity and was encouraged to regard itself as such. Tremendous rivalry existed between crews, with the happiest results to efficiency. If, through casualties in action, sickness, promotion, or any other cause, a tank crew lost one or more of its members, some little time elapsed before that crew regained its previous standard of efficiency and the mutual confidence which was essential for its welfare.'

One development that was not conducive to this increasing *esprit de corps* was yet another reorganisation. There were now 18 tank battalions, and they would soon run out of letters of the alphabet by which to the name them. So the letters now became numbers, and G Battalion became the 7th. The First Brigade was reorganised, too, and now comprised what had been G, K and L battalions, newly-designated as the 7th, 11th, and 12th. A corresponding change was made to the names of the individual companies, with numbers replaced by letters. Baker's 20 Company now became B Company under the command of Major C.G. Rossi-Ashton.

The tank men didn't like it. The change did not sit comfortably with the growing feeling that they were ever more closely bound together. As the history of G complained: 'In all that went to foster *esprit de corps*, the spirit was wedded to the letter, and unofficially and in the affections of its constituent members the Battalion is still G and as such still spoken and thought of and acclaimed at sports. There is a sort of character in the letters that has never attached itself to the numbers, and a mental translation to the old designation seems still necessary for the identification of a Battalion referred to in the new style.'

Baker recorded the change, but passed no comment on it. Douglas Browne, of course, could not let it pass without voicing an opinion, and he was at one with the battalion historian: 'This reform, however necessary, was painful to the victims. It might mean nothing to the new battalions forming in England but we in France felt that we had lost our individuality. It was as if the law, without obtaining my consent had decreed that I was to be called Smith or Jones. The old names however are not dead. In any gathering of officers or men from the first three brigades, you will find the battalions still spoken of as A or B, F or G and so on, as the case may be.'

It was true. Colonel Fernie, as he now was, sent a card to 'Charles' at Christmas 1918, six weeks after the end of the war. The message inside read: 'Good Old "G"!'

So Baker was now a member of B Company, 7th Tank Battalion, First Tank Brigade. And in mid-February 1918, the 7th was on the move to positions 40 miles north, to the west of Lens, to be ready for a new attack or to counter the expected German offensive. The latter seemed the more likely. The Germans were about to make peace with the new Bolshevik government in Moscow, releasing a vast number of resources that could be thrown instead into a massive attack on the Western Front. They were desperate to launch it before the arrival of American reinforcements on the Allied side tilted the balance back the other way.

As Haig and his generals planned their response, there would be a new application for the tanks. 'A huge German onslaught was expected, and people began to think of the tanks as a defensive as well as an offensive weapon,' Baker-Carr recalled. There was a new respect for the calibre of the crews as well as the potential of the tanks themselves. 'The members of a tank crew were the most highly and the most widely-trained men in the British Army. Every man was a skilled machine-gunner; most of them were trained 6-pounder gunners; most were fully competent drivers; most if not all were able to read a map and steer by compass; every single man was, to a greater or lesser degree, a mechanic.'

The winter had been spent salvaging and patching up as many tanks as possible, to make them ready for the new campaign. In the early spring their numbers were swelled by new machines arriving from England. These were the Mark Vs, built to revised specifications and notably superior to the Mark IVs that had been in action in 1917. Sadly for the First Brigade, none of the Mark Vs were headed in their direction. Industrial action and shortages at home meant the new tanks were not arriving at the promised rate of 50 a week. Other brigades were given priority. First Brigade was in this respect a victim of its own success. Because its losses had been smaller than those of other brigades, it was last in line for the new model, and did not receive any until near the end of the war. The 7th never took the Mark Vs into action.

Browne, with his customary loyalty to his battalion, reckoned that G with its Mark IVs could outperform anyone else with their Mark Vs: 'If any battalion could make the Mark IV capable in the field of rivalling its more powerful and handy successor, it was G; and in the end both the 12th and ourselves I think not only rivalled but excelled the performances of most of the Mark V battalions.'

Mark V Tank
No made 400 (200 male, 200 female)
Weight 29 tons (m), 28 tons (f)
Length 26ft 5in/8m
Width 13ft 6in/4m
Height 8ft 8in/2.64m

Crew 6
Engine Ricardo 19-litre 150hp petrol engine
Fuel capacity 93gals/420 litres
Consumption 2mpg
Max Speed 5mph/8kmh
Trench Crossing 11ft 6in/3.5m
Armament
Male 2 x Hotchkiss 6pdr (57mm) 40-calibre quick-firing, maximum range 7,500yds/6,858m
4 x .303 Hotchkiss Mk 1 machine-guns
Female 6 x .303 Hotchkiss Mk 1 machine-guns
Ammunition
Male 332 x 6pdr round; 6,272 machine-gun rounds
Female 24,000 rounds

The Mark Vs represented a big advance on their predecessors in a number of respects. The gearing expert, Walter Wilson, had created an epicyclic gearbox that meant the driver could now control all aspects of transmission. At a stroke, this did away with the need for the two gearsmen, and the commander was no longer required to operate the brakes. It also allowed for the removal of the differential gear mechanism, creating much more space at the rear of the machine.

Mark Vs were equipped with a new and more powerful 150hp six-cylinder engine designed by Harry Ricardo. The tank was capable of moving up to twice as fast, at around 5–6mph, and had an operational range of about 45 miles. A new machine-gun mount was fitted at the rear, and the unsatisfactory Lewis guns were replaced with Hotchkiss guns. The unditching gear could now be released from inside the tank.

Although it was a far superior machine to the Mark IV, some of the problems that had dogged the earlier model remained unresolved. The new engine still occupied most of the centre of the tank and generated even more heat. The din was still prodigious. Worst of all, the ventilation was wholly inadequate, worse in some ways that that of the Mark IV. After running for an hour or so, the exhaust pipes were white hot. Once they reached a certain temperature the joints warped and neat carbon monoxide fumes were pumped into the cabin. The air did not circulate properly inside, and many of the crew became ill. Some of them passed out altogether.

The Fifth Tank Brigade were among those to be issued with the Mark Vs, and produced a report on them in September 1918, a few weeks after their introduction. The report made it clear that the effectiveness of the tanks was limited by the capacity of the crews to endure these horrific operating conditions. 'When a tank is in good condition with a new engine, favourable weather, not exposed to hostile shelling or very severe fighting, the crew may be counted on for twelve hours in action. The average time however is about eight hours – but very hot weather, hard fighting, and engines requiring overhaul considerably lessen this.

In the action of 23 August, some crews were physically ill after two hours.' Once released from this ghastly experience, it was reckoned the crews needed 36 hours fully to recover.

For the 7th Battalion and their Mark IVs, the early days outside Lens were spent rehearsing with soldiers of the Canadian Corps. 'Have to train some Canadians,' Baker reported at the end of February. 'Grand fellows. Terrific frosts – engines a worry.' A few days later, he added: 'Preparations for wedding in May!' He did not elaborate further, perhaps because events on the ground crowded such thoughts out of his mind. On 21 March 1918, the German offensive began.

A satisfactory defensive strategy had still to be developed for the tanks. Elles wanted them kept together as 'a sword behind the shield', while Fuller thought they could be used in a series of pre-emptive strikes. The idea that prevailed came to be called the 'savage rabbit' plan, so styled by Elles. In the event of the Germans pushing forward and compelling the infantry to retreat, the tanks would be strung out in hiding places along the defensive line, emerging to harass the enemy and attempt to disrupt and delay his advance. The crews thought the scheme suicidal.

The sector allotted to the 7th was a 20-mile stretch of road between Béthune and Arras. In the event, there was no frontal attack in this area, but the tanks were kept busy shoring up defences as the Allied line was breached in other places. During these detachments the tanks lost 11 men, with 20 wounded. One such deployment was to Merville, where the Germans had broken through. It seems that Baker was part of the tank force sent to face them there, because he sent Miriam a brief message after the action saying simply 'Am safe – in case you work out this morning's news'.

It was as gruelling in its own way as operating in offensive mode. There are few other entries in the Tablet for this period bar one reference to 'much fighting' and another to the fact that he hadn't removed his clothes for a week. For two months, the game of cat and mouse continued, with the tanks on permanent standby to reinforce breaches in the line. In practice, they do not appear to have been very effective, and the number of serviceable machines steadily dwindled. Often, they simply ran out of fuel and had to be abandoned, the crew scuttling the tanks and taking the machine-guns with them.

By the end of May, the men of the 7th were back near Lens rehearsing with the Canadians, and a few weeks later they were withdrawn from the front and returned their tanks to the workshops at Érin. There followed a fortnight's gunnery practice and downtime by the seaside at Merlimont, before the battalion went back to Érin and drew new tanks. Baker's B Company then headed for Hersin, west of Lens.

By now the talk was not of the German offensive but of a massive Allied effort under the joint command of General Foch. After coming within 75 miles of Paris and making huge inroads into Allied territories, the German advance had steadily lost momentum. Just like the British at Cambrai, they did not have the resources to consolidate their positions and press the advance further. The Allies began to score small but important victories. One such came at the village of Le Hamel in early July, of strategic importance to both sides because it sat on high ground. That gave the Germans a good observation point and a springboard for a push towards Amiens, ten miles away. Mark V tanks were deployed for the first time, and combined with Australian and newly-arrived American infantry to capture the village, achieved all their objectives in only 90 minutes. The Australians who had so mistrusted the tanks since Bullecourt, now had nothing but praise for them. The action did not turn the tide of the war, but it demonstrated that it was beginning to turn – and that the tanks were now an influential factor. Fuller's view was that, 'Hamel was a minor action, but the result was that from now on the war became a tank war.'

The Allies now began planning an attack in early August outside Amiens. It would mark the beginning of the Hundred Days Offensive, the campaign that finally gave one side a decisive advantage over the other, and led to the end of the war.

The 7th Battalion was not part of the plan for Amiens, perhaps because it was still operating with Mark IV tanks. Although the crews did not know it, their turn would come later in August, in the battles for Albert and Bapaume. For now, there was a window that allowed Baker's thoughts to return to his wedding. He told Miriam he had been promised leave for early July. On 11 July, he sent a message via another man going home on leave to confirm that he would be back within a few days:

> Tuesday night.
> Dear Miriam,
> Am just back with Bn. Sending this by man going on leave. I'm coming certain on Saturday crossing Channel that day. Wedding on 16th shall we say? More later, your own Bert.

That left Miriam just five days to make all the arrangements for her wedding. Photographs of that day show that she succeeded in organising a substantial event within that time. The newspaper report called it 'a very pretty wedding'. The pictures were taken outside Oaklands, the house in Chellaston where Miriam lived with her mother and sisters. About 25 people are in the main picture, all standing save for a seated figure in the foreground who is probably Miriam's mother. Bert was in his army uniform, his bride in white. There were two bridesmaids – Miriam's sister Annie and Bert's youngest sister, Winnie, who is standing next to her husband-to-be Ted Woodhams. Ted was the best man. Bert's parents, George and Emma, do not seem to be present.

There was time for a short honeymoon in Llandudno. But by 31 July, a few days before the start of the Battle of Amiens, Bert was back with his company in France. As a section commander, he had a wide range of administrative duties associated with the management of his group of tanks and their crews and other rankers – around 30 men in all. Documents that survive among his papers, show how varied and detailed these commitments could be. A few examples serve to make the point:

To o/c B Coy VII Tank Bn June 3 – 18
No 302544 Pte Maher E W is to go on leave before the return f 8 Section from Merlicourt.
May I take 302903 Pte Kellett H in his place.
A G Baker, Capt, o/c 8 Sectn.

To o/c B Coy VII Tank Bn June 3 – 18
70000 Pte Thomas A G – this man's pay book is in Coy office and I have struck him off the pay roll accordingly.
A G Baker, Capt, o/c 8 Sectn.

To o/c B Coy VII Tank Bn
Attached is my programme of work for week ending June 11th. I regret the delay in forwarding same but a great many difficulties cropped up in connection with the allocation of ranges – the gunnery School being very busy. All Hotchkiss gun instruction and firing has had to be omitted owing to the lack of guns and qualified instructors.
A G Baker, Capt, o/c 8 Sectn.

To o/c B Coy VII Tank Bn June 26 – 18.
No 8 Section.
Report on reinforcements
95221 Pte Bartlett R (Gunner)
An intelligent man and likely to make an excellent gunner.

77244 Pte Rumsey R (Driver)
A good driver and quite above the average in regard to maintenance work. A very good all round crew.

305830 Pte Robinson W (Gunner)
Likely to make a good gunner. Poor at tank maintenance work. A hard-working man.

306096 Pte Baudains A (Gunner)
I should like to see another week's work before reporting on this man.
A G Baker, Capt, o/c 8 Sectn.

To o/c B Coy VII Bn Tank
No 8 Section Aug 2 – 18
Roll of officers, batmen and supernumeraries.
No 8 Section.
Capt A G Baker

Lt W R Beatson
Lt H S Bishop
2/Lt O Ross
2/Lt E E Peak
2/Lt W B Duncan

201446 Pte Spearman J W
302544 Pte Mahers E W [?]Batmen
302731 Pte Whiteford J
70004 Pte Parkin T W Cook

301224 Pte Bartlett R H
306496 ~~Pte Baudains A~~x Orderlies
~~309191 Pte Holloway G~~
Gloster H

201288 Cpl Churchill W J
40324 Pte Wells H E Officers Mess
302903 Pte Kellett H

A G Baker, Capt.

To o/c B Coy VII Tank Bn Aug 3 – 18
Herewith amended roll of crews of No 8 Section.

36 Crew
201429 Cpl Cormack A
70002 L/Cpl Robinson??
201300 Pte Stansfield H
300830 Pte Robinson W
Pte Clarkson
304234 Pte Kirkwood A

37 Crew
201453 L/Cpl Luscombe E J
95561 Pte Spencer G W
96681 Pte Smith H E
96680 Pte Perkins S
78780 Pte White A
309166 Pte Baker P W

38 Crew
201412 Cpl Evans H A
77244 Pte Rumsey R

45323 Pte Prideaux E J
95110 Pte Clark D
306867 Pte Inglis E
95221 Pte Brooks T
302274 Pte Dennis J R

Events began moving swiftly as soon as Baker returned from his wedding leave. A week-long engine course he was due to begin the following day was cancelled, and the three companies of the battalion were back together at Bienvillers-au-Bois, south-west of Arras, by the middle of August. They were only 30 miles west of Cambrai, where they had so distinguished themselves nine months earlier.

Outside Amiens, a force of 120,000 men and 400 tanks was preparing to launch Foch's great offensive. There had been no debate this time about the involvement of the tanks, as Baker-Carr noted approvingly: 'Every report from the army commander downwards paid eloquent tributes to its services. From now on, no question ever again arose concerning its merits; indeed the only question was how many of them each commander could manage to obtain for cooperation with his infantry.'

Daniel Hickey, a section commander in H Battalion, was in the fighting at Amiens, and he too noted the discernible difference in the attitudes that now prevailed regarding the tanks. He reported that a week into the Amiens offensive, General Haig had made a personal visit to the battlefield to inspect them. According to Hickey, it was the first time he had done so in the two years since he had first sent them out on their doomed mission into the sucking mud of the Somme. Hickey had himself arrived in France a year earlier, when the tanks were on the point of being scrapped after their poor performances. 'Now, after they had been properly used, their value in action was appreciated,' he said. Haig, whom Hickey described as looking very old and worried, acknowledged as much in his despatch after Amiens, writing that the whole scheme of the attack had been dependent upon tanks.

The very first day of the Battle of Amiens, 8 August 1918, signalled the beginning of the end for the Germans. Allied forces blasted open a gap in the German lines that was 15 miles long. The German commander, General Ludendorff called it 'a black day', and within three days the Kaiser was reportedly accepting that his armies had reached the limit of their resistance, and that the war would have to be brought to an end.

Haig and Foch now had a new tactical approach up their sleeves. The well-established pattern of the fighting to date had been one side making gains, the other resisting and countering, and then a return to the status quo, with little achieved and many dead on both sides. This time, instead of keeping up the attack outside Amiens, the Allies held their positions there and switched their focus further north, and a line between Albert – near the 7th's winter camp at Méaulte – and Bapaume. The first phase, the Battle of Albert, involved an attack on the railway line between Albert and Arras. The second phase, in which the 7th Battalion would support the Third Army's 4th Corps, would pass through the breach and capture the village of Ablainzevelle and the high ground nearby, east of Bucquoy. Once this had been achieved, they were to advance another mile or so to join a larger force in the capture of Bapaume itself, and advance further east if possible.

Major Rossi-Ashton, commanding B Company, which included Baker, issued detailed instructions for the order of battle two days before the action was due to begin. They told the section commanders exactly what they had to do, and how they fitted into the wider plan.

SECRET B Coy VII Tank Bn order No 1 from
Rossi-Ashton commanding B Coy 7 Tank Battalion

18 AUGUST
Ref. map
ERVILLERS Special Sheet

1 The 37th Division (Maj Gen Bruce Williams CB) has been warned to be ready to attack the enemy with a view to gaining and holding the high ground east of ABLAINZEVILLE and BUCQUOY, the objectives being roughly a line drawn from F24 cent to L9 cent.

2 4 Tanks under Capt FitzHerbert and 4 Tanks under Capt Baker have been allotted to the left and right Bns respectively of the 63 Bde for the capture of 1st objective. The remaining 6 Tanks of the Coy are under the command of Capt Gregory.

3 Tanks will lie up Y Day [the day before Zero Hour] in positions already notified.
4 Zero hour and Z day will be notified later.

5 The barrage will consist of a rolling barrage advancing at a rate of 100 yds in 4 mins. Tanks will keep as close to the barrage as possible.

6 12 Spuds per tank will be carried also horn covers and camouflage nets. Tarpaulins will be dumped at lying-up places before going into action.

7 Tanks will leave starting points completely filled up.

8 Tanks will cross infantry forming up line at points already notified at Zero hour.

9 SIGNALS
Flags waved from Tank
Tanks to Infantry –

White and Green Flag... Come to me
Red and Yellow Flag... Am out of action go on without me
Red White and Blue Flag) Am withdrawing
(and to Artillery)
Infantry to Tanks –
Helmets waved on rifles... Come to me.

10 Objectives and boundaries of the 1st and 2nd phases have been notified to all Officers.

11 12 Tanks (7 under Capt Baker on left and 5 under Capt Gregory on right) have been allotted to the 13th and 14th Brigades of the 5th Div for the capture and consolidation of the 2nd objective [Bucquoy]. These tanks will leave 1st objective [Ablainzevelle] followed by the Infantry at Z plus 1 hr 30 mins. Capt FitzHerbert will report to 13th Bde HQ as soon as possible after Z plus 1 hr 30 mins.

12 Coy Rallying Point after capture of 2nd objective will be L16 b 7 7.

13 2/Lt Mathias (G 4)) will collect tarpaulins which have been left behind at lying up points and will convey them to Coy Rallying Point by Zero plus 6 hours.

14 Tank commanders will ensure that Infantry are well consolidated before withdrawing from objectives.

15 Coy HQ for 1st phase will be at 63rd Bde HQ (F 26 a 8 0).

16 Great care will be taken to see that no noise or lights are allowed during approach marches. Tanks will move at very slow speed during approach marches when close to the line.

17 Section commanders will report as soon as possible to Coy HQ how many Tanks have started into action in each phase.

18 <u>WITHDRAWAL OF TANK CREWS FROM ACTION</u>
(i) Whenever a crew is withdrawn from a derelict tank they will bring back the Lewis guns and their spare parts. Everything else will be left in the tanks which will be locked up. In the case of a Male tank, however, the crew will bring back the firing mechanism of the 6-Pdr guns.
(ii) If a tank is out of action and the crew has been withdrawn the Crew Commander is responsible that the equipment of the tank is salved as soon as possible.

19 Tank routes and objectives have been notified to all concerned.

20 Lt Ritchie and 1 Orderly will report 63rd Bde HQ as liaison Officer by midnight on Y/Z night.

The operation began at 4.55am on the morning of 21 August 1918. The 14 tanks of A Company, and B Company's eight, moved forward under a creeping barrage and in near-zero visibility because of heavy ground mist. They quickly took the first objective without meeting much resistance. At 6.25am, the advance was resumed. They reached the second objective by 7.30am. The History of G says that all the tanks then withdrew to their rallying points, where three were later disabled by enemy artillery fire. The advance would be resumed the following day.

It sounds like a textbook operation, but it was a particularly eventful day for Albert Baker. Details are frustratingly scarce, but at some point during the morning he distinguished himself once again on the battlefield. The evidence for this is that Colonel Fernie subsequently recommended him for a second bar to his MC, although in the event this did not materialise. Baker also sustained gunshot wounds that would bring his active service to an end. As a section commander, directing his tanks in the open and on foot, he would have been particularly vulnerable to enemy gunners. But we know nothing about how he came by his wounds.

Douglas Browne, by now battalion reconnaissance officer, provided the most detailed narrative of the action on 21 August, but there was nothing in his account to shed light on what happened to Baker on that day, in terms of either heroics or injuries. Browne recalled the dense early morning mist that reduced visibility to a matter of feet. Even when it was full daylight, they could see no more than 3–400 yards. Even so, the tanks achieved their early objectives without much trouble. Browne recalled that at about 7.00am, two hours into the operation, he and Major Rossi-Ashton began walking up the road towards Ablainzevelle. They hadn't gone very far when they met the first of the tanks returning. 'There had been little or no fighting in the village. The fog had caused far more trouble than the Germans, of whom hardly any had been seen. One machine-gun had kept firing from a ruined house until a tank drove over it, one or two officers had loosed a few bursts before their crews fled, and then proceedings had degenerated into a hunt for souvenirs. There were plenty of these, for the attack had come as a complete surprise.'

Browne and Rossi-Ashton returned with the tanks to their rallying point outside Bucquoy, where Browne reported that all the machines deployed to Ablainzevelle were accounted for. One had been disabled with a broken track. Its commander, slightly wounded by a stray bullet 'in an unromantic part of his person', was the only casualty to date. The nature of this injury – thankfully – does not tally with what we know of Baker's wounds. In any case, Baker was not in a tank, but on foot directing the operations of a section of tanks. The relative ease with which the objectives had been attained does not appear to have offered much scope for the kind of gallantry that had earned him his previous two decorations. Comrades from another tank battalion were finding the action hotter in the next village, but

Browne reported no further incidents involving the 7th on that day.

All we can say then, in the absence of any record, is that Baker did well on that morning, but was wounded in the process, or subsequently. To follow what happened next, we have to rely on understandably brief entries in the Tablet. It is evident that after being hit he was taken back to a Casualty Clearing Station and given painkillers. 'Just out of ether at CCS near Bucquoy,' he wrote that same day. The wounds were not severe enough to stop him writing, but too serious to allow him to return to combat duties. Within two days he was on his way home. 'On hospital train. Several of my section also on train – one dying.'

From the train he embarked on the 23rd on a ship called the *Panama*, bound for Southampton. The docket accompanying him said he was suffering from gunshot wounds to his chest and hands, but they were classified as 'slight'.

He arrived at Southampton on the 24th and at 1.45pm sent a telegraph to his wife of barely six weeks. We must assume that she already knew that he was wounded but safe, since it said only: 'Going to First Southern General Hospital Birmingham.' It was delivered to her at Oaklands two and half hours later. The news of his injuries had also reached his family in East Dulwich. That same evening, perhaps worried that Miriam was unaware of what had happened, his sister Winnie also telegraphed Chellaston. Her message was delivered soon after seven, but her news was a little out of date or had got twisted in transit: 'Bert slightly wounded gunshot wounds chest and hand admitted General Hospital Rouen.'

From Southampton, Baker was taken to the Mayfield Auxiliary Hospital for Officers in Edgbaston, Birmingham, and thence to the First Southern General Hospital. Just over a week after being wounded, it seemed to be his hand that was causing most concern. 'Saw doctor this am – hand not going together very nicely. Forefinger gone dead but they say it will come better.'

He somehow managed to make contact with his company commander Major Rossi-Ashton, who told him all about the fighting after his own premature withdrawal from the fray. The infantry and their supporting tanks had made steady progress to the outskirts of Bapaume, which they took on 29 August after three days of fighting. Over the two weeks that followed, the infantry continued to push eastwards as far as the Hindenburg Line, where the attack on Cambrai had begun in November 1917, and from where the Germans had launched their Spring Offensive in March.

At about this time, Baker was discharged from hospital and sent to Catterick Camp in Yorkshire for what he described as 'light duties'. He was having electrical massage on his hand. He walked the five miles into Richmond – 'pretty town, posh castle' and went halfway to Darlington, 15 miles away, to visit the father of one of his fellow G officers, Close, who had commanded a tank at the Cockcroft. On 24 September, he reported that his treatment was finished. A couple of days later he had a letter from Spearman, his batman, which contained 'much news of G' as he was still calling it. He then seems to have had an extended period of leave, during which he made no entries.

Perhaps he was at Chellaston. In any case, his thoughts no doubt strayed often to the comrades he had left behind in France, who were still very closely involved in pushing the Germans back east. The Allied advance moved ever closer to Cambrai, and by late September the tanks of the 7th Battalion were once again on the fringes of Bourlon Wood, the graveyard of British hopes in the battle ten months previously. This time they found the going much easier. By 8 October, more than 300 tanks had been massed to join an attack on Cambrai. There was sporadic and light resistance, but when the soldiers entered the town two days later, they found it deserted, with buildings ablaze. The German retreat became so rapid that the tanks, lumbering along at their leisurely walking pace, could not keep up with it. At the same time, it appears they were breaking down or being disabled in larger numbers than previously. The Germans had developed a number of anti-tank armaments, and they were taking their toll. The workshops could not keep pace with the repair work, and not enough new tanks were arriving to make good all the losses.

Baker-Carr judged his First Brigade to be 'on its last legs'. On 12 October, the 7th Battalion was withdrawn, and the tanks made their way to Havrincourt, also familiar territory from the previous November. From there they were taken by train back to the workshops at Érin, while the crews went to Blingel Camp, not far away. Here they were issued with eight of the new Mark V tanks, but they never took them into action. They were still being instructed in the driving and maintenance of the new machines when the fighting came to an end. In its final few weeks of action, the battalion lost four officers and 13 other ranks. Another 133 officers and men were wounded, and ten were reported missing.

Major Rossi-Ashton wrote to Baker in mid-October. 'Letter from my major saying Company and majority for me if I can get back to Bn soon.' But this prospect of further promotion and the command of a company was but fleeting. On 18 October, Rossi-Ashton relinquished his command and returned to England. If Baker had been on active service, he might have been considered for the post, although one of his champions, Colonel Fernie, had also left by this time to take over a new battalion in England. The window of opportunity closed. Baker went before a medical board on 6 November and was on leave when, at the eleventh hour of the eleventh day of the eleventh month, the Armistice signed a few hours earlier in a railway carriage north-east of Paris, came into effect. For him, and for everyone else, the war was over.

10
'GALLANT AND DEVOTED'

With the end of the fighting, entries in the Tablet understandably fell away, and finished entirely on 24 January 1919, with momentous news: 'Last night in the army proper. Leave, pending demob.' The couple of months since the Armistice had been occupied by some lecturing on tank work at various depots. He reported Colonel Fernie telling him he had been recommended for a further bar to his MC, but heard no more of it. There was a B Company dinner in London, of which one of the organisers was his friend Loxley, who had been seriously wounded at Cambrai and lost a leg. Bert, Lox and three others went to see the celebrated Bing Boys revue at the Alhambra Theatre, which was now close to the end of a three-year wartime run. Bert enjoyed seeing its two stars, George Robey and Violet Lorraine, whose duet *If You Were the Only Girl in the World* was one of the highlights of the show. It was a convivial reunion for the veterans of B Company. A week later, Bert finished his last working day as a member of His Majesty's Armed Forces. Before leaving he obtained a brief reference from Colonel Fernie. It read: 'A sound, hardworking and reliable officer who has done excellent work in every respect. Thoroughly fit for promotion. Physically fit.'

Colonel Fernie also added a handwritten message in Bert's Service Book, on the section left blank for comments from the commanding officer. It read: 'Led his tank most successfully on 19 Aug 17 in operations in Ypres Salient – awarded MC. In Battle of Cambrai commanded a section most gallantly 20–23 Nov (especially at Graincourt). Awarded bar to MC. F.H. Fernie.'

The days of the 7th Battalion itself were also coming to an end. It was about to be broken up as part of a post-war reorganisation. Most of the battalion was demobilised at the end of January at the same time as Bert Baker, the rest leaving in dribs and drabs over the weeks that followed. What was left – the 'cadre' – was formally disbanded on 24 May 1919. Its last commander, Lieutenant-Colonel H.O.C. Thorp, spent much of the final weeks compiling a short history of the battalion. He wrote the preface to his 30-page booklet on this last day. He concluded it by suggesting that there should be a reunion dinner on Saturday 8 November 1919, just before the anniversary of the Armistice, and hoped it would become an annual event.

A dinner was indeed held later in the year, on 20 November rather than the 8th. Bert Baker was there and his papers contain a menu, although it does not indicate the venue or the occasion. As was the custom, Bert invited some of his fellow diners to sign his menu, and the autographs he collected suggest that this might have been an occasion for the Tank Corps as a whole, rather than just G/7th Battalion. Many of the most prominent players in the story of the early tanks were there, and signed their names for him: Swinton, Fuller, Elles and Stern. A heavyweight guest list indeed.

Thorp's history was a narrative account of the activities of G and the 7th Battalion from formation to disbandment. It stuck to the facts, without opinions or gloss. But Thorp relaxed sufficiently at the conclusion of his work to express his pride at what the tanks had achieved. 'In the fighting which brought about the downfall of our enemies and the final triumph of the Allies – a consummation devoutly and long desired – the Tank Corps had the honour to play an important and effective part, and may claim to have abundantly justified the hopes in which it was formed and developed.'

G and the 7th had performed with particular distinction, and Thorp could not resist pointing out one last time that they had excelled in the 'old' Mark IV tanks even when others had the benefit of more sophisticated machines: 'Among the Tank battalions... [the 7th] has not been the least conspicuous in achievement, notwithstanding that in the final series of attacks it appeared in rivalry with Battalions equipped with newer and swifter weapons than the Mark IV Tank with which the 7th Battalion worked throughout its fighting days.' In the short span of its existence, which was by no means a period of unbroken triumph for the tanks, the battalion had still managed to establish an enviable reputation. In Baker-Carr's admiring words: 'G Battalion proved to be one of the very best in the whole Tank Corps.'

It was well over a year before Bert Baker received formal notification that his commission was at an end:

War Office
Whitehall
29 October 1920
133555/8

Sir
I am commanded by the Army Council to inform you that in consequence of the demobilization of the Army, a notification will be published in the London Gazette at an early date, to the effect that you relinquish your commission on completion of service.

You will be granted the rank of Captain but such grant does not confer the right to wear uniform except on appropriate occasions of a military nature.

I am to take this opportunity of conveying the thanks of the Army Council for your services during the late war, and for having done all in your power to assist in bringing it to a successful conclusion.

I am SIR your obedient servant
B.B. Cubitt

For all his chafing that the end of the war had cost him his opportunity for promotion to major, Bert was fortunate to have been in England when the Armistice was signed. Many still in France or in other theatres had to endure lengthy delays before they straggled back to Blighty and a return to civilian life. It must have been a frustrating delay for men who by then wanted nothing more than to get home. The giddy sense of jingoistic enthusiasm that had characterised the early weeks of the war were long gone. After all the sacrifices and the grievous losses, the mood now was of relief, weariness and a desire to put the whole experience behind them. The returning soldiers had the satisfaction of knowing that they had fought and won what everyone believed would be the war to end all wars. Now it was over, all that most of them wanted was to pick up the pieces of their lives.

But of course, life would never again be the same for anyone. There were too many young men lying dead in Flanders and on other battlefields, too many survivors who were physically and mentally broken, and whose lives could never be repaired. The war had left no life untouched. Women had more than done their bit on the home front. The production lines that built the tanks at Foster's workshops in Lincoln were staffed entirely by women.

Bert Baker was one of the lucky ones. He had sustained minor injuries on the battlefield, but had come through largely unscathed. He had faced the terrors and horrors of war, in the trenches and from inside the cacophonous oven of a tank, but he seems to have escaped permanent after-effects. It would be crass to be even remotely dismissive of the traumatic nature of what so many millions suffered, on all sides; but there is no doubt that Bert had enjoyed much of the experience, in spite of the privations and some of the terrible things he had seen and been through. He had emerged with credit. The dairyman volunteer had been commissioned as an officer and risen to the rank of captain. He had led men in battle and twice been decorated for gallantry. He had played his part in the revolution brought about by the mechanisation of warfare. On a personal level, he had stepped outside the relatively narrow confines of his previous life, made many friends, shown qualities of leadership and courage, and seen and heard much that would shape and influence the course of the rest of his life.

Now peace had come, he was luckier than many of his brothers in arms in other ways too. For one thing, he had a job to return to. Although F.W. Gilbert had been taken over in his absence, his new employers, United Dairies, had kept his job open for him. He could return to Derby and resume his nascent career as an industrial chemist where he had left off. It was a benefit and a degree of security that so many others did not enjoy.

And his girl, his wife of a few months, was still waiting for him at home. Now they had the opportunity to begin a proper married life together. Countless other relationships and marriages, many forged in the urgency of wartime, did not survive the peace. The returning soldiers were changed men. The letters of their sweethearts had sustained many of them during the ordeal. But for those wives and girlfriends, the returning soldiers were like strangers. They had been too close to death for too long, and found it hard to re-assimilate easily into the mundanities of everyday life. They were numbed and traumatised in many cases, and felt emotionally detached from what felt like a humdrum or even unreal civilian existence. These feelings were captured by the German writer Erich Maria

Remarque in his book *All Quiet on the Western Front.* There had been a decade of peace by the time it was published, but within months it had sold more than two million copies. The publication of the work of soldier poets such as Edward Thomas, Rupert Brooke, Wilfred Owen and Siegfried Sassoon, and memoirs such as Robert Graves' *Goodbye To All That* reflected something of the same sense of futility, banality, emptiness and lack of direction. The hostilities had put intolerable strain on many relationships and on the physical and mental resources of men who had survived the war. Now it was over, they found it hard to handle the peace.

These writings were part of a huge volume of war literature to emerge in the early years of peace, fact as well as fiction. Dozens of military memoirs jostled with each other on the shelves of bookshops. The men who had created the tanks were among those speedily getting into print, anxious to be first in the field with their versions of history.

All of them considered how far the tanks had changed or decided the course of the war – an active question in November 1918 and still a lively matter of debate to this day. The consensus seemed to be that the tanks had not won the war, but had done much to bring it to a conclusion sooner than might otherwise have been the case. In fact the Germans gave more weight to the effectiveness of the tanks than the British did, both during the war and after it. Baker-Carr wrote: 'The Germans had no hesitation in attributing the defeat which they suffered solely to the use of the tanks. Their despatches, orders and memoranda were filled with references to the tanks. Stringent orders were issued on the subject, and Ludendorff in his memoirs refers to the "tank panic" which seized the German troops when attacked by these machines.' The German general Hans von Zwehl, who became a military historian after the war, wrote: 'It was not the genius of Marshal Foch that defeated us, but General Tank.'

Haig himself, an early convert and steadfast supporter of the tanks – even if his deployment of them was often problematic – was never in any doubt as to the significance of their impact. His despatches made frequent reference to their value, and he was particularly fulsome about them once victory had been achieved. 'Since the opening of our offensive on August 8 [1918], tanks have been employed in every battle, and the importance of the part played by them in breaking the resistance of the German infantry can scarcely be exaggerated. The whole scheme of the attack of August 8 was dependent upon tanks, and ever since that date on numberless occasions the success of our infantry has been powerfully assisted or confirmed by their timely arrival... It is no disparagement of the courage of our infantry, or of the skill and devotion of our artillery, to say that the achievements of those essential arms would have fallen short of the full measure of success achieved by our armies had it not been for the very gallant and devoted work of the Tank Corps under the command of Major-General H.J. Elles.'

It was generally accepted that the emergence of the tank had changed the nature of warfare for ever. We have already heard Fuller's reflection after Cambrai, that the bells of St Paul's, however prematurely they had sounded, had rung in the age of mechanised warfare. Only the oldest of the old guard were yet to be convinced. On the very afternoon the war ended, Fuller encountered an old officer acquaintance who said to him: 'Thank God we can now get back to real soldiering!'

Fuller was one of the first into print after the war ended, publishing his *Tanks in the Great War* in 1920. He had not been part of the creation of the tanks. But after he joined the Tank Corps as chief of staff he had emerged as one of the primary theorists and strategists when it came to their use in the field, and he was one of the chief architects of the Cambrai battle plan. He had no doubts that his old soldier friend was on the wrong side of history: 'The tank has come not only to stay but to revolutionise, and I for one, enthusiastic as I am, do not for a minute doubt that my wildest dreams about its future will be realised and surpassed, and that from its clumsy endeavours in the Great War will arise a completely new direction in the art of warfare itself. Before the Great War, I was a believer in conscription; I was an 1870 soldier. My sojourn in the Tank Corps has dissipated these ideas. Today I am a believer in war mechanics, that is, in a mechanical army which requires few men and powerful machines.'

'Boney' Fuller retired with the rank of major-general in 1930 to devote himself to writing, and expanding ideas such as this. He became an increasingly influential thinker on the future of mechanised warfare. Short of stature and with the angular features that gave him his nickname, the brilliance of his thinking was often overshadowed by his controversial public persona. He was clearly a difficult man, for one thing: condescending, overbearing, pedantic and irritable. Apart from his published writings, he kept a detailed journal from 1917, in which he roundly criticised almost everyone in the military establishment, and beyond, with whom he came into contact. He was not a man to suffer fools gladly: and his definition of a fool was drawn very broadly. Beyond this, his reputation was tainted by unsavoury acquaintances. He kept company with the scandalous Aleister Crowley, who was notorious for his interest in the occult – Satanism according to some – and founded his own religion, with himself as its prophet. Fuller also shared Crowley's enthusiasm for fascism. As late as April 1939 he was attending Hitler's birthday parade in Berlin and chatting to the Führer about tanks. Hitler was a willing listener: the Germans paid more attention to Fuller's military insights than did the British, who tended to regard him as too clever by half. The great panzer commander Heinz Guderian paid out of his own pocket to have Fuller's *Provisional Instructions for Tank and Armoured Car Training* translated into German. Guderian would soon be demonstrating just how devastating a weapon the tanks could be in the next generation of warfare.

Among others who were quickly into print after the end of the war was the newly-knighted Albert Stern, the banker who had been brought in to run the Landships Committee and drive the production of the tanks. His *Tanks 1914–18: the Log-Book of a Pioneer*, came out in 1919. There were also personal accounts from men who had been closer to the tanks in battle – William Watson's *A Company of Tanks* and Clough Williams-Ellis' *The Tank Corps*. Williams-Ellis had been an intelligence officer in the Corps and would later become an architect, best known for creating the Italianate village of Portmeirion in North Wales. The stylistic flourishes that characterise his book were probably the work of his co-author, his wife Annabel, who was a member of the literary Strachey family and a luminary of the Bloomsbury Group.

Although Williams-Ellis had been closely involved with the tanks and had been awarded the Military Cross, his book was peculiar in that none of it was written from a first-person viewpoint. At no point did he share any of his personal experiences or thoughts, or his own part in any of the actions that he described. His was a detailed but dispassionate history. In an Epilogue, he attempted an assessment of how far the tanks had contributed to the defeat of the Germans, and looked ahead to its possible role in the army of the future. Citing the post-war views of British, French and German generals, he concluded that the tanks had indeed been a decisive factor. There was, he said, 'a good deal of evidence which makes it certain that, every other factor having cancelled out, the fact that the French and the British possessed tanks and the Germans did not was just enough to win the last war for the Allies.' He hoped that the lead the British had established in the field 'in our agony of striving' would be built upon and not squandered. With considerable prescience, he predicted that there might be another war within a generation. 'Let us not abandon that lead in the production and use of a vital weapon,' was his final plea.

Williams-Ellis pulled off a small coup by persuading Hugh Elles to write a foreword for his book, and to offer his own judgement on the contribution made by the tanks. Elles obliged, but said events were still too recent for him to come to any firm conclusions. He confined himself to a rather ponderous comparison with rugby union, the sport that, he suggested, 'offers the closest analogy to war'. He recalled a rule change in the game some years previously, which had reduced the number of defenders in a team by one, in order to allow for an extra attacker – in rugby parlance, a fourth 'three quarter'.

Elles drew a parallel between this and the birth of the tank. 'What we may claim is that the fourth three-quarter, after a nervous start, in which he was perhaps sometimes out of his place, nevertheless on more than one occasion got away unmarked; and that he ran straight even when he was being heavily tackled and drew the opposition for his side; that he went down well to the rushes of German forwards; and that finally, he more than once handled the ball in the great combined run which took his team from within its own twenty-five over the opponents' goal line.' Some of the jargon might have been lost on non-rugby aficionados, but the thrust was clear enough. The tanks had more than played their part in driving the Allies to victory.

Perhaps the most magisterial contribution to the tank literature in the immediate aftermath of the war came from Douglas Browne. He must have started writing his *The Tank in Action* practically on Armistice Day, since it ran to nearly 600 pages and was in the shops by 1920. We have heard much from Browne in these pages. His account is of particular interest, because he had been a tank commander and later reconnaissance officer in G Battalion and was well-known to Bert Baker. They had commanded two of the eight tanks that had carried out the Cockcroft raid, and subsequently went together to brief General Gough about it. Browne's book contains a very comprehensive account of the action. He insisted that his book was a first-person account and not a history of the tank, but it is so detailed and wide-ranging that it has become a major source book for tank historians. It is also pacily written and entertainingly opinionated. Bert Baker bought a copy. Like Fuller, Browne did not hesitate to call out incompetence higher up the chain of command, and his account still makes for compelling reading.

Browne's verdict on the tanks was similar to that of Fuller: 'It is certain that future warfare on land will be dominated by the successors of the Mark I tank which struggled through the mud of the Somme battlefields.' And he echoed Williams-Ellis in his scepticism about whether the will or imagination existed fully to exploit what had literally been a ground-breaking invention. 'For once, this country has taken the lead in military invention; and it has now at its disposal a preponderant body of experience in this new method. It remains to be seen whether the advantage will be maintained or whether it will be lost by diversion to political schemes of even the comparatively small annual outlay of money which is essential to adequate experimentation.' Sadly, the events of 1940 would demonstrate that these misgivings were fully justified.

Another ten years would pass before Christopher Baker-Carr committed his memories to paper. *From Chauffeur to Brigadier* was a racy account of his wartime journey from civilian driver to founder of the Machine Gun Corps and a pioneer of the tanks as commander of the First Brigade. Baker-Carr relished recounting his confrontations with the 'Military Mind', but remained astonished, nearly 15 years later, that it had been so hard to persuade the top brass of the potential of the new weapons. He acknowledged that the Great War was still too recent to be treated as history, but found such pig-headedness and narrow-mindedness difficult to forgive: 'Today perhaps it will seem incredible that the High Command failed to appreciate the true value of the machine gun and tank in the early stages of their development. It will seem even more incredible that, at a later period, it was necessary to scheme and struggle against official lukewarmness, at times almost indistinguishable from hostility, in order to secure the increase in the numbers of these arms which, as was evident to everybody else, had proved themselves to be the greatest preservers of life yet discovered.'

A couple of years later, Swinton entered the fray with *Eyewitness* – the title taken from his by-line as an erstwhile war correspondent. It was ponderously subtitled *'Being personal reminiscences of certain phases of the Great War, including the Genesis of the Tank'.* It came out in 1932, and Bert Baker was among those who bought a copy – the same copy I have used as a work of reference in this book. It was detailed, a little dry, and slightly self-serving in its account of his struggles to get the tank up and running, and his frustrations with the various obstacles he had to overcome in doing so. His account ended abruptly at the moment of his removal from the project, perhaps out of pique, perhaps a punctilious reluctance not to write about events of which he had not had first-hand experience.

Swinton had retired from the army in 1919 with the rank of major-general, and later worked for the Air Ministry and became a director of the car maker Citroën. He wrote *Eyewitness*, and a number of other books, while a Professor of Military History at the University of Oxford. He was also Colonel Commandant of the Royal Tank Corps from 1934 to 1938. Even then, as we shall see, he was not yet quite done with the tanks.

Two more notable volumes of reminiscences were published in the 1930s before the growing prospect of another great conflict concentrated minds elsewhere. Daniel Hickey was one of those writing from personal experience in his *Rolling into Action: Memoirs of a Tank Corps Section Commander*, a copy of which was also purchased by Bert Baker, and from which I have quoted extensively in these pages. Hickey had been with the tanks of H Battalion outside Ypres and was part of the great thrust that briefly occupied Fontaine-Notre-Dame on the outskirts of Cambrai on the first day of the battle in 1917. He was in all the important actions of the following year as well. With a preface by Fuller, who described it as 'thrilling', the book painted a powerful picture of those early days. Hickey later qualified as a chartered accountant, but put his writing skills to good use as the author of several plays, and later as a wartime sub-editor at BBC Southern European News.

The final work of note was written by Basil Henriques, the man who had delivered that jolting reality check in his lecture to the trainee tank crews at Bovington Camp early in 1917. His talk that night had been based on his experiences in the first tank action, at Flers-Courcelette the previous year. His book about that period, *The Indiscretions of a Warden*, was published in 1934. Leaving the army with the rank of captain, Henriques devoted the rest of his life to establishing clubs for deprived Jewish children in East London, travelling widely to lecture about his work. He was knighted in 1955.

Bert Baker does not seem to have been interested in emulating these authors by setting out his own experiences, and was content to transcribe selected extracts of his diaries and letters into the Tablet. He even appears to have passed up a tempting invitation to see his name in print. In April 1929, the secretary of the Ypres League wrote to ask if he was interested in contributing an article to its journal, the *Ypres Times*. 'I hope you receive the *Ypres Times* regularly and find it interesting,' the letter ran. 'As time goes on we find it difficult in obtaining suitable articles, so we are wondering if you can help us in contributing an article on some of your experiences in the Tank Corps. We have always been wanting to receive a Tank Corps article for our journal.'

We do not have Bert's reply, but no such article ever appeared in the *Ypres Times*, so we must assume that he declined the offer. It wasn't that he wanted to put his army years behind him – he made strenuous efforts to keep in touch with former comrades, and he went to reunions when he could. Perhaps he thought his exploits unexceptional, or his writing talents limited. Perhaps he did not want to appear boastful. For whatever reason, no article was ever submitted.

After the war, Bert and Miriam bought or rented a house named Walden in Manor Road, Chellaston – a short walk both from Bert's place of work and Oaklands, where Miriam's mother lived. They settled down to a peaceful middle-class life. At the end of 1919, Miriam gave birth to their first child, a boy – my father. He was christened John Charles Holland. His godfather was Colonel Fernie, the former commander of the 7th Battalion. My father said he never met or had any contact with Fernie, but it was evident that Bert kept in touch with his old commander after the war, at least for a time, and was on terms of some cordiality with him. My father always believed that the 'Charles' in his name was a nod to the pet name by which Bert had been known throughout the war. The 'Holland' came from Miriam's side of the family, a maiden name that had been passed down through several generations. John passed the Holland on to his own first son, and the Charles to his second.

Bert might not have been inclined to write about the war, but he remained passionately interested in anything to do with the tank, buying tank books as they were published and making strenuous efforts to keep in touch with former comrades. When he and Miriam moved house at the end of 1923, he sent a number of letters informing old friends of his new address and wishing them a Happy New Year for 1924. Several of them wrote back: their letters showed just how far flung the former members of G Battalion had become in only a few years of peace. The replies – all addressed to 'Charles' – came from as far afield as Glasgow, Hull, Wakefield, and Bury St Edmunds.

As is to be expected, the letters were full of references to the old days. 'My mind often goes back to the one and only "G" Battn and the jolly times we had together,' said one. 'I never seem to meet any of the old school – "Will R", "Tubby", "Bony", "Bish" and others no less popular because their pet names are not brought to mind. I have forwarded your post card to Hal who will smile when he receives it. Who could forget your smile? You will be interested to hear that I now have a family of two, "a pigeon pair".'

'It is very kind of you to think of me,' said another. 'I note your new address and if ever I am near would like to meet you. I had lunch with Tommy Morgan a short time ago and had a good talk about the old crowd.' Morgan was a veteran of the Cockcroft action, and like Bert, had been awarded an MC for his part in it.

Jack Brown, writing from Glasgow, had bumped into another hero of the Cockcroft: 'Last summer I was on holiday at Carnoustie in Forfar and who of all people should I bump into on the beach but Claughton! We just looked at each other for a moment and then spoke. After that we had a jolly fortnight. He's the cricket pro for Forfarshire. He was just his same old self – telling his same old stories – remember the one about "Thomas, Thomas, mark you"? We had it served up nearly all the time until it became a standing joke.'

Brown regretted that he had lost touch with other old friends. 'I'm sorry I've never managed to get down to any of the dinners, but we have had little ones on our own here – up until last year. You see, we are all so scattered up here – it's difficult collecting people. I haven't been down in England since the war. And it's such a while since that now, one can scarcely realise that it ever happened.

And that one lived so happily in France with so many fine friends for such a long time! However, there are innumerable little incidents I'll never forget. I've just finished reading D.G. Browne's "Tank in Action" and it recalled to my memory many little happenings that I had completely forgotten. I suppose you have read it? I thought it exceedingly well-written and so like him! I did enjoy it!" Bert had indeed read it, and we still have his copy of it.

There was also a response from Ted Loxley, Bert's best friend through the war years.

> My dear Charles,
> I was delighted to get your postcard and I am sorry I have not replied before, but I have been so busy at the office during the day and out late in the evening so that I don't seem to have any time to attend to my correspondence.
>
> I believe you are as much to blame for not writing as I am, and as for calling, I have never been anywhere in your district but I believe you have been in Wakefield on one occasion but couldn't find the time to slip up and see me. I have seen Carby once or twice during the last twelve months when he has happened to be in Wakefield on business. Well, Charles, I have at last joined the army of Benedicts. I was married on 20th November last, the anniversary of the great Cambrai show and the day on which I was wounded.
>
> I wish we could arrange to meet somewhere. I should like to have a chat with you about old times.

Loxley had been able to meet to chat over old times with another of Bert's correspondents, writing from the Midland Bank in Hull and signing himself A. Bristow:

> You will think I am an awful rotter not having replied to your PC ere this, but I am not much good at writing. So please excuse. I was glad indeed to hear from you, as it is not very often any of the 'boys' write. Thanks very much for new year's greeting and if not too late, I reciprocate.
>
> Well, Charles my lad, I am an old married man now having been wed in 1921, as yet have no family. I am living in Hull where I am employed at the above office. What are you doing with yourself? What about another war? We should be able to visit Charlie's Bar again, amongst other things!! I dropped across Ted Loxley in Leeds some time ago. Am quite out of touch with tanks these days, having settled down into a very matter-of-fact existence.

Bert was also still in contact with Jack Spearman, his batman. Spearman set himself up as a photographer after the war, and opened a shop in Eton High Street, a stone's throw from Windsor Castle.

For all this, Bert spoke very little at home about his wartime experiences. But he did take his son John on a trip to Belgium in 1936. Tours of the Western Front had been established soon after the end of the conflict. 'He and I went on a bus tour of the old battlefields,' John recalled. 'He got very excited, and took over from the official guide at several points.'

By then, the wreck of *Gorgonzola 1* would have been removed from the side of the road out of St Julien. But Bert had a picture of it there, sent to him in 1920 by his friend Gregory, who had been in action with him on the day he was wounded, as section commander of the adjacent group of tanks. Gregory had been on one of the earliest battlefield tours, and the photographs he sent Bert also included some from their earlier days together, at Elveden and Bovington.

It is evident from Bert's correspondence that there were regular opportunities to catch up at reunion dinners. He saved some menus, so it is fair to assume that he attended regularly. One menu is from a reunion of his old colleagues in the Royal Fusiliers, which was held in the Russell Hotel, London, in March 1930. As far as his tank associations went, the most memorable occasion of all took place in June 1938, when Bert was reunited not only with many old friends, but also with his celebrated battlefield trophy: the Graincourt gun.

We last saw the gun being hitched to the back of *Gorgonzola 2* and hauled back to Havrincourt, as the tanks were withdrawn from the Battle of Cambrai. It became a sort of Corps mascot, and when G Battalion moved back to Méaulte for the winter in late 1917, the gun went too. According to the battalion history, 'the trophy was often the prize in joyous inter-Company tussles.' Just what these tussles involved was not specified.

The collection of trophies and 'souvenirs' from the battlefield was common. The Graincourt gun was one of the larger mementos, but by no means the oddest. At about the time Baker and his crew were silencing the guns at Graincourt, tanks of the 6th Battalion were helping clear the Germans from a town on the eastern flank of the advance. As a sign of gratitude, the town's French mayor presented the company commander with two cows, which became cherished mascots and accompanied the battalion for the rest of the campaign.

It is not clear what happened to the gun in the months after the winter camp. But when the commander of the 7th, Colonel Fernie, left France at the end of August 1918 to assume command of a new battalion in England, he seems to have taken it with him. How he managed this is anyone's guess, but various accounts use words like 'smuggled' and 'by devious means' to describe what happened, so its removal seems to have been both unofficial and far from straightforward. Fernie was senior enough to pull a few strings. And he was clearly keen to keep the gun. Once he had it back in England, he held on to it for the next 18 years.

What prompted him to restore it to the Tank Corps at Catterick Camp in the mid-1930s is another unanswered question. Perhaps Mrs Fernie had eventually persuaded him that a disabled German field gun was not entirely suitable as a garden ornament. Fernie was a Liverpudlian by birth, but when he died in 1952, he was living on the Isle of Wight: perhaps when he moved there he thought it would be too much trouble to transport the gun. Whatever the reason, he handed it over, and it sat in a shed at Catterick for a couple of years attracting no attention whatever.

That changed as the result of a conversation between Fernie and his former second-in-command of 7th Battalion, Arthur Kenchington, at a Corps Dinner in 1937. The 7th Battalion, disbanded in 1919, had just been re-formed, and with a pleasing symmetry, Kenchington had rejoined it as its commander. Fernie and Kenchington yarned about the old days over the cigars and port, and Fernie told him that he had donated a gun to the Corps some time earlier. And not just any gun. *The* gun. The Graincourt gun.

Kenchington would have understood the significance of this at once, and either he or someone else at the new 7th Battalion clearly had a keen sense of history and occasion. Here was a great opportunity to bring some of the old comrades together for a reunion and a formal handover of a legendary piece of battalion history.

Like other veterans, former members of the Tank Corps were known as the Old Comrades, perhaps after the marching tune of that name. Every summer, members of their northern branches were invited to visit the Corps at Catterick. The last weekend in June was set for the 1938 event. Proceedings would include a special feature: the ceremonial presentation of the gun to the battalion. Formally handing it over would be the man who had captured it, former Captain Albert Baker.

There was a great turnout – around 120 of the wartime brothers in arms were there, including Kenchington, Baker and seven other officers of 7th Battalion from the Western Front: Major Gregory – who had sent Bert the photograph of *Gorgonzola 1*, still stranded in the mud outside St Julien, in 1920; Captain Tommy Morgan, who had captured Maison du Hibou alongside Baker during that action; Baker's other great friend Ted Loxley, who had lost a leg at Cambrai; and four others: George Ritchie, who had won a Military Cross outside Bourlon Wood; and Wain, Rigg and Bancroft. Also there was Gunner D.T. Philip MM, whose accuracy with the 6pdr from his perilous perch inside *Gorgonzola 2* had put the Graincourt gun out of action. So, too, was the father of the tank himself, Major-General Ernest Dunlop Swinton KBE, KB, DSO, in his capacity as Colonel Commandant of the Tank Corps.

The battalion pulled out all the stops to make it a memorable weekend for the legends of G and their comrades. On the Saturday morning, General Swinton inspected the battalion. The Old Comrades began to arrive in the afternoon, and were given tea, before refreshing themselves at a bar run by the Sergeants. 'The beer, thank God, was British,' said the report of the day. The drinking and reminiscing went on until past midnight.

On Sunday morning, the Old Comrades formed up behind Colonel Dundas of the Scottish branch and followed the Corps Band, resplendent in new uniforms, to the Garrison Church. When they came out, officers and men of the new 7th Battalion led the way back to the barracks, followed by the Old Comrades. Swinton took the salute and the band played 'My Boy Willie', the quick march of

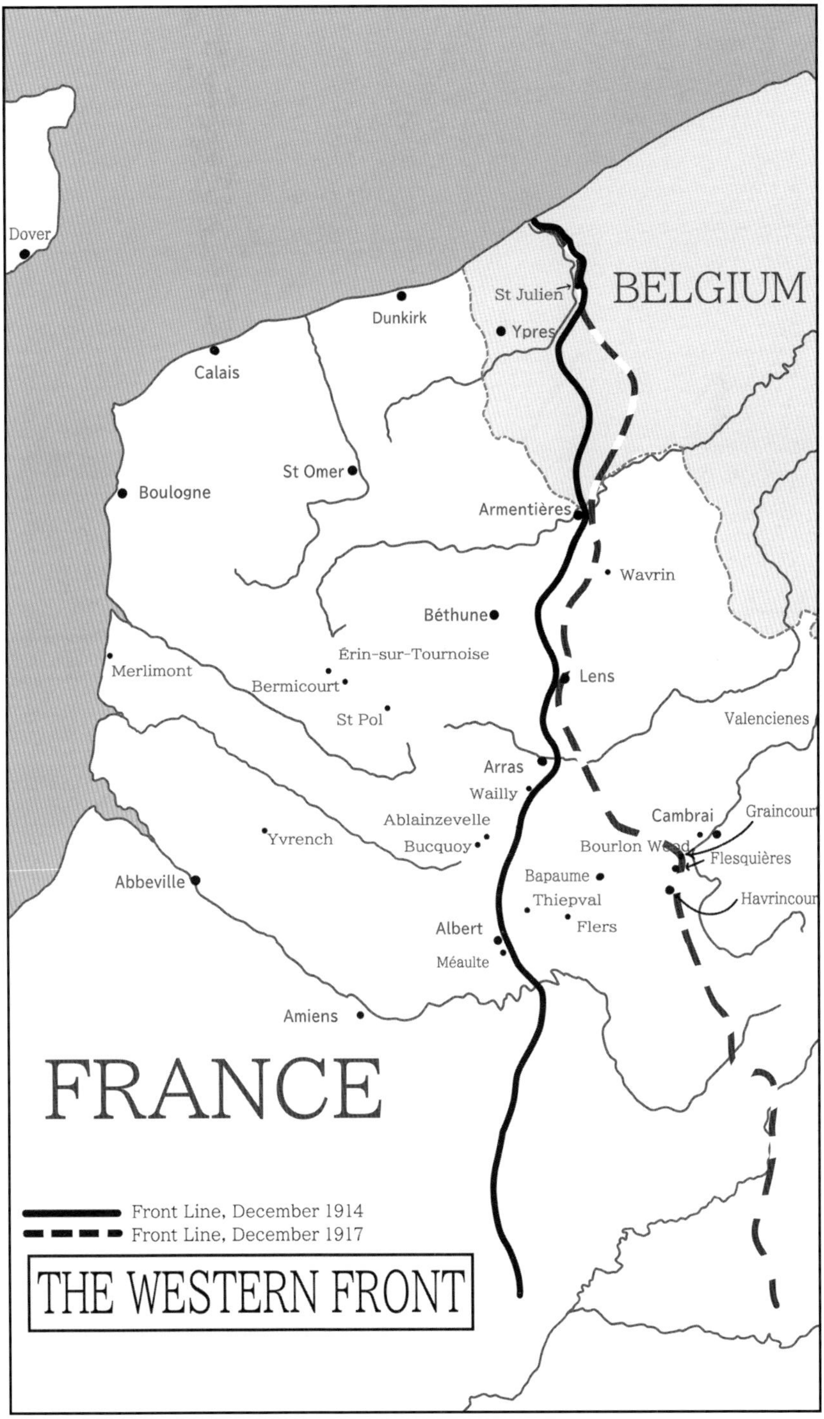
BELGIUM
Dover
Dunkirk
St Julien
Ypres
Calais
St Omer
Boulogne
Armentières
Wavrin
Béthune
Érin-sur-Tournoise
Merlimont
Bermicourt
Lens
St Pol
Valencienes
Arras
Wailly
Cambrai
Graincourt
Ablainzevelle
Yvrench
Bucquoy
Bourlon Wood
Flesquières
Bapaume
Abbeville
Thiepval
Havrincourt
Albert
Flers
Méaulte
Amiens
FRANCE
Front Line, December 1914
Front Line, December 1917
THE WESTERN FRONT

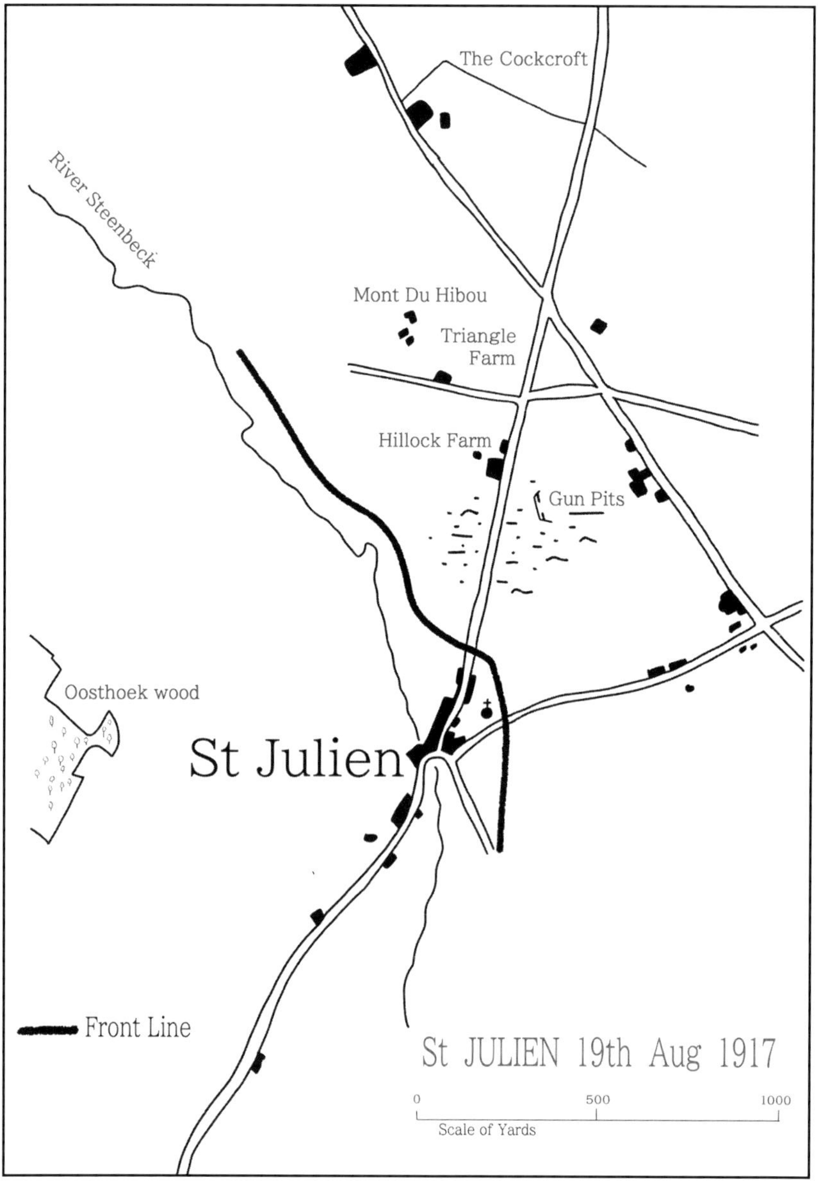
The Cockcroft
River Steenbeck
Mont Du Hibou
Triangle Farm
Hillock Farm
Gun Pits
Oosthoek wood
St Julien
Front Line
St JULIEN 19th Aug 1917
0
500
1000
Scale of Yards

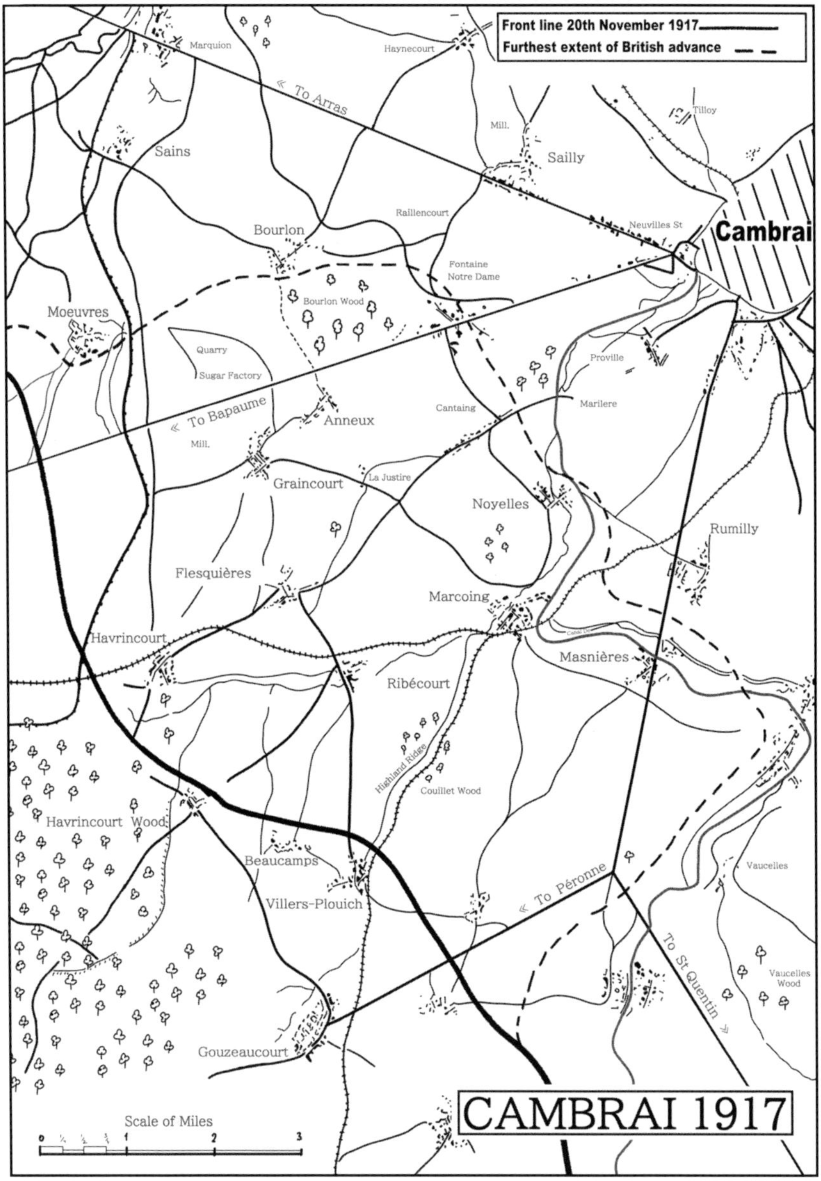
Front line 20th November 1917
Furthest extent of British advance
Marquion
Haynecourt
« To Arras
Tilloy
Mill.
Sains
Sailly
Raillencourt
Bourlon
Neuvilles St
Cambrai
Fontaine
Notre Dame
Bourlon Wood
Moeuvres
Quarry
Sugar Factory
Proville
« To Bapaume
Cantaing
Anneux
Marilere
Mill.
Graincourt
La Justire
Noyelles
Rumilly
Flesquières
Marcoing
Havrincourt
Masnières
Ribécourt
Highland Ridge
Couillet Wood
Havrincourt Wood
Beaucamps
Vaucelles
« To Péronne
Villers-Plouich
To St Quentin »
Vaucelles
Wood
Gouzeaucourt
CAMBRAI 1917
Scale of Miles
0 ¼ ½ ¾ 1 2 3

Bert Baker in uniform as a lieutenant in the Machine Gun Corps.

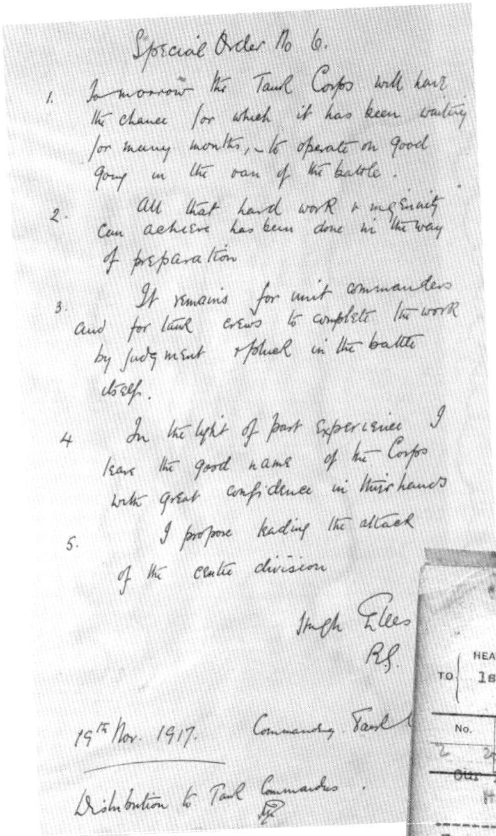

Special Order No 6.

1. Tomorrow the Tank Corps will have the chance for which it has been waiting for many months, – to operate on good going in the van of the battle.

2. All that hard work & ingenuity can achieve has been done in the way of preparation.

3. It remains for unit commanders and for tank crews to complete the work by judgment & pluck in the battle itself.

4. In the light of past experience I leave the good name of the Corps with great confidence in their hands.

5. I propose leading the attack of the centre division.

Hugh Elles
B.G.

19th Nov. 1917. Commanding Tank [illegible]

Distribution to Tank Commanders.

Special Order No 6 sent by General Elles to the tank crews on the eve of Cambrai.

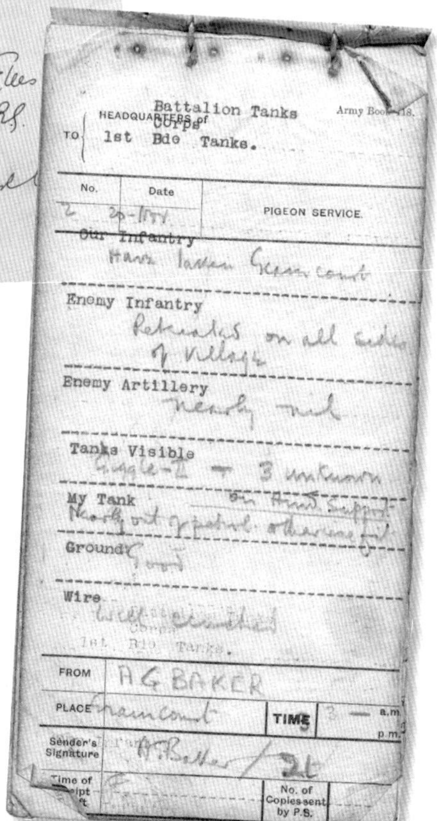

HEADQUARTERS of Battalion Tanks Corps — Army Book [illegible]

TO 1st Bde Tanks.

No.	Date	PIGEON SERVICE.
2	20-11-17	

Our Infantry: Have taken Graincourt

Enemy Infantry: Retreating on all sides of village

Enemy Artillery: Nearly nil

Tanks Visible: Giggle-II + 3 unknown

My Tank: [illegible] Nearly out of petrol otherwise fit

Ground: Good

Wire: Well crushed

1st Bde Tanks.

FROM: A G BAKER

PLACE: Graincourt — TIME: 3 — p.m.

Sender's Signature: A.G.Baker / 2Lt

Time of receipt — No. of Copies sent by P.S.

Bert Baker's pigeon message reporting the capture of Graincourt at the Battle of Cambrai.

The unditching beam, designed to help tanks extricate themselves from the mud.

Tank loaded with fascine on its way to Cambrai.

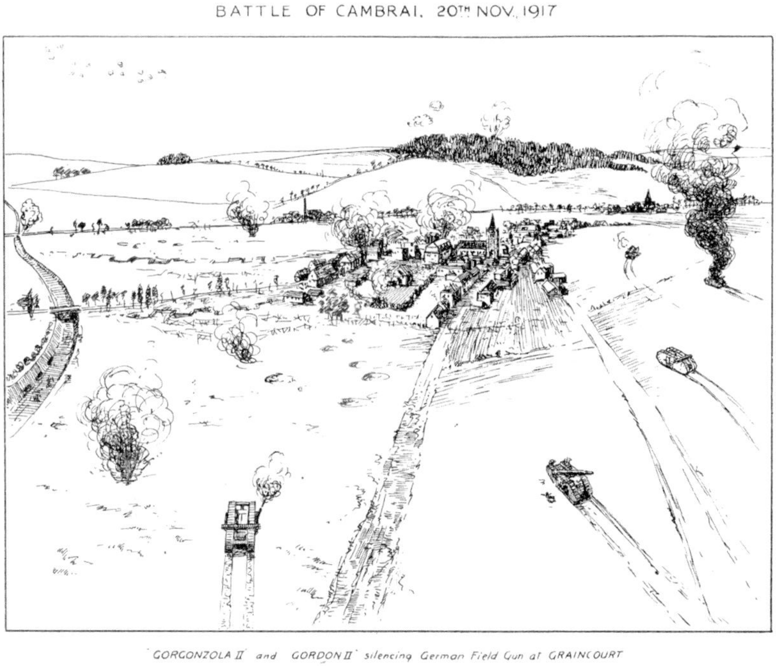

Sketch by an unknown artist of *Gorgonzola 2* and *Gordon* disabling the German field guns at Graincourt.

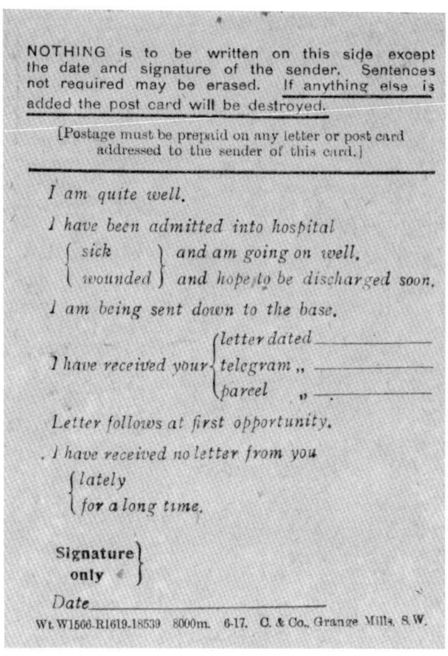

NOTHING is to be written on this side except the date and signature of the sender. Sentences not required may be erased. If anything else is added the post card will be destroyed.

[Postage must be prepaid on any letter or post card addressed to the sender of this card.]

I am quite well.

I have been admitted into hospital

{ sick } and am going on well.
{ wounded } and hope to be discharged soon.

I am being sent down to the base.

I have received your { letter dated ______
{ telegram " ______
{ parcel " ______

Letter follows at first opportunity.

I have received no letter from you
{ lately
{ for a long time.

Signature only

Date ______

Wt. W1566-R1619-18539 8000m. 6-17. C. & Co., Grange Mills, S.W.

A field postcard.

These two photographs are believed to show *Gorgonzola 2* and the captured German field gun outside Graincourt.

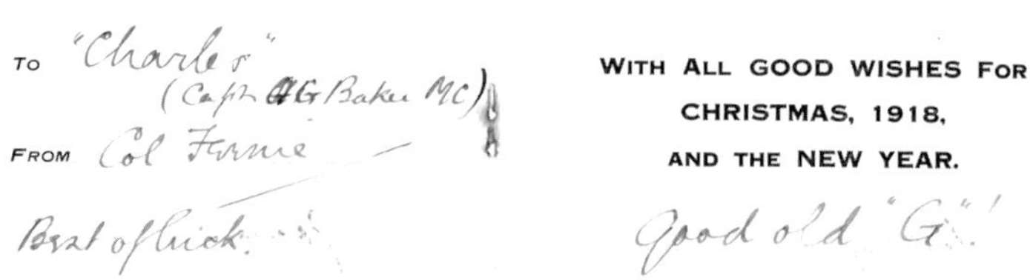

To "Charles"
(Capt. G G Baker MC)

From Col Fernie

Best of luck.

WITH ALL GOOD WISHES FOR
CHRISTMAS, 1918,
AND THE NEW YEAR.

Good old "G"!

'Good old "G"!' Colonel Fernie's Christmas card to Bert Baker a few weeks after the Armistice.

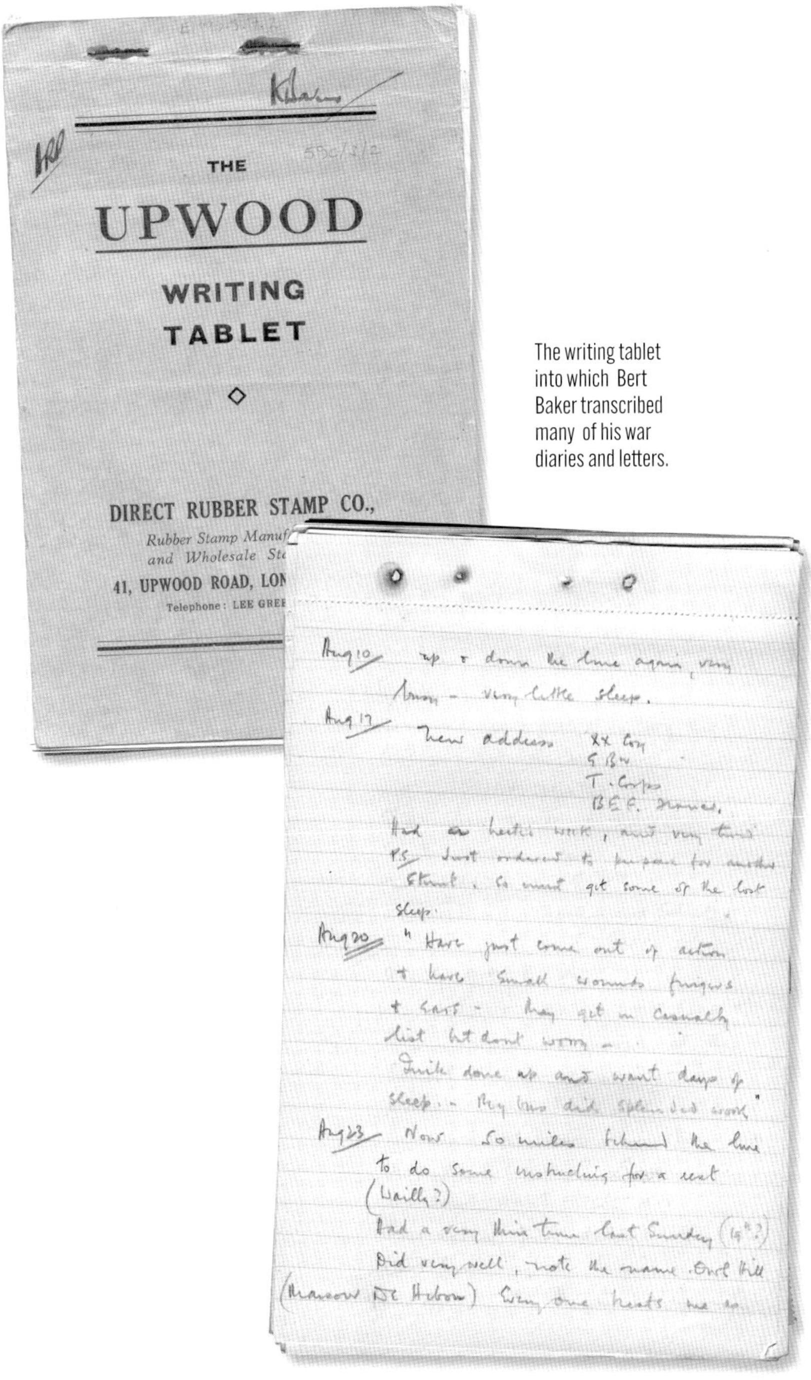

The writing tablet into which Bert Baker transcribed many of his war diaries and letters.

BAKER FAMILY TREE

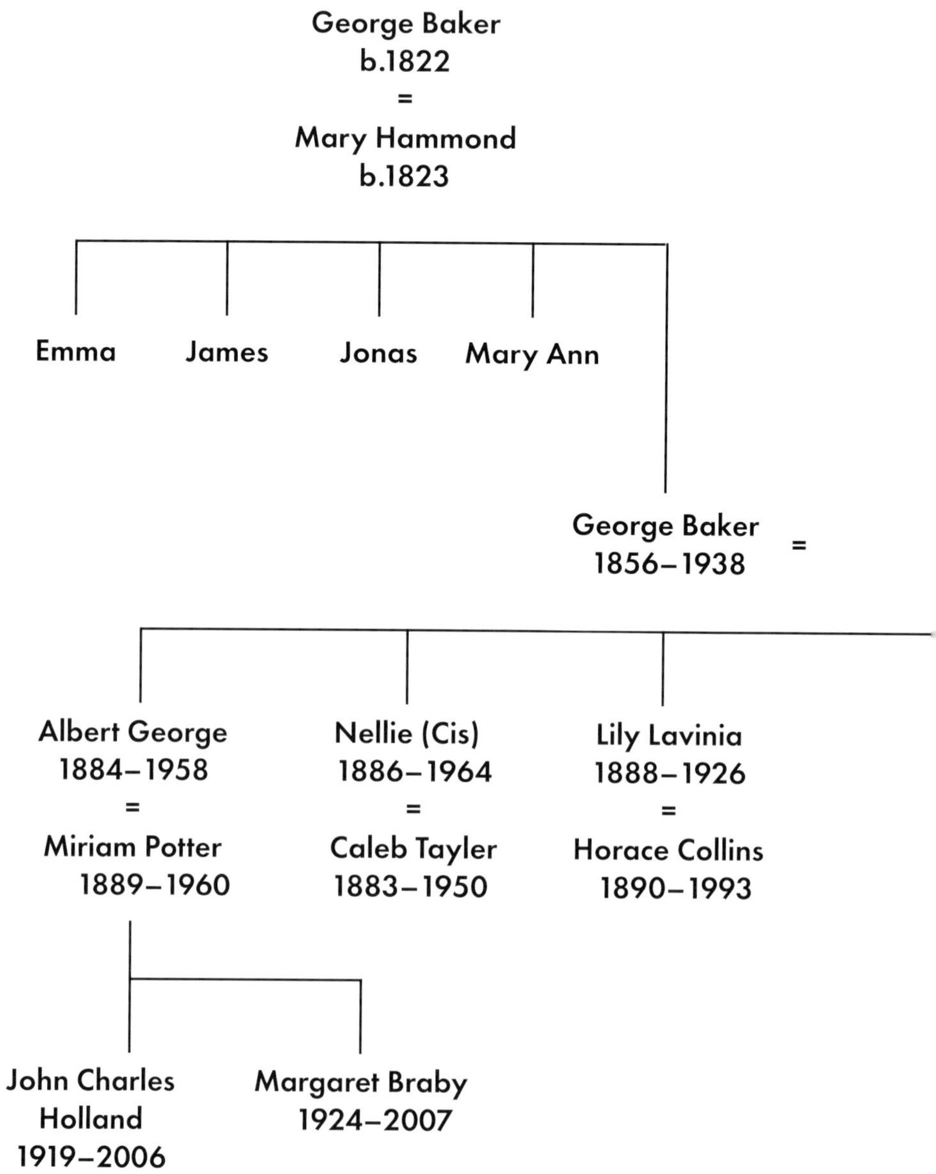

George Braby
b.1832
=
Elizabeth Peachey
b.1834

George

Ellen

James

= Emma Braby
1858–1924

Ernest Reginald
1890–1975
=
Isabella
Hetherington
1895–1965

Leonard
1893–1982
=
Lillie Yeo
1894–1969

Winifred Emma
1895–1981
=
Charles
Woodhams
1896–1992

Bert and Miriam's wedding, 1918.

Bert and Miriam with their young family

General Swinton with Gunner Philip and Bert Baker at Catterick Camp for the handing over of the Graincourt gun.

Bert poses with the Graincourt gun.

A family at war, 1939–45: Margaret, Bert, Miriam and John in their wartime uniforms.

Bert Baker in middle age.

Bert and Miriam at John's wedding, 1947.

Bert with Margaret on her wedding day, 1948.

Bert and Miriam in later life, with Morris.

United Dairies, Uttoxeter, where Bert worked for 30 years.

Bert Baker's staff testing milk supplies in the United Dairies laboratory, 1930s.

The milk train running on the North Staffordshire lines at Uttoxeter, 1925.

the Royal Tank Regiment.

At the entrance to the barracks, the new battalion formed lines on both sides of the road for the old soldiers to march through to the tune of 'Old Comrades'. On the parade ground, a hollow square was formed by soldiers young and old, and a sense of expectation descended.

Slowly, a modern tank, named *Gorgonzola 3* in honour of the occasion, towed the Graincourt gun into the middle of the human square. Accompanying it were Baker and Philip from the crew of *Gorgonzola 2*, with Gregory, Morgan and Ritchie.

This was Bert Baker's moment. He had been asked to make the formal presentation of the gun to the battalion, and perhaps no one had a better claim to the honour. He stepped forward and made a short speech. If he found the task daunting, he does not seem to have shown it. He described briefly the circumstances in which the gun had been knocked out and captured, laying particular emphasis on the marksmanship of Gunner Philip. He then turned to General Swinton. Apart from the Tank Corps dinner in 1919, it was the first time they had met since Swinton had interviewed him for a commission with the tanks in Oxford in April 1916. Baker asked Swinton to accept the gun as a Corps trophy and requested that it might be entrusted to his old battalion again. He hoped that for the young soldiers it would be 'a reminder of the former high standard of efficiency, high endeavour, determination and good comradeship they are to uphold'. It is one of the few reports we have of him speaking, and in his words we can hear again the soldier who stood up to thank Frank Gilbert and his staff for the gift of the suitcase in January 1918.

One of the national newspapers thought the event newsworthy enough to send its military correspondent to Catterick to report on proceedings. Bert kept the cutting containing his account. It began with a highly coloured description of the gun's capture in 1917, setting the scene outside Graincourt as the German field guns held up the British advance and *Gorgonzola 2* prepared to engage them.

The first task, the report said, had been to pinpoint their location. 'Taking the risk under heavy fire, Philip got out of the tank and by watching the smoke of the German firing positions succeeded in locating their position.' In the margin next to this assertion, Bert Baker wrote the single word 'NO!'.

The report continued: 'He got back into the tank and indicating the position to the subaltern, got behind his six-pounder gun. As the tank moved towards the German guns he opened fire. Six shells fell in the compound and silenced the guns. "Good shooting Philip," said Lieutenant Baker." Here Bert added three more exclamation marks. It would have been impossible to hold a conversation inside a tank.

'Yesterday at Catterick Camp,' the report went on, 'appropriately enough in Cambrai Lines, headquarters of the 7th Battalion Royal Tank Corps, I saw the finale to this story.

'In the middle of the square, towed by a modern tank named *Gorgonzola III*, trundled the captured German gun. Twenty-one years before, a tank called

Gorgonzola II had hauled the gun over the battlefield. Standing watching were the former young subaltern and gunner.

'On the jacket of the retired officer, now Captain A.G. Baker, businessman of Uttoxeter, Staffordshire, was the Military Cross and bar and other war medals, while Gunner D.T. Philip of Castle Street, Brechin, Scotland, wore the Military Medal in front of his war medals.

'They had not met since that memorable incident at Cambrai. The whole parade saw them walk towards each other and shake hands.

'The young men of 1917 had grown into grey-haired men – "the grandfathers of the Tank Corps" as they were described by the Colonel Commandant.' Bert appended a large question mark next to the reference to 'grey-haired men'.

The correspondent also recorded the words of General Swinton, accepting the trophy on behalf of the battalion. He had begun by reminding the young and old soldiers that the British Empire was still the biggest force in the world.

'I am not going to talk politics,' Swinton had continued. 'But we hear these days quite a lot about the power of others. Don't forget that we are powerful. There are those who think we haven't got the guts to fight. We are told about other marvellous anti-tank weapons of other nations. Well, we fought against them during the Great War and we beat them, and with the modern tank we could fight against them again and beat them.'

The event, the report concluded, was 'a splendid gesture from the young army to the old'.

With the speeches done, Colonel Kenchington formally took over stewardship of the gun. A tank crew of the 7th Battalion placed it at the foot of the battalion flagstaff.

After the formalities, according to the battalion's report, the band delighted Catterick with 'a really first-rate concert' in the Officers' Club. 'The old soldiers, after due proof that they are by no means dying yet, faded away in parties during Sunday and Monday, leaving behind a warm memory of the Corps' old fellowship and good cheer. It was a good party. It was more: it was Corps tradition. Passed alive from old comrade to new, to keep alive and build up. We owe the Old Comrades our thanks for their part – and we think they enjoyed it as much as we did.'

We can be sure that it was a day Bert Baker would never forget. He had taken his copy of Swinton's book *Eyewitness* to Catterick, and like any starstruck autograph hunter had got the great man to sign it.

Bert continued to keep tabs on the gun. When there was a reference to it ten years later in the journal *The Tank*, a letter from him – signed 'A.G. (Charles) Baker' – appeared on the front page of the next edition. He wanted to know whether the gun was still at Catterick. His letter concluded: 'One loses touch with old friends. Perhaps you will allow me to send greetings to those of the old Mark IV days, particularly those of "G" Battalion.' A note from the editor assured him that the gun was still standing outside the Regimental Headquarters at Catterick Camp. It would eventually be moved to The Tank Museum at Bovington, where it remains on permanent display. The gun was taken back to Cambrai in November 1987 to attend the 70th anniversary commemorations of the battle.

Bert also continued to stay in touch with his former comrades, but an exchange with Esmond Finnegan in February 1942 reveals that they had recently heard of the death of Loxley. 'I was ever so pleased to get your letter and hear all about your activities,' Finnegan wrote. 'But poor old Lox, I am really dreadfully sorry, but not entirely surprised because he seemed to lose his luck. I think the shot was called near Havrincourt. Up till then he had had a happy life, things were always made easy for him. Then came the change.' This presumably was a reference to Loxley having lost his leg. Finnegan's next comments seemed to suggest that Loxley had relied heavily on Bert Baker to get him through the challenges of commanding a section. 'When he got back to his job was it a big one? Was he really a good businessman? Or did he, as in the old 7th, try and wangle his way through? Poor old chap, he was likeable but at the same time was unreliable. He could never have run his Section without you.'

Swinton's comments at the Catterick ceremony were a clear reflection of the growing concern about the spread of fascism in Europe and the rapid rearming that was going on in Hitler's Germany. The British were now rearming too, but had much ground to make up. General Guderian had evidently made a close study of Fuller's book, and acted upon its contents. The British, as usual, had failed to exploit the potential of their own invention. When, belatedly, this dawned on them, they wondered what to do about it. So it was that within a year of the Catterick event, and more than 20 years after being considered surplus to requirements in the Tank Corps, Ernest Swinton found himself pitchforked back into the tank story.

It happened courtesy of Albert Stern, a fellow veteran of the arguments with the War Office in 1915 and 1916. Stern had returned to banking after the war, and was on the boards of several big institutions, but he had always maintained his interest in the development of the tank. In 1939, he was approached by the Minister of Supply, Leslie Burgin, for some expert advice, and he jumped at the chance. With an eye on Hitler's military expansion, Burgin wanted to understand better what the British Army would need in a future conflict. Better late than never: British strategy was lagging well behind.

Stern was made head of a Special Vehicle Development Committee, and wasted no time in rounding up some of the old guard. He brought together Swinton, Eustace d'Eyncourt, the former Director of Naval Construction, Harry Ricardo, the designer of the Mark V engine, and Walter Wilson, the brains behind the design of the early tanks, and especially their gearboxes. They called themselves TOG – The Old Gang – and between them developed a design for a heavy tank they called Tog 1. Another name from the early days, William Tritton from Foster's in Lincoln, was commissioned to produce it. But the committee lacked the power to drive the plans through, and the project was torpedoed when Winston Churchill – with whom Stern had had a major falling out in 1917 – became Prime Minister. Burgin was sacked, and in a subsequent blame game was identified as one of those who had failed to respond appropriately to the Nazi threat. The tank problem turned out to be a critical issue when the Second World War broke out. Perhaps TOG could have done something to help solve it. As it was, they were side-lined.

The Old Gang were not the only ones dismayed at how dilatory the British military had been in developing the tanks. Doubtless it reminded them of all the frustrations of trying to overcome the complacency and hostility of 1915 and 1916. It was galling, too, for the old tank men, if the latter half of Esmond Finnegan's letter to Bert is anything to go by. It developed into something of a rant: 'What a mess our designers have made of our tanks. I have had for long very strong views about them and voiced them here. One thing I think is that the new man, and that means the ex-cavalry man, has had too much say in the matter and worked on horse cavalry tactics, quick mobile attack and run and back again. All very well but the infantry are no longer shock troops so the tanks must be larger, stronger and have more fire power. They must be the spearhead of an attack, then come the cavalry tanks and the infantry to mop up. I could enlarge and write pages.' The tank men had been arguing along these lines for more than 20 years. Boney Fuller of course had written plenty of pages, with exactly this message. The more far-sighted German generals like Guderian and Rommel had listened to him; his own countrymen had largely failed to do so.

11
UTTOXETER

The industry to which Bert Baker had returned was in a state of flux. The mergers that had swallowed F.W. Gilbert of Derby had involved many larger companies as well. United Dairies, formed in 1915, was a coming together of Wiltshire United Dairies, Metropolitan and Great Western Dairies and the Dairy Supply Company. It was partly an act of self-preservation: the war effort meant that men, vehicles and horses were in short supply, a real problem for a business reliant on the regular distribution of a highly perishable product. The larger group was able to pool and maximise resources. It was further swollen in 1917 by the addition of a number of London retailers. Expansion continued after the war. By 1920, United Dairies employed 12,000 people across 750 outlets and handled a third of the total milk supply.

By now, much more was known about the potential health issues surrounding milk, and the technology was available to do something about it. Pasteurisation made it possible to kill the harmful bacteria in milk without diminishing its taste or quality; refrigeration meant it could be transported further and kept fresh for longer.

These developments contributed to the growth of big operations with the resources and the scale to invest in the new technology and to process and distribute very large quantities of milk. But they were highly ominous for the small dairyman. While the companies were all for pasteurisation, the cow keeping producer-retailers like George Baker of East Dulwich could be forgiven for being less enthusiastic. There were still plenty of them: more than a dozen local dairies were still going strong in Camberwell by the time of the Great War. At least one thought the fact that cows were kept on the premises was a big enough selling point to be a prominent feature of its advertisements. But the days of the independent urban dairymen were numbered. They could not afford to keep pace with the march of science, and to instal costly pasteurisation or refrigeration facilities.

They clung to their local markets though, and George soldiered on after the war, now with only one of his children left to help him. This was Len, who had served in the army, and by 1921 was back at 75 Pellatt Road with his new wife, Lillie. Bert was now settled in Derby, Ernie who now preferred to be known as Reg was in the Far East, and the three girls were all married. The house must have seemed quiet after the hustle and bustle of 20 years earlier. Soon George was to lose another mainstay. Emma died in 1924, and although he kept going for a while longer, his mind turned towards retirement. In 1925, he bought a plot of land on the south coast at Bosham. Over time he built a house on it, and seems to have started living there in 1928. His sister in-law Ellen and her husband James Kent lived not far away in Emsworth, which might have influenced his choice of location. He named his new house Kilsham, after the farm that Emma's parents had occupied outside Petworth.

George's working life more or less spanned the age of the small suburban dairy, which had sprung up in answer to a need among expanding towns and cities in the 1870s and 1880s. They were now being undercut by big companies with whom they could not compete on price or quality. George was by now over 70, and must have been pleased to be getting out. He had built a successful business, but its best days were behind it. He was proud, though, of what he had achieved, and his Will gave a hint of the effort that had gone into it. He described his 'small estate' as the result of 'many years of careful living and hard work'.

George's new home in Bosham was but a short step from a pub, the Berkeley Arms, and he was wont to refresh himself there of an evening. A story passed down in the family is that on his walk home from the pub every evening, he would pick up a handful of white pebbles from the roadside. Over a period of years, according to the story, he laid an entire path from his gate to his front door.

His father's home in Bosham provided a holiday destination for Bert and his family, which suggests that relations between father and son were cordial. It is likely that others of his children would have visited him there too. George died in Bosham in March 1938 at the age of 82. Bert, and George's solicitor, were executors of the will. His estate was worth £3,745.14s.11d, the equivalent of perhaps £250,000 today. He made some individual bequests to his children and shared the rest between them. Nothing was left outside the family – George's Will specified that this was his 'most earnest wish', and it urged his children to follow suit when their time came. The family brought his body back to London so that he could be buried alongside Emma in Camberwell Old Cemetery. Their graves are in a part of the cemetery that was allowed to grow wild, and are now lost deep in the woodland.

Bert too had had to struggle with the changes that were sweeping through the dairy industry, although not in the same way as his father. The war had slowed the already halting take-up of the new methods of sanitation and purification, and it took the founding of the National Clean Milk Society in 1915 to provide the necessary push towards the general adoption of higher standards.

Even so, under the Milk (Special Designation) Orders of 1922 and 1923, the grading of the bacteriological quality of milk was still only voluntary. It was also confusing, based on a series of different grades, depending on the level of tuberculin testing that had taken place, and whether or not churns had been sealed before leaving the farm. The graded milk was dearer than the traditional raw milk, which was good news for the remaining small dairymen, if not for the consumer. Thousands of small producers took no heed of the new voluntary regulations.

The Milk and Dairy Order of 1926 was designed to prevent contamination while the milk was in transit, and the Sale of Milk Act of 1927 brought in the licensing of Grade A Tuberculin Tested milk. But the piecemeal nature and varying speed of adoption meant that milk remained a significant spreader of infectious diseases. By 1939, most milk on retail sale in the United Kingdom was still unpasteurised. It was not yet the clean and healthy food that is a staple of today's diets.

A stark assessment of how serious the situation was even as late as 1943 was published early in that year in the *British Medical Journal*, in an article entitled 'The Pasteurisation of Milk'. Its author was G.S. Wilson, Professor of Bacteriology as Applied to Hygiene at the London School of Hygiene and Tropical Medicine. Professor Wilson did not mince his words:

> About 5–10 per cent of farms in this country are sending out milk containing tubercle bacilli. About 20–40 per cent Brucella abortus; and a much higher proportion mastitis streptococci, which although not usually infective to man may cause undesirable changes in the milk. Bulked milk reaching our large towns usually contains all three organisms and it can be affected with other organisms, eg scarlet fever streptococci, diphtheria bacilli and bacilli of the typhoid paratyphoid food poisoning and dysentery groups.
>
> The first three come from the cow's udder; the others either from the infected fingers of those handling the milk, or from water used for washing the udders, cleaning the utensils or watering the milk.

All this was a nightmare for the distributors, who mixed together supplies from many sources. One infected batch could contaminate a much larger quantity. Wilson said that up to 2,000 people were dying in England and Wales every year as the result of tuberculosis of bovine origin. He estimated that in the 25 years from 1912, 65,000 lives had been lost in this way. The so-called Victorian killer was still claiming significant numbers of victims almost a century later. It was clear to Wilson that these deaths could be avoided if only pasteurisation were fully adopted. 'The only practicable method at present of ensuring that the human population is supplied with milk free from pathogenic organisms is by some form of heat treatment, of which pasteurisation, if carried out under proper conditions, is undoubtedly the most satisfactory.' But it would be 1949 before compulsory pasteurisation was introduced with the Milk (Special Designations) Act.

The snail's pace at which this process of producing safe milk progressed makes clear the importance of the work of analytical chemists like Bert Baker. United Dairies were early adopters of pasteurisation, but keeping their milk fresh and free of disease and infection required constant vigilance, with continuous sampling and testing. Bert must have applied himself to this with his usual assiduity, because in 1923 he was appointed chief analytical chemist for the whole Northern Area of United Dairies. The new job meant a move: the company's main laboratories were in the market town of Uttoxeter, 20 miles from Chellaston and just across the Derbyshire border into Staffordshire. Bert and Miriam and young John moved to a spacious house a few minutes' walk from the dairy. It is to be presumed that they bought rather than rented it, because they chose its name. It was a name that recalled for Bert his wartime sojourn in the Norfolk countryside that he had found so attractive: Elveden. In early 1924, Bert and Miriam had a second child, a daughter. She was christened Margaret Braby, the latter being her grandmother's maiden name.

Bert's new job made him responsible for the daily sampling and analysis of milk from United Dairies depots across the Midlands and the north of England. Over time, a vast amount of data was collected, and Bert began to wonder whether any use might be made of it. As far as he was aware, no comparable data collated anywhere else had ever been subjected to any statistical analysis that might contribute to the field of dairy education and research. He thought it would be of particular interest to map the volume and composition of milk produced over a period, and to see whether connections could be made to external factors, such as the level of rainfall.

The academic paper that resulted from this was written in collaboration with H.T. Cranfield of the Midland Agricultural College at Loughborough in Leicestershire. Cranfield had been involved in the production of a number of other papers, and probably contributed thoughts about the methodology while Bert Baker provided the data. The paper was called *Variation in the Composition of Milk in certain Midland Districts of England during the years 1923–31*.

The data related to samples taken from bulking or balancing tanks, into which the milk was placed when it arrived at the depots from the farms. The fat percentage and solids-not-fat percentages were measured, and average figures compiled. Bert's paper estimated that around 1,800 farms and 20,000 cows across Cheshire, Staffordshire, Derbyshire and Leicestershire had contributed to the data that had been collected over the nine-year period, with the number of individual samples standing at about 300,000. Rainfall and temperature data were taken from the records of weather stations across the four counties.

His purpose in analysing this vast databank was to see if any conclusions might be drawn about variations between districts, between different years and between different months within a year. The results were rendered in a series of a dozen graphs setting out and comparing fat percentages, solids-not-fat percentages, rainfall, and mean air temperatures. The writers were modest – and very brief – in the conclusions they drew from an interpretation of the graphs. Their main finding was that there appeared to be a direct correlation between quality of milk and level of rainfall. In sum: the more it rained, the better the milk. Not altogether surprising perhaps, but this kind of work had not been done before, and Bert had the satisfaction of seeing his paper published in the *Journal of Dairy Research* in May 1933.

His son John also grew up with an interest in the land, and as a young man his ambition in life was to become a farmer. One of his earliest memories was of pedigree British Friesian cattle that Gilbert's kept at Chellaston and exhibited at County Shows all over the country. John remembered herds of 20–30 cattle being led down the road to Chellaston station to be loaded on to the trains *en route* to one or other of the shows. Each animal was accompanied by a herdsman in a long white coat, with the bulls escorted by a man on either side.

After leaving school, John had spent a year working on a farm near Derby and thoroughly enjoyed the experience. But he could not afford to buy or rent a farm of his own. Becoming a farm inspector looked like the next best option, and he won a place at the Midland Agricultural College at Sutton Bonnington in Leicestershire. He travelled to Reading to take his final exams on the day war was declared in 1939. His career plans ground to a halt. He was 19.

His father pulled what strings he could, and after a couple of false alarms, John was duly posted to the 7th Battalion, the Royal Tank Regiment (RTR). It was Bert's old battalion, disbanded after the first war and reconstituted in the run-up to the second. John's war would take him and the RTR with the Eighth Army through Palestine, Persia, Iraq, Egypt – including Alamein – and finally to Italy and Austria in the last days of the conflict. He learned how to drive a tank, but although he served in the regiment for nearly six years, and was away from home more or less continuously for that time, he did not see any direct action. One period of leave at the end of 1940 saw him back in Uttoxeter for a party to celebrate his 21st birthday. He set tongues wagging by spending most of the evening dancing with Doreen Bagnall, the daughter of a local businessman who had established laundries in Leek and Uttoxeter.

Bert himself was not idle during the war years, becoming training officer for the Home Guard in Uttoxeter, although as the town was just about as far from the sea as it was possible to get, there would have been no imminent fear of German invasion. Nor were there any particularly obvious targets for the German bombers in the near vicinity. Even so, the town had Air Raid Precautions as well as the Home Guard, and Miriam served as an ARP warden. All the family were in uniform: a photograph of the four of them shows Bert in the uniform of the Home Guard, Miriam in that of the ARP, John in that of the Royal Tank Regiment, and Margaret in that of a nurse. Bert also kept up his military connections as secretary of the local branch of the armed forces' charity SSAFA, the Soldiers, Sailors, Airmen and Families Association, which provided support to past and present members of the military and their families. He was always to be seen helping with the annual Poppy Day appeal organised by the British Legion. Bert had devoted considerable energy to the Legion, and played a leading role in the search for a headquarters for the newly-formed Uttoxeter branch. These efforts duly bore fruit, and the Uttoxeter Ex-Servicemen's Club was established in Bradley Street in 1938. It became a favourite haunt for him. As it was more or less on the way between United Dairies and Elveden, he would often drop in for a drink on his way home from work.

By now he was a well-established figure in the town he had called home since 1923. He was active in the Rotary Cub and served as its President, and also as Worshipful Master of the local lodge of Freemasons. He was a season ticket holder at Derby County Football Club. Miriam, too, was active in local organisations and was also a keen golfer, winning a number of prizes at Uttoxeter Golf Club. She featured in a report in the local newspaper as the first lady member to score a hole in one.

Bert's siblings were by this time scattered across various parts of the country, and we do not know how closely he kept in touch with them. There were two opportunities for family reunions in Uttoxeter soon after the war, when the Baker children were married. John married Doreen Bagnall in 1947, and Margaret married John Statham, whose family had a farm in Bramshall just outside Uttoxeter, in 1948.

Only one of Bert's siblings, Nellie, the oldest of his sisters, stayed close to East Dulwich. She was always known as Cis or Cissie – perhaps Bert had called her 'Sis' when they were children. Cis married Caleb Tayler in 1912 and they lived in Elfindale Road, Herne Hill.

Cally, as Caleb was known, had evidently seen his life panning out differently as a young man, because in 1909, at the age of 26, he had boarded a boat from Liverpool to Quebec with the apparent intention of settling in Canada. On arrival, he gave his occupation as clerk, but his intended occupation in Canada as farmer. His plans did not work out. By the time of the 1911 Census, he was back in London and once again working as a clerk. He and Cis married the following year. I remember meeting Auntie Cis only once, when she came to stay with us, and my abiding memory of her is how small she was – barely five feet tall. Cis died in 1964.

The next sister, christened Lily but sometimes called Lilian, married Horace Collins, an upholsterer and fabric worker from Hackney in north London. They were married in 1916, the same year Horace joined the Royal Naval Air Service. In 1918, the RNAS merged with the Royal Flying Corps to become the Royal Air Force, and Horace served as an air mechanic. Horace and Lily had a son, Dennis, but Lily died from complications a few days after giving birth to their second child, Stancia. She was 37. Horace was later married again, to Rose Powell, known as Nettie, and he lived to be more than a hundred.

Ernie, or Reg, the son in whose education George and Emma had invested what money they had, took full advantage of the benefit bestowed on him. He attended Dulwich High School and went on to study civil engineering at Battersea Polytechnic. This led to a job with the firm of J. Watt Sandeman in Newcastle-on-Tyne, where he worked largely on the surveying and construction of harbours.

Like his older brother Bert, Reg clearly had a sense of adventure, although he did not satisfy it with a military career. A few months before war broke out in 1914, he sailed from Southampton to Singapore, and on to the town of Sandakan in British North Borneo. There he was employed by the Public Works Department as an assistant engineer, working on the construction of roads, bridges, drains, culverts and sewers – even, at one time, a lighthouse.

Reg came back to England for several months every five years or so. At the time of the 1921 Census, he was staying with Bert and Miriam at Chellaston. He was back again in 1926, this time in Newcastle where he married Isabella Hetherington, whom he had presumably met while he was working there some years earlier.

Reg and Belle lived the privileged lives of expats in Borneo until Reg retired from the Public Works Department in 1939 and returned to England for good. His colleagues presented him with an autographed silver salver, which is still in the family. Reg worked as an engineer for the Air Ministry during the Second World

War, and in 1949 he and Belle bought a large house in Yapton near Bognor Regis on the south coast. They named it Sandakan and set about turning it into a guesthouse. It does not seem to have been a conspicuous success, and they spent their later lives at various addresses in Sussex and Hampshire. Reg died in 1975.

Next came Len, who returned from service in France to resume work in his father's dairy and to live at Pellatt Road. He married Lillie Yeo in 1921, and they later moved to a house of their own a few streets away. Little is known about Len's activities between the wars, though a family legend suggests that he was for some time involved in the clothing business, and supplied the firm that made clothes for the young princesses, Elizabeth and Margaret. The enterprise is said to have folded when Len's partner absconded. He was back in the dairy industry by the time of the 1939 Register, where his occupation is given as Clerk (Dairy). By then, he and Lillie were living not far from East Dulwich in Forest Hill with Lillie's widowed father, a retired railway clerk, and her younger brother Charles, an insurance clerk. Later they would move to a house in Cheam.

Len and Lillie had one child, a son, Alan. Alan was an usher at John Baker's wedding in 1947, which suggests that the cousins must have seen a fair bit of each other, in spite of the geographical distance between them. By then, Alan had just graduated from the University of Southampton – the first member of the family to go to university. He embarked on a scientific career as a physicist with the Safety in Mines Research Establishment in Sheffield. In the early 1960s he led the team that invented a device that could detect combustible and other hazardous gases in mines. Until then, colliers had relied on a canary in a cage to warn them of potential dangers from poisonous gases. The 'Baker Pellistor' consisted of small ceramic pellets within a cylinder, the resistance of which changed if gas was present. The name was a conflation of 'pellet' and 'resistor'. The device made a major contribution to improving safety in mining and other hazardous environments.

Alan Baker's status as one of the foremost experts in his field was reflected in his leadership of investigations into major industrial accidents. He led inquiries into the Flixborough chemical plant disaster in Lincolnshire in 1974, in which 28 people died. Ten years later, he investigated an explosion at a newly-opened water treatment plant at Abbeystead in Lancashire, which killed 16 people.

When Lillie died in 1969, Len moved to Sheffield to be near to Alan and his family. Like his sister Cis, Len was diminutive in height but remained fit and active into his eighties. He was always full of chat and good humour. Len died in 1982.

The youngest of the six Baker children was Winifred Emma, or Winnie. Winnie was married in 1921 within a few weeks of the wedding of Len and Lillie. Her husband was Charles Edward Woodhams, known as Ted. They might have met as the result of Ted's friendship with Bert, who had chosen him to be best man at his wedding. Ted was the son of a watchmaker, and lived a few streets away from Pellatt Road. He had served in the Great War, first as an infantryman, and later in the Royal Flying Corps. Ted and Winnie lived in various addresses in the Camberwell area, and were still there in 1939, Ted giving his occupation in the

Register as bank clerk. Later they moved to Sevenoaks, where Winnie emulated her father by naming her house Kilsham. Later still, they moved in with their daughter Beryl and her husband Derek, also in Sevenoaks. Beryl's son Richard remembers his grandmother as a pleasant but rather reserved person, and he did not feel he really got to know her even when they were living in the same house, albeit in separate accommodation. Although she had been outgoing as a young woman, she became more withdrawn in later life and did not attend family events, although the dapper Ted was always present. Winnie died in 1981.

In the early 1950s, Bert retired from his job at United Dairies, and then worked for a short time at Elkes and Sons in Uttoxeter. Elkes were biscuit makers, and we do not know in what capacity Bert was employed there. He and Miriam bought a small house on the outskirts of Uttoxeter. Bert died in January 1958 after a short illness, just after his 73rd birthday.

Nearly every local organisation in the district was represented at his funeral at St Mary's Church in Uttoxeter. His surviving sisters, Cis and Winnie, were there, Cis also representing his brother Len. The coffin was covered with the Union Jack and borne by members of the Uttoxeter branch of the British Legion, whose home in the town Bert had done so much to establish.

Miriam was not in good health either. After Bert's death, she went to live with John and Margaret on the farm in Bramshall and died in August 1960 at the age of 72. She and Bert are buried in Bramshall churchyard.

Although we have learned much about Albert George Baker from his writings, actions and achievements, it has been difficult to pinpoint what he was really like. There is no one left alive with any clear memory of how he spoke, what he liked to do, what made him laugh. We must rely then on the evidence set out in this book, and the eulogy delivered at a meeting of the Rotary Club of Uttoxeter soon after his death. The President, C.E. Herbert, endeavoured to sum up the man, as well as what he had achieved in life. At this distance, his address is the closest we can get to an understanding of the sort of person he was.

> We are met this morning in the shadow of the death, within the last 48 hours, of one of our senior members, Past President A.G. Baker.
> He served in the Great War of 1914–18 and was awarded the Military Cross, and he was one of the first ex-Servicemen to join the British Legion; indeed, during the difficult years between the two wars, it was largely the work and enthusiasm of Rotarian Baker that kept the Legion alive in this town. It was, I think, significant that last November was the first time he had to tell me that through failing health and advancing years he could no longer help me with Poppy Day – up to then he had invariably given me invaluable assistance.
>
> He was not a man who sought the limelight, or, indeed, the glare of publicity, but went about his work with a quiet efficiency and carried out services for the community in a manner which will long remain an example to us all.

UTTOXETER

SOURCES

KIRDFORD

Austin, Janet, *Kirdford: The Old Parish Rediscovered* (Ifold and District Local History Society)
Bruce, Pamela, *Northchapel: A Parish History* (Northchapel Parish Council, 2000)
Kirdford Parish Council records

EAST DULWICH

Almeroth-Williams, Thomas, *City of Beasts* (Manchester University Press, 2019)
Green, Brian, *Victorian and Edwardian Dulwich* (Barracuda Books, 1988)
Booth, Charles, *Life and Labour of the People in London* (London School of Economics Library)

DAIRYMAN

Joy, Dave, *Liverpool Cowkeepers* (Amberley, 2016)
Velten, Hannah, *Milk: A Global History* (Reaktion Books, 2010)

TANKS

Some of these books are available as more recent imprints.

Baker, Albert George, Personal papers, The Tank Museum
Baker-Carr, Christopher, *From Chauffeur to Brigadier* (Ernest Benn, 1930)
Browne, D.G., *The Tank in Action* (Blackwood, 1920)
Campbell, Christy, *Band of Brigands: the first men in tanks* (Harper Press, 2007)
Fuller, J.F.C., *Tanks in the Great War, 1914–1918* (John Murray, 1920)
Fletcher, David and Tait, Janice, *Tracing Your Tank Ancestors* (Pen and Sword Books, 2011)
Fletcher, David (editor), *Tanks and Trenches: first-hand accounts of tank warfare in the First World War* (Sutton Publishing, 1994)
Fletcher, David, *British Mark I Tank 1916* (Osprey, 2004)
Fletcher, David, *Great War Tank Mark IV: Owner's Workshop Manual* (Haynes Publishing, 2013)
Hickey, Daniel, *Rolling into Action: Memoirs of a Tank Corps Section Commander* (Hutchinson, 1936)
Horsfall, Jack and Cave, Nigel, *Cambrai: Bourlon Wood* (Pen and Sword Books, 2002)
Horsfall, Jack and Cave, Nigel, *Cambrai: Flesquières* (Pen and Sword Books, 2003)
Maurice, R.F.G. (editor), *Tank Corps Book of Honour* (Naval and Military Press)
McNab, Chris, *Cambrai 1917: Battle Story* (Spellmount, 2012)
Spagnoly, Tony and Smith, Ted, *Cameos of the Western Front: Salient Points*

Three (Pen and Sword Books, 2001)
Smithers, A.J., *The New Excalibur: the Development of the Tank 1909–1939* (Secker and Warburg, 1986)
Swinton, Ernest, *Eyewitness. Being personal reminiscences of certain phases of the Great War, including the genesis of the tank* (Hodder and Stoughton, 1932)
Thorp, H.O.C., *Narrative History of 'G' and 7th Battalion 1919* (Gale and Polden, 1919)
Turner, Alexander, *Cambrai 1917: the birth of armoured warfare* (Osprey, 2007)
Williams-Ellis, Clough and Annabel, *The Tanks Corps* (Country Life, 1919)

ARTICLES

Arscott, Peter, 'G Battalion 1st Tank Brigade at St Julien on 19 August 1917', *Stand To!* (the magazine of the Western Front Association), Spring 1993
Atkins, P.J., 'White Poison? The Social Consequences of Milk Consumption, 1850–1930', *Social History of Medicine*, 1992
Atkins, P.J., 'The Retail Milk Trade in London c1790–1914', *The Economic History Review*, 1980
Atkins, P.J., 'London's Intra-Urban Milk Supply, circa 1790–1914', *Transactions of the Institute of British Geographers*, 1977
Fletcher, David, 'The First Tanks at Elveden', *Stand To!* (the magazine of the Western Front Association), September 2015
Taylor, David, 'The English Dairy Industry 1860–1930 – the need for a reassessment', *The Agricultural History Review*, 1974
Taylor, David, 'London's Milk Supply 1850–1900: A reinterpretation', *Agricultural History*, 1971
Wilson, G.S., 'The Pasteurisation of Milk', *British Medical Journal*, February 1943